Eben-Emael and the Defence of Fortress Belgium, 1940

Eben-Emael and the Defence of Fortress Belgium, 1940

Clayton Donnell

Pen & Sword
MILITARY

First published in Great Britain in 2021 by
Pen & Sword Military
An imprint of
Pen & Sword Books Ltd
Yorkshire – Philadelphia

ISBN 978 1 52677 982 3

A CIP catalogue record for this book is
available from the British Library.

Typeset by Mac Style
Printed and bound by CPI Group (UK) Ltd, Croydon, CR0 4YY

Pen & Sword Books Limited incorporates the imprints of Atlas,
Archaeology, Aviation, Discovery, Family History, Fiction, History,
Maritime, Military, Military Classics, Politics, Select, Transport,
True Crime, Air World, Frontline Publishing, Leo Cooper, Remember
When, Seaforth Publishing, The Praetorian Press, Wharncliffe
Local History, Wharncliffe Transport, Wharncliffe True Crime
and White Owl.

For a complete list of Pen & Sword titles please contact

PEN & SWORD BOOKS LIMITED
47 Church Street, Barnsley, South Yorkshire, S70 2AS, England
E-mail: enquiries@pen-and-sword.co.uk
Website: www.pen-and-sword.co.uk

Or

PEN AND SWORD BOOKS
1950 Lawrence Rd, Havertown, PA 19083, USA
E-mail: Uspen-and-sword@casematepublishers.com
Website: www.penandswordbooks.com

Contents

Author's Notes and Acknowledgements

This book is, in some respects, a follow-on to *Breaking the Fortress Line 1914*, published in 2013. That book follows the progress of the German Army siege corps as they move through Belgium and into France. It begins at Liège in Belgium where a two-week stand by Belgian fortress troops altered the fate of the Germans who had hoped to quickly smash the Allied armies. Along the way to the Marne the Germans encountered the fortress garrisons of Liège, Namur, Maubeuge, Longwy, the Trouée de Charmes, the Heights of the Meuse, and finally Fortress Antwerp. This current book concentrates only on the forts of Liège and Namur during Belgium's 18-day campaign of May 1940. The attack on the Maginot Line is covered in another volume.

I had the good fortune to live in Liège from April 1970 to August 1972. My parents loved to go on rides around the countryside at the weekend and one day we drove north to a large concrete bunker, which had a small museum along the main tunnel inside the fort. I didn't know it at the time but this was Fort Eben-Emael. On other days I took my racing bike and rode up and down the hills that surrounded this industrial city. My journeys took me to the old Citadelle and to the ring of forts around Liège. They were still army property and mostly closed up with the exception of Fort Embourg, next to the village where most of my American friends lived. It was possible to walk right through the open gate of the fort and explore the tunnels. One very long tunnel ended at a ladder that led up to one of the observation positions overlooking the Vesdre Valley. I had no idea what happened there in August 1914 and May 1940 but I have spent the years ever since learning and writing about it.

I do not speak fluent French or German. I can read most French texts with 90 per cent understanding but I still need to check the translation for quite a few unfamiliar words. All of the text I used to research this book, with the exception of Tim Saunders' *Fort Eben-Emael*, was in French and German. The captured German records, all original source documents, are typed and handwritten messages. Forget the handwritten ones as I could not read them at all – unfortunate because I probably missed some good details. But most of the messages were typed by a clerk in whatever headquarters staff office he was assigned to throughout May 1940. While translating some documents, i.e., retyping them and copying to a translation application, I realized I was copying words originally put to paper in May 1940. I hope the translations do some credit to the original authors, both Belgian and German. That is the intent, to tell their story and to relay the emotions and experiences they felt both on the giving and receiving end.

I had help writing this book from quite a few folks in Belgium. Emil (Milou) Coenen and Franck Vernier, authors of a series of books on the Belgian forts of Liège and Namur, provided lots of details and photos. Françoise Legros, of the *Fondation Emile Legros* at Fort Saint-Héribert in Namur, provided me with written materials and photos that are high class. Marc Romanych of Digital History Archive, who has spent what seems like half his life at the National Archives, supplied the captured German documents and photos from Army Group down to battalion level, including Sixth Army, and 223rd, 253rd and 211th Infantry Divisions which launched the main attacks on the forts. Thanks to *Amicale du Fort d'Aubin Neufchâteau* for two magnificent vintage photos taken during the surrender of the fort. Bunkerfreaks Antwerpen allowed me to use 'as many photos as I wanted to', and I used quite a few. Photos were also provided by Reynaud Mayers and Fortif.be. Thanks to the associations that spend so much time inside these old forts making repairs and leading thousands of visitors through the tunnels and preserving the *Patrimoine Militaire*. Finally, thanks to my daughter for editing photos, my brother for encouraging me to press on, and my wife for her continued support to my 39-year long hobby.

List of Abbreviations

AA		Anti-aircraft
AP		Armour-piercing
AT		Anti-tank
FM	*Fusil-Mitrailleur*	Automatic rifle/light machine gun
FRC	*Fonderie Royale des Canons*	Royal Gun Foundry (Belgian)
GP	*Grande Portée*	Long range (guns)
HE		High explosive
ID		Infantry Division (German)
IR		Infantry Regiment (German)
KW Line		Konigshookt-Wavre Line
LG	*lance grenades*	Grenade launcher
MG		Machine gun
Mi/LG	*Mitrailleuse/Lance Grenade*	Machine gun/grenade launcher (turret)
OKH	*Oberkommando des Heeres*	German Army High Command
PAK	*Panzer Abwehr Kanone*	Anti-tank gun (German)
PFL	*Position Fortifiée de Liège*	Fortified Position of Liège
PFN	*Position Fortifiée de Namur*	Fortified Position of Namur
PL		Pontisse-Lixhe (sector)
PO	*Posts d'Observation*	Observation post (artillery)
POC	*Post d'Observation Cuirassée*	Armoured observation post
RFL	*Régiment de Forteresse de Liège*	Fortress Regiment of Liège
RFN	*Régiment de Forteresse de Namur*	Fortress Regiment of Namur
rpm		Rounds per minute
TSF	*Télégraphie sans fil*	Wireless

Glossary

Abri – Shelter: can refer to any of the small concrete bunkers built along the fortified Belgian lines between the main forts, equipped with observation capabilities, or light guns or machine guns, manned by small crews.

Air tower – A tall concrete structure resembling a water tower that served as an air intake shaft for a fort's ventilation system; also served as an observatory, close-defence gun chamber and secondary exit of the fort.

Bangalore Torpedo – An explosive charge placed inside one or more connected tubes, used by combat engineers to clear obstacles, such as barbed wire.

Bloc – A concrete surface component of a fort, armed with long-range guns, howitzers, anti-tank guns, mortars or machine guns.

Boîtes-à-Balles – A projectile containing small lead pellets that scatter when the shell leaves the muzzle; used for close defence against enemy infantry. Similar to canister shot.

Bunker – An independent concrete fortification equipped with small arms or guns, also referred to as a blockhouse.

Bureau de Coordination de Tirs (*Bureau de Tir*) – A fire-control command post inside a fort, where decisions are made as to which guns to use to fire on a reported target, including type of projectile, range, azimuth and elevation.

Caisson – A metal container for transporting munitions from storage to the gun chambers.

Casemate – A large concrete chamber with one or more openings for guns or small arms, designed to protect the flanks of a position.

Central Massif – In a Belgian fort, a large concrete structure in the centre of the fort, surrounded on all sides by a ditch, containing all of the fort's artillery.

Chasseurs – Belgian light infantry.

Chevaux-de-frises – Anti-personnel obstacle made of a row of pointed steel spikes intertwined with barbed wire.

Cloche – A bell-shaped observation or small-arms post embedded into the top of a concrete casemate or artillery bloc.

Coffer – See Casemate.

Corps de Garde – A bombproof chamber with machine guns adjacent to the postern that defended the ramp of a fort.

Council of Defence – Met to discuss and vote on the fate of a fort, typically after a long period of siege or attack; composed of the commander, the oldest officer, the youngest officer and the doctor.

Counterbattery – Artillery fire intended to silence an enemy gun battery.

Counterscarp – The outer wall of a ditch below the glacis, faces inwards.

(Denkschrift) – (Photo source) Oberkommando des Heeres, General der Pioniere und Festungen, *Denkschrift über die belgische Landesbefestigung*, 1941.

(Digital History Archive, 'Bunkers of the Blitzkrieg') – (Photo source) US National Archives (NARA) Captured German Records Collection. 'Bunkers of the Blitzkrieg Photograph Collection 1939-40'. (Digital History Archive – Marc Romanych).

(Digital History Archive, German Military Study P-203) – (Photo source) US National Archives (NARA) Captured German Records Collection. German Military Study P-203, 'German Attacks Against Permanent and Reinforced Field-Type Positions in World War II' (*Deutsche Angriffe gegen Festungen im 2. Weltkrieg*) by General Rudolf Hofmann.

(Digital History Archive, Microcopy No. T-315) – (Photo source) US National Archives (NARA), Records of German Field Commands – Divisions (National Archives Microcopy No. T-315, 223. *Infanterie-Division* (223rd Infantry Division). 2 Apr–19 May 1940, Ia, *Anlage zum Kriegstagebuch Nr. 1. Anlagen Nr.* 188-264. Division Orders and combat reports relating to the capture of enemy fortifications. T-315 Roll 1689.

Ditch – The dry moat of a fort, an obstacle several metres deep and wide, defended by casemate guns.

Embrasure – A small opening in a fortification for a gun, machine gun or rifle.

Escarp – The inner wall of a ditch below the central part of a fort.

Galerie de Bombardment – A section of the *Galeries de Grande Profondeur* (q.v.) where the troops can take shelter from heavy bombardment.

Galeries de Grande Profondeur – A series of tunnels built beneath the quadrilateral of a fort that includes a ventilation tunnel leading to the air intake.

Glacis – The gradual slope on all sides of a fort leading up to the counterscarp.

Gorge Front – The unexposed side of a fort. In the Belgian forts, they are immediately inside the postern.

Grande Portée – Long range.

Head Casemate – The casemate defending the ditches that meet at the head of the fort, the Salient angle closest to the enemy.

Interdiction Fire – Artillery fire directed at predetermined targets where the passage of the enemy is detected or suspected.

Lances Grenades – Grenade Launcher: a light infantry weapon with a fixed elevation, installed in a turret also equipped with machine guns; used to target the glacis of the fort.

Lateral – The area between two Salients, identified as Salient I – II, etc.

Obus de Rupture – Armour-piercing shell.

Panzerjäger – Anti-tank arm of the German army; equipped with weapons that could also be used against fortifications.

Parapet – An embankment of a fortified position designed to protect a rifleman from enemy fire.

Pioneer – German equivalent of combat engineers consisting of small demolition or flamethrower squads which attack key enemy positions, such as fortifications, in advance of a main attack.

Post d'Observation Cuirassée – An armoured observation post built inside the former searchlight turret in the centre of the massif of the Brialmont forts of Liège and Namur.

Postern – The rear entrance of a fort.

Posts d'Observations: – An observation post typically located outside of a fort, but subordinate to the commander of the fort, the mission of which was to keep watch on the approaches to the fort and report the presence of enemy troops or vehicles.

Quadrilateral – Bombproof tunnels built beneath the older section of a refurbished Brialmont fort of Liège or Namur.

Ramp – A roadway leading to the postern of a fort.

Salient Angle – The inner points of a triangular or quadrangular fort where the ditches meet, identified by Roman numerals and beginning with the first point to the left of the postern.

Schwere Artillerie-Abteilung – German heavy artillery 'department'.

Shaped charge – An explosive charge shaped to focus the energy of the explosive in a downwards direction, and used to penetrate a thick steel surface, such as a turret or cloche.

Télégraphie sans fil – Wireless.

Table of Equivalent Ranks

Belgian	German	US	UK
N/A	Generalfeldmarschall	General of the Army	Field Marshal
General	Generaloberst	General	General
Lieutenant Général	General	Lieutenant General	Lieutenant General
Général-Major	Generalleutnant	Major General	Major General
Général de Brigade	Generalmajor	Brigadier General	Brigadier
Colonel	Oberst	Colonel	Colonel
Lieutenant Colonel	Oberstleutnant	Lieutenant Colonel	Lieutenant Colonel
Major	Major	Major	Major
Capitaine-Commandant	N/A	N/A	N/A
Capitaine	Hauptmann	Captain	Captain
Lieutenant	Oberleutnant	First Lieutenant	First Lieutenant
Sous-Lieutenant	Leutnant	Second Lieutenant	Second Lieutenant
1er Sergent-Chef	Stabsfeldwebel	Master Sergeant	Master Sergeant
1er Sergent-Major	Oberfeldwebel	Technical Sergeant	Sergeant Major
1er Sergent	Feldwebel	Staff Sergeant	First Sergeant
Maréchal des Logis	Unterfeldwebel	Sergeant	Sergeant
Caporal	Unteroffizier (Oberjäger)	Corporal	Corporal
Brigadier	Gefreiter	Private First Class	Lance Corporal
Private	Obersoldat (Obergrenadier)	Private	Private
	Soldat (Grenadier)		

Prologue

In the darkest hours of 10 May 1940, forty-two Junkers Ju 52 transport aircraft, each towing a DFS 230 glider, took off from two airfields outside of Cologne in Germany and headed west. The Ju 52 pilots followed ground beacons, looking for a triple beacon on the Vetschauer Berg, about 5km north-west of Aachen and 1km from the Dutch border. Here they reached an altitude of 2,500m and uncoupled their towing tethers from the gliders, allowing them to drift silently to their intended targets. This part of the operation required silence during the flight, the main reason gliders were chosen for this ultra-secret mission. Having no radar capability at the time, the Belgian and Dutch armies used ground listening stations to detect the presence of enemy aircraft overhead, but on this night they heard nothing that set off any alarms. The 2-ton gliders, each carrying eight to ten men, drifted on the wind towards four objectives: three bridges spanning the Albert Canal west of Maastricht, and what was described as the most powerful fortress in the world, Fort Eben-Emael.

German victory in the West depended on a rapid advance into Belgium. German infantry and armoured units of Sixth Army needed to quickly cross the Meuse River and the Albert Canal and establish a bridgehead in Belgian territory. The bridges had to be seized in an undamaged condition in order to sustain the rapid pace of the invasion force. There were two problems: the bridges could be blown up by the Belgians at a moment's notice, and the crossing sites were in range of the guns of Fort Eben-Emael. Ground forces would first have to cross 30km of Dutch territory, then the Meuse River at Maastricht, then advance through the sizeable defended city before they even reached the canal bridges. It was a certainty that the Belgians and Dutch would blow up the bridges over both waterways long before the Germans arrived. Their forces would then become bogged down, giving the Allies time to move up additional troops and attempt to block their advance into central Belgium. The only way to avoid this outcome was to launch a surprise attack by Special Forces to seize the bridges before they could be destroyed, and to take out the guns and eyes of Fort Eben-Emael. An airborne operation was possible but would require engine-driven transports which could be detected by the listening posts. The Germans needed stealth and silence. The solution was a glider-borne task force.

VII *Flieger* (Airborne) Division, which had operational control of parachute and transport units, was ordered to look into the feasibility of using gliders for tactical missions. The Luftwaffe had in its inventory the DFS 230 assault glider, developed by the *Deutsche Forschungsanstalt für Segelflug* (German Research Institute for Sailplane Flight). The DFS 230 could carry ten men plus explosive charges and equipment. The glider troops did not have to struggle with parachutes after landing so they could organize on the ground more quickly than paratroopers. Test results were positive and concluded that, to reach the Belgian targets, the gliders had to be released by the transports at an altitude of 2,500m over German territory. They would then cruise at an air speed of 120kph and arrive high enough over the targets to remain undetected and to descend in a spiral to their landing points. A surprise attack on the canal bridges and Fort Eben-Emael was now possible. The operation received Adolf Hitler's blessing.

On 3 November 1939, *Sturmabteilung* (Storm Division) Koch, a top-secret unit, was assembled to plan and train for the operation. It was made up of the 1st Company of 1st Parachute Regiment, one parachute engineer platoon, and the experimental troop-carrying glider detachment. No one knew the true purpose of the unit; not even the members were informed of the target. Hitler's directive ordered the task force to conduct the following mission:

1. In a surprise attack, seize intact the Albert Canal bridges at Veldwezelt, Vroenhoven, and Canne, and hold them until ground forces arrived; and
2. Silence Fort Eben-Emael by destroying the guns in the artillery casemates and turrets, and its observation capabilities.

Intelligence operations revealed that the gliders could land very close to the bridges at Veldwezelt and Vroenhoven, but no closer than 200m to the Canne Bridge. The gliders could easily land in the open space on top of Fort Eben-Emael. Gliders could not land close enough to the Meuse bridges at Maastricht because the area was too built up. Other Special Forces units would be called upon to seize the bridges at Maastricht.

Sturmabteilung Koch was organized as follows:

- Veldwezelt Bridge – Operation *Stahl* (Steel) – Ten gliders, 92 men, led by Oberleutnant Altmann.
- Vroenhoven – Operation *Beton* (Concrete) – Eleven gliders, 117 men, led by Oberleutnant Schacht.

- Canne – Operation *Eisen* (Ice) – Ten gliders, 92 men, led by Oberleutnant Schächter.
- Eben-Emael – Operation *Granit* (Granite) – Eleven gliders, 84 men, led by Leutnant Witzig.

The mission of the Veldwezelt, Vroenhoven and Canne glider teams was to move directly to and seize the control bunkers at each bridge where they would find and dismantle the demolitions detonators, then defend the bridges against Belgian counter-attacks until the arrival of German reinforcements. Each glider destined for Fort Eben-Emael had its own objective on top of the fort, primarily the turrets, casemates and observation cloches. Pioneer teams were tasked with moving directly from the glider to the target and placing explosive charges to destroy the objective. If the mission was successful each team had secondary missions.

Sixth Army was commanded by Generalfeldmarschall Walter von Reichenau. His Chief of Staff was Generalmajor Friedrich Paulus, future commander of Sixth Army during the Battle of Stalingrad. Sixth Army was subordinate to *Heeresgruppe* (Army Group) B, commanded by Generalfeldmarschall Fedor von Bock. The mission of Sixth Army was to move out from the region of Aachen into Belgium and the Netherlands, cross the Meuse and Albert Canal, and tie up Allied armies in the centre of Belgium. 4th Panzer Division, led by Generalleutnant Johann Joachim Stever, was subordinate to Sixth Army and led the advance through Dutch territory. *Kampfgruppe* (Battle Group) A, commanded by Oberstleutnant Hans Mikosch, consisting of 51st Pioneer Battalion and 2nd Battalion of 151st Infantry Regiment, was tasked with crossing the Canne Bridge and relieving the glider teams on Eben-Emael. German infantry, artillery and pioneer units would follow the vanguard and lay siege to the remaining eleven forts of Liège.

Objectives of the initial attack:

1. 100th *Bataillon zur Besonderen Verwendung* (Special Purpose Battalion) to capture the three bridges over the Meuse at Maastricht.
2. *Sturmabteilung* Koch to capture the bridges of Veldwezelt, Vroenhoven and Canne, and silence Fort Eben-Emael.
3. *Kampfgruppe* A to relieve troops on the surface of Fort Eben-Emael and complete the capture of the fort – relief troops expected to arrive six hours after the commencement of the assault.
4. 4th Panzer Division to form and enlarge the bridgeheads of Veldwezelt, Vroenhoven and Canne.
5. VIII *Fliegerkorps* to provide air support.

Mission details:

Objective 1: Capture the Maastricht bridges. Because the bridges could not be captured by gliders or paratroops, the 100th Special Purpose Battalion, a unit of the Counter-intelligence Service, was instructed to take the Meuse River bridges at Maastricht in a surprise raid and prevent their destruction.

Objective 2: Capture the bridges of Veldwezelt, Vroenhoven and Canne, and Fort Eben-Emael.

Objective 3: Relief of troops at the fort: 151st Infantry Regiment, reinforced by 51st Pioneer Battalion, was scheduled to march on the first line of 4th Panzer Division, and upon reaching Maastricht, head south towards Canne and Eben-Emael.

Objective 4: Enlargement of the bridgeheads to begin by 1000hrs.

Objective 5: Aerial support of *Sturmabteilung* Koch to begin 15 minutes after the landings to maintain the element of surprise. Support would last for 60 minutes by which time additional troops would arrive and support would shift to field artillery batteries.

Fall Gelb, or Case Yellow, the invasion of France and the Low Countries, was set to begin on 10 May 1940. At noon on 9 May *Sturmabteilung* Koch received the alert to prep for the operation. During the afternoon the men were taken to the airfields of Ostheim and Butzweiler, the former located 3.5km south-east of Cologne on the east bank of the Rhine and the latter 3.5km north-west of Cologne. The layout of the two airfields permitted forty-two Ju 52s to take off at intervals of 45 seconds; thirty-one tow trains from two runways at Ostheim carrying the men from *Granit*, *Eisen* and *Beton*, and eleven from Butzweiler carrying the *Stahl* team. Four Junkers were in reserve. The squadrons needed 25 minutes to take off and assemble in the air and 31 minutes for the steep climb to an altitude of 2500m. The distance from Cologne to the canal was about 90km. Two separate routes marked the path from Cologne to Aachen, one with rotating beacons, the other with 60cm searchlights, six markers in all along the 73km route to the release point. The gliders would be released from the tow planes when the pilots spotted the terminal beacon – a cluster of three lights – on the Vetschauer Berg. From there the gliders would then travel the remaining 28km over Dutch Limburg. Landing time was scheduled for 0525hrs (0425hrs Belgian time), 90 minutes before sunrise.

At 2105hrs, a rope was unrolled behind each Ju 52 and attached to the DFS 230. After midnight the teams loaded up their designated aircraft and at precisely 0325hrs the Junkers began to move down the runway. Fifteen minutes later all eighty-four aircraft (transports and gliders) were airborne. Weather conditions were good. The ground beacons were switched on, leading the way to the release point. Two of the gliders, one carrying Witzig, leader of the *Granit* group, lost contact with the main group at some point during the flight. The Ju 52 towing Witzig's glider became uncoupled from the glider over Aachen when it was forced to avoid hitting a faster aircraft. Witzig's glider was too low to fly long enough to reach Eben-Emael so the pilot turned back towards Cologne. Fortunately Witzig commandeered one of the reserve Ju 52s and resumed the flight. His arrival at Eben-Emael was delayed by two hours.

At 0032hrs (Belgian time), while Koch's men were loading up the gliders and making final preparations, Fort Eben-Emael received the war alert order from Belgian III Corps. Eben-Emael's commander, Major Jean Jottrand was called at his residence and directed to report to the fort. Jottrand, with more of an administrative than combat background in the Belgian army, was sceptical, suspecting it was probably another of many false alarms that had taken place over the past few months. He reported quickly to the fort but until he was sure there was an actual and confirmed danger to the fort, hesitated to take immediate defensive action which, to be fair, was quite drastic and final, and included ordering the demolition of the Canne bridge and the Lanaye locks, evacuating the peacetime barracks and setting up anti-tank obstacles to block access to the fort. At 0300hrs Jottrand received the confirmation message he was waiting for that German ground units were moving west. Observers also reported the sound of heavy gunfire coming from the north. Emergency actions were thus put into effect, but the demolition of the bridge and the locks was delayed. Soon after the alert message was received the command post switched on the fort's warning siren that echoed throughout the tunnels.

The mission of Eben-Emael's two MG blocs, Mi-Nord and Mi-Sud, was to defend against an infantry attack against the top of the fort. The likelihood of that taking place was just about zero, so the crews of the two blocs were sent to assist in the process of evacuating the external wooden barracks, located just outside the entrance to the fort. This included moving supplies and bunks into the fort and then setting fire to the barracks to remove cover for enemy infantry. The crew of the twin 75mm turret designated as *Cupola Nord* (North Gun Turret), was tasked at some point with firing a series of warning shots using blank shells in all directions to alert Belgian infantry troops stationed along the canal of an impending attack. However, the *Cupola Nord* crew was also helping to evacuate the barracks. Jottrand ordered *Cupola Sud* (South Gun Turret) to fire the warning shots but in the process, the guns malfunctioned and they were unable to fire until after 0300hrs.

The men not on duty were awakened by the sirens and immediately proceeded to their assigned posts or were given other duties to perform. The gun crews, while placing the turret and casemate guns into combat mode, encountered a number of delays and problems. The 75mm rounds were stored in magazines on the intermediate level of the fort. The shells were stored in caissons which needed to be moved into small elevators and delivered to the turrets and casemates on the surface. There was nothing extraordinary about this but it took a considerable amount of time to complete the delivery so that each gun position would have a sufficient supply of shells ready to fire. The *Cupola Nord* crew was finally relieved of the detail at the outer barracks. Upon arrival at the bloc around 0400hrs they ran into an immediate problem. The door to the shell storage magazine at the base of the bloc was locked and they could not find the custodian to give them the key. After the door was finally opened, the elevator loaded with the first caissons failed to move. The shells then had to be carried by hand up the stairs to the bloc. There was no sense of panic at this point. As far as the Belgians knew, the Germans were hours away so there was plenty of time to prepare for their arrival, or so they thought. In reality the gliders were now soaring silently over Dutch territory, ready to begin their final descent.

As they approached the four targets the gliders dropped to an altitude of 300m. Belgian troops along the Albert Canal could hear the Dutch anti-aircraft guns firing in the distance. They started to see strange shadows overhead but weren't exactly sure what they were looking at. Some of the men fired into the air with rifles but didn't cause any damage. Just before 0425hrs, Jottrand was standing outside the entrance to the fort to see how the movement of supplies from the outer barracks was proceeding when he spotted the outline of an aircraft circling the fort and realized it intended to land on top. There was now no doubt in his mind whatsoever that Belgium, and Fort Eben-Emael, was under attack. He immediately ran inside to the command post and ordered the demolition of the Canne bridge and the Lanaye locks. *Sturmgruppe Granit* had arrived.

Chapter 1

10 and 11 May 1940:
The Tragedy of Fort Eben-Emael

Fort Eben-Emael was built between 1932 and 1935 at a cost of 24 million francs. The fort was located 200m from the Dutch border, east of the village of Eben-Emael. It was 17km north of the *Citadelle de Liège*, on the western edge of the *Montagne Saint-Pierre*, also known as the Caestert Plateau (Caster in French) situated between the Albert Canal and the Geer Creek. The fort was triangular in shape. The canal, built between 1930 and 1939, was cut through the middle of the mountain, to create the *Tranchée de Caster*, which conveniently served as a deep 800m-long moat along the eastern edge of the fort. The canal was 3.5m deep and is currently 100m wide.[1] The southern flank of the fort consisted of an anti-tank ditch that ran about 400m from the canal bank to Bloc 5, then 350m to Bloc 6, and finally 115m to Bloc 1. The ditch's counterscarp was formed by a steep slope that angled downwards to a flat floor that ran across the base of the ditch to a concrete wall on the escarp side. The ditch casemates were built into that wall. The west flank of the fort consisted of a steep slope about 800m long that ran from Bloc 1, through Bloc 2, then above a water-filled ditch to the canal bank. The fort's surface area was 75 hectares, 45 of which comprised the superstructure.

Fort Eben-Emael was built in an excellent location from which it primarily covered the Visé gap 6km to the south, and the canal bridges at Canne (1.7km), Vroenhoven (4.3km) and Veldwezelt (7.25km) to the north. Belgium had no control of the Meuse bridges at Maastricht but Eben-Emael's guns were in range and the commander of the fort had the go-ahead from the Belgian High Command to destroy them if necessary. Fort Eben-Emael added a significant degree of protection north of Liège that was missing in 1914. Its guns could reach as far as the Liège forts of Barchon, Pontisse and Aubin-Neufchâteau, and well into the south-west salient of The Netherlands. The Belgian 7th Infantry Division guarded the roads leading into Belgium from the Albert Canal crossings. 2nd Carabinier Regiment defended the section between the Gellik Railway Bridge and Veldwezelt (a 4km-long sector).

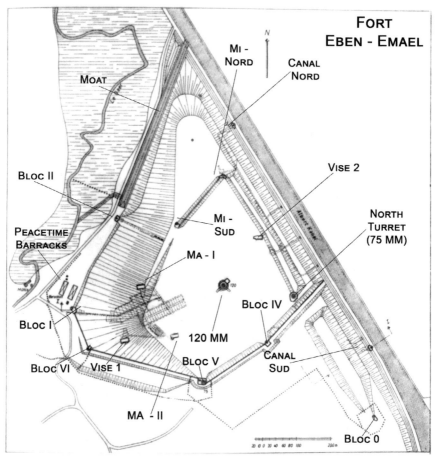

Plan of Fort Eben-Emael. (Denkschrift)

18th Infantry Regiment defended Vroenhoven Bridge and 2nd Grenadier Regiment was positioned to defend Canne. The bunkers built into the bridges themselves were guarded by the Frontier Cyclists Battalion. The *Chasseurs Ardennais* were in reserve.

The fort was organized into two batteries:

- Battery 1, commanded by Captain G. Vamecq, included the gun turrets and the artillery casemates.
- Battery 2, commanded by Captain Alfred Hagermans, included the defensive (infantry) bunkers.

Combat Blocs Assigned to Each Battery

Battery 1:

- **120mm Bloc**: artillery bloc with a non-retractable,[2] rotating turret with twin 120mm long-range guns (range 17.5km). The bloc was located in the centre of the superstructure and its approaches were defended by the machine-gun (MG) blocs (see below).
- *Cupole Sud* – South Turret – see Bloc 5 below.
- *Cupole Nord* – North Turret: artillery bloc with retractable turret for twin 75mm Model 1934 guns. Included an infantry patrol exit defended by an automatic rifle/light machine gun called the *Fusil-Mitrailleur* (FM), similar to the American Browning Automatic Rifle.
- **Maastricht-1** (Ma-1) and **Maastricht-2** (Ma-2) and **Visé-1** (Vi-1) and **Visé-2** (Vi-2): Four identical artillery casemates, each with three 75mm GP (*Grande Portée* – long range) guns (field of fire 70° and range of 11km). Ma-1 and Ma-2 covered the north in the direction of Maastricht; Vi-1 and Vi-2 in the direction of Visé to the south. An artillery observation cloche (in the shape of a bell or cloche) designated **EBEN 3** was built on top of Ma-2. The cloche was equipped with a periscope that could be raised and lowered through a hole in the top of the cloche, much like a submarine periscope.

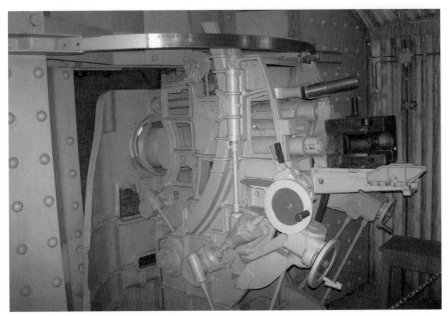

75mm gun in Maastricht-1 at Fort Eben-Emael. (Bunkerfreaks Antwerpen)

Battery 2:

- **Bloc 1**: this was the main entrance to the fort. The bloc also defended the approaches from the west and the intervals between Blocs 2 and 6. The entry postern was defended by an iron gate and a drawbridge that rolled laterally into a pocket off to the side, and by an internal blockhouse equipped with an FM. An observation cloche on top of the bloc provided a view of the approaches to the fort and in the direction of Blocs 2 and 6. Armaments included two 60mm anti-tank (AT) guns, one covering the approaches, the other towards Bloc 2; three twin Maxim MGs mounted on reversible carriages. The MGs were paired in sets of two and the reversible carriage allowed the guns to be swapped over to prevent one barrel from overheating. One set of MGs was on the lower level and pointed in the direction of Bloc 6, and two on the upper level, one towards Bloc 2 and the other the approaches, the FM in the blockhouse guarded the entry, and there were two searchlights to light up the outside of the bloc.
- **Bloc 2**: guarded the western side of the fort and the water-filled ditch. It crossed fire with Bloc 1 and included an observation cloche and an exit door for patrols on the Bloc 1 side. An interior blockhouse with FM guarded the exit. Armament pointed in two directions, towards Bloc 1 and towards the moat and included two 60mm AT guns, two twin MGs and two searchlights.
- **Bloc 3**: The fort did not have a Bloc 3. Reason unknown.
- *Bloc Canal Nord*: built into the cliff face below the fort along the canal. This bloc guarded the canal in the direction of Canne and Lanaye. It was equipped with one 60mm AT gun in the lower level pointing towards Canne, three twin MGs, one on the lower level pointing towards Lanaye and two in the upper level pointing in both directions, and a cloche with FM.
- *Bloc Canal Sud*: same configuration as *Bloc Canal Nord* but the 60mm gun pointed towards Lanaye. This bloc was destroyed after the war when the canal was widened.
- **Bloc 4**: a casemate that guarded the anti-tank ditch on the south flank of the fort between the canal and Bloc 5. Included an observation cloche. Armament included two 60mm AT guns, two twin MGs and two searchlights. The guns and searchlights pointed along the ditch in both direction.
- **Bloc 5 – *Coupole Sud*** (South Turret): between Blocs 4 and 6, on the extreme southern angle of the anti-tank ditch. It was unique in that it

Looking north along the Albert Canal in the Caster Trench. Eben-Emael's Bloc Canal Sud is on the left. Additional Cointet gates, like the ones on the left, would have blocked the canal road. ((Digital History Archive, German Military Study P-203)

also included a 75mm Model 34 turret that could fire in all directions – this turret was considered part of Battery 1. An observation cloche kept watch over the ditch approaches. Armaments included one retractable 75mm FRC (*Fonderie Royale des Canons*) Model 34 twin gun turret, one 60mm AT gun pointed towards Bloc 6, one twin MG and one searchlight.

- **Bloc 6**: a casemate located along the anti-tank ditch that defended the approaches to the fort in the direction of Bloc 1, with an observation cloche on top and an emergency exit. Armament included two 60mm AT guns, one twin MG and one searchlight.
- *Bloc Mitrailleuse Mi-Nord* (MG bloc): a casemate located on the superstructure equipped with MG to defend against an attack taking place on top of the fort. Its armoured cloche served as an artillery observation post, designated **EBEN 2**. The bloc included an infantry patrol exit defended by an FM in an internal blockhouse. Armament included three twin MGs, one pointed towards Canne, the other two to the south, and two searchlights.
- **Bloc Mi-Sud**: the same mission as Mi-Nord, with a regular observation cloche, three twin MGs, and three searchlights.

- **Bloc O-1** (Observation): This enormous bloc was located outside the perimeter of the fort but was connected to it by an underground tunnel. It perched on top of the cliff overlooking the canal, the Lanaye locks and the Meuse River. It included an artillery observation cloche with periscope, designated **EBEN 1**. Armament included one 60mm AT gun pointed in the direction of the locks, three twin MGs pointing north, south and east, and two searchlights

To guard against an attack by paratroopers or aerial bombardment, four anti-aircraft (AA) gun positions were located on top of the fort, in the open between Bloc 4 and the North Turret. The four gun pits were equipped with Maxim 08/15s, First World War-era model MGs. Protection for the AA gun crews was weak, consisting of sandbag parapets.

Finally, two external observation posts fell under the command of Eben-Emael:

- *Abri* O: equipped with a 47mm AT gun and a machine gun, to defend the Canne Bridge. The detonator to blow up the bridge was located here. Permission to blow the bridge came from the commander of Eben-Emael.
- *Abri* PL 19, armed with a machine gun only, was located on the hill between Hallembaye and Loën, 1.5km west of the canal.[3]

Interior of the Fort

The ground level of the fort (same level as the Geer Valley) was 60m below the surface of the plateau. The main entrance to the fort (Bloc 1 – see above) was on this level. The entry postern led to a 200m-long corridor that headed east to the troop support facilities (barracks, latrines, kitchen, etc.) and the power plant, ventilation, water storage and supply rooms. A set of stairs at the end of the corridor, protected by a set of airlock doors, led up to the intermediate level of the fort.

The intermediate level was about 40m below the surface and included 4km of tunnels. All of the combat blocs located on the surface of the fort were accessible by staircase from this level. Munitions storage rooms were located below each combat bloc. A vertical shaft housed two small elevators to move the ammunition caissons to the combat blocs. The elevators were surrounded by a spiral metal staircase with about 100 to 120 steps. If the enemy accessed the interior of the fort through one of the combat blocs and attempted to penetrate to the lower levels, a system was in place at the base of the stairs to block access to the main tunnel system. The entrance to each bloc and to the staircase and elevator was defended by a double set of two armoured doors. A concrete column with slots was placed between the two sets of doors. Steel beams could be dropped into the slots to provide additional protection. Sandbags were loaded between the beam barricade and the doors to create an impenetrable barrier.

Three *Bureau de Coordination des Tirs* – artillery and infantry command posts – were located at this level, one for the turrets, one for the casemates and one for the close-range defence blocs. There was also a central command post with telephone switchboard and a radio room for use by the commander of the fort.

The turrets, casemates and MG blocs were located on the surface of the fort. Movement of the turrets was driven by electric motors and hydraulics. Each turret bloc had bunk rooms for the troops and an additional munitions storage room. The 75mm casemates consisted of two levels, the upper level for the guns, the lower for the troops and for storage. The air to and from the turret blocs and casemates could be kept in suppression by a ventilator, causing the smoke from the guns to be forced outside through the gun barrels.

The surface area of the fort was not protected by barbed wire or land mines or ditches in front of the casemates to keep attackers away from the embrasures and exit doors. This would prove to be a major omission on 10 May 1940.

* * *

When the alert sounded at 30 minutes past midnight on 10 May 1940, Warrant Officer Dieudonné Longdoz, the chief of the anti-aircraft machine gun (*Mitrailleuse Contre-Avion* – Mi-CA – hereinafter referred to as AA) crews, appeared in the barracks to notify the men that this was a 'real alert'. In the corridors of the fort, the alert sirens wailed. The men murmured among themselves, no one really believing this was the 'real thing'; more likely another false alarm like the previous ones. But then Commander Van der Auwera, second-in-command of Eben-Emael, arrived and confirmed that it was really war.

The crews of the four AA positions were initially tasked with helping to evacuate the wooden barracks located outside of the fort. Furniture, administrative and personnel documents, food, beds, everything needed to be moved inside the fort. The crews of Mi-Nord and Mi-Sud were also part of the barracks work detail, which would have serious consequences in the hours to come. Everywhere, officers and soldiers were rushing to their assigned posts, or wherever they were told to go, and the activity was intense. The barbed wire network was inspected and damaged areas were repaired; previously-prepared *chevaux-de-frise* and anti-tank tetrahedrons were moved into place to block access to the entrance.

It was still calm outside the fort and there was no sound or light coming from the nearby village of Eben-Emael. Everything seemed like normal. Warrant Officer Longdoz left his men to go inside to get them something to eat. Suddenly, a loud bang like thunder tore through the silence of the night. All eyes shifted to Bloc 5 as the 75mm guns of the south turret fired warning shots in all four directions, twenty rounds in total. There was no longer any doubt: war had come. The time was 0325hrs.

The AA crews finished their job at the barracks and, carrying their bulky personal equipment, began the trek up the hill behind Bloc 1 to the top of the fort to the four machine guns. During the firing of the warning shots, some of the brush surrounding the south turret caught fire. Maréchal des Logis Franco, Brigadier Boussier and Private Paque put out the fire and, while returning to the fort's entrance, bumped into the AA crews heading up to the top. A few friendly words and 'Good lucks' were exchanged. The gunners arrived at their posts. Four gun positions were carved into the corners of a square, 25m on each side. The AA guns were mounted on tripods in each of the four gun pits. There was also a small shelter in the centre reserved for the warrant officer and telephone operator. The shelter

A twin 75mm turret, this one at Bloc 4 of Fort Battice. The viewing port is in the centre. (Bunkerfreaks Antwerpen)

also served as a storage place for the men's personal gear, two spare machine guns and reserve ammunition.

A little after 0400hrs Longdoz phoned the duty officer inside the fort to announce '*Mi prêtes*' – machine guns ready. The men now waited. For what, they had no idea. Bombers? Recon aircraft? Large puddles of mist covered the ground. In their gun pits, the soldiers kept their eyes peeled on the night sky, sunrise still two hours away. Gun No. 1 was manned by Joseph Morelle, Jean Frédéric, Joseph Parmentier, Pierre Pasques and Pierre Pire. Around the second weapon stood Robert Servais, Léon Sluismans, Arthur Willems, Marcel Seret and Emile Prévôt. Charles Antoine, José Pairoux, Auguste Reichert and Georges Kips manned the third gun. Finally, René Fonbonne, Marcel Boîte and Adrien Heine were in the last pit. Warrant Officer Albert Remy manned the phone in the shelter. The time was 0425hrs.

Suddenly, against the dark sky, a shadow filled the air over the fort, but it was impossible to determine what the men were seeing. Then someone shouted: 'Aircraft are overhead. Their engines have stopped! They stand motionless in the air.' And the German gliders were there, about 250m above the fort. Another man shouted: 'Nine gray shapes with no distinctive markings, swooped down in large circles like vultures.' Major Jottrand, from the mouth of the postern, spotted the gliders making their turns and asked Captain Hotermans why the AA guns were not firing. The telephone rang on top of the fort in the AA shelter. Remy picked it up and handed it to Longdoz. It was Captain Hotermans:

Hotermans: 'Longdoz, what's going on?'
Longdoz: 'Planes are flying over the fort.'
Hotermans: 'Can you identify them?'
Longdoz: 'No.'
Hotermans: 'What are you going to do?'
Longdoz: 'I'm going to shoot.'

Longdoz rushed outside and blew loudly on a shrill whistle, the signal to open fire. There was no hesitation and dozens of strings of tracer bullets immediately flew from the gun barrels towards the enemy aircraft. They appeared to be everywhere; the sky full. The MG fire was sporadic. Weapons jammed and the gliders were already starting to land. One landed near the *Cupola Nord* bloc. Another soared in and landed right next to the AA position, so close that its left wing clipped gun No. 3, knocking it over. The gunner, Charles Antoine, had only enough time to flatten himself in the bottom of the gun pit. The plane continued to slide and then came to a stop. The aircraft door flew off and German troops emerged. The surprise was complete.

* * *

The Albert Canal was considered the key to keeping an enemy from breaking out of Dutch Limburg. The defences included bunkers built into the bridges and flanking bunkers between the bridges on the Belgian side of the canal. If the enemy got past Maastricht, the brunt of the attack would have to be absorbed at the first three bridges above Fort Eben-Emael – Canne, Vroenhoven and Veldwezelt. Bunker M at Vroenhoven and Bunker N at Veldwezelt were built next to and guarded the road leading across each bridge. They were equipped with 47mm AT guns, machine guns and searchlights. The bridge piers were mined with dynamite and the detonators were located in Bunkers M and N. Bunkers A, B, B', C, and D flanked Vroenhoven and Veldwezelt. Bunker C was built into Veldwezelt's support pier, eighty steps below the road. Bunkers E and F flanked Canne and Bunker O, built on a hill at Opcanne overlooking the bridge, defended the bridge directly. It was also equipped with a 47mm AT gun and machine gun.

Bunkers M and N were connected by telephone to the army barracks at Lanaken via overhead cables. Captain Giddelo of the Border Cyclists was

Veldwezelt Bridge over the Albert Canal, taken from the Netherlands towards Belgium. (Digital History Archive, 'Bunkers of the Blitzkrieg')

stationed at the barracks and had the authority to grant permission to blow the two upper bridges. If the detonations failed, Giddelo had a direct line to Fort Eben-Emael, which would then destroy the bridges with its guns.

Troops of the 2nd Carabinier Regiment at Veldwezelt Bridge heard the warning shots from the south turret and went straight away to connect the demolition detonators. Corporal Cornée was responsible for setting off the charges. The radioman, Private Gustaaf Van Driessche, thought it was best to destroy the bridge right away, but the rest of the crew thought it best to wait for permission from Captain Giddelo. To blow the bridge for a false alarm would be unforgivable.

At Vroenhoven Bridge, Sergeant Crauwels, responsible for destroying that bridge, left his bunker to gaze at the spectacle of the arrival of the gliders. By the time someone started firing up at them, the first glider teams had already landed.

*   *   *

The AA position at Eben-Emael was quickly overrun by Germans pouring out of the glider. Grenades were exploding and mixed with bursts from MP 38 sub-machine guns. A German leapt over the top of the parapet of gun pit 4 and fired on the Belgians at point-blank range. The three occupants of the position were hit. Marcel Boîte was hit twice but fled in the direction of the fort to report what was happening. René Fonbonne was taken prisoner and Adrien Heine was left for dead at the bottom of his trench. The communications shelter was machine-gunned and Longdoz came crawling out. Remy was killed. The tragedy at the AA position quickly came to an end, but the agony of the fort was just beginning.

Glider Team 5, commanded by Feldwebel Erwin Haug, was assigned to destroy what was designated by the *Sturmabteilung* planners as 'Objective 29', the anti-aircraft guns above Bloc 4, and as we have seen, that objective was swiftly dealt with. Team 5 then moved on to its secondary objective, the observation cloche of Bloc 4. A shaped charge blew a hole in the top, killing the observer, Private Furnelle.

Granit's Glider Team 8 was actually the first to arrive at Eben-Emael. At 300m altitude the glider began to fly in a large circle to shed height and landed at 0424hrs, 30m from 'Objective 31', *Cupola Nord*. The squad leader was Oberjäger Karl Unger. He and two of his team, Bruno Hooge and Ernst Hierlaender, moved swiftly out of the aircraft and ran to the turret with their explosive charges.[4] Unfortunately, *Cupola Nord* had not yet received its provision of *boîtes-à-balles* (case shot for close-range targets) shells, otherwise it could have swept the surface and pinned down the approaching pioneers. But no one was expecting to have to use close-range weapons at this early stage. High-explosive rounds, mostly ineffective at this range, were quickly delivered to the gun chamber but by then it was too late. As the turret started its vertical movement into the battery position a powerful explosion blew a hole through the turret cap, destroying the two guns and the turret controls and causing severe injury to the crew. The blast was caused by the explosion of a 50kg shaped charge. Its powerful downward force blew a hole through the thick steel. The turret was out of action less than two minutes after the glider landed. A 12.5kg shaped charge was placed against the outer door of the combat bloc's infantry exit. The ensuing explosion blew the door off and caused large chunks of concrete to fall into the opening. The bloc's FM, located in a blockhouse facing the door, continued to fire and the Germans were unable to knock it out. However, at 0445hrs Jottrand ordered the evacuation of the bloc. The Belgians rushed down the stairs and the airlock doors at the foot of the bloc were closed and sealed with steel beams and sandbags. The Germans did not pursue to the lower level.

Leutnant Egon Delica's Glider Team 1 attacked 'Objective 18', Maastricht-2, whose guns, along with Ma-1, were pointed in the direction of the three other glider landing sites to the north. The glider landed cleanly

75mm turret at Fort Eben-Emael damaged by a shaped charge. (Bunkerfreaks Antwerpen)

in an open area between Ma-2 and the 120mm turret bloc at 0425hrs. The observers at post EBEN 3 atop Ma-2 did not see the Germans until they were on top of the bloc and had placed a shaped charge on the cloche. The concentrated downward explosion of the shaped charge blew a hole in the top of the cloche, sending steel splinters into the space below and blowing the inside of the cloche to bits. Both observers were killed. A 12.5kg conventional charge was placed in the embrasure of the first 75mm gun. The explosion blew the gun off of its carriage and sent it flying into the back of the gun chamber. The hole in the embrasure caused by the explosion was 60cm x 60cm, large enough for a man to crawl through. The Germans peered inside and as the smoke cleared, could see bodies lying on the floor. Privates Philippe and Férrire were dead and Corporal Verbois wounded. Gunners at the remaining guns were also thrown against the rear wall and were wounded or stunned. As the wounded were being attended to, another explosion blew up the barrel of the second gun. The rest of the bloc's crew were ordered by Sergeant Poncelet to evacuate to the lower level. They were followed inside and down the stairs by the pursuing Germans. The lower airlock doors and access to the intermediate level were quickly sealed by Poncelet's men.

Glider Team 3's 'Objective 12' was Maastricht-1. The glider landed 25m from it. Oberjäger Peter Arent was in command. Once again the bloc's three 75mm gun embrasures were the main target. A 50kg charge proved to be too large to fit across the embrasure of gun No. 1 so it was substituted with a 12.5kg charge which was placed against the steel collar of the embrasure. The charge exploded with the same effect as at Ma-2, blowing a hole in the embrasure and wounding the crew inside. The heavy gun was torn from its carriage and flew across the casemate, killing Private Borman before it came to rest in the stairwell. The blast ignited the propellant charges of the 75mm shells, filling the casemate with thick black smoke. The remaining crew, facing more explosions, grenades and German sub-machine gun fire, fled down to the lower level. Arent climbed inside the casemate through the newly-blasted hole. Except for some wounded men, the casemate was clear. Arent came to the staircase and from below, he could hear the Belgians making their way back up the stairs, so he threw another charge down the stairwell. The blast stopped the Belgians but at the same time, knocked his own men, fortunately unharmed, onto the floor of the casemate.

As soon as Glider Team 9 landed the men headed for Mi-Sud ('Objective 13'). Oberjäger Ewald Neuhaus had to cut through barbed wire to get to the bloc, which appeared to be abandoned. The crew of the bloc had been helping to evacuate the outer barracks, but just minutes after the gliders were spotted the crew moved up to the bloc and started firing the MGs.

Ernst Schlosser, one of the German squad members, fired his flamethrower at the MG embrasure and the firing stopped. A 12.5kg charge was then placed against the embrasure. The Belgians spotted the charge and pushed it to the ground where it exploded. More charges were placed and finally the Germans were successful in blowing up the embrasure. A 50kg shaped charge blew in the top of the observation cloche. Grenades were tossed inside and any Belgians still capable of doing so headed down the stairs. Neuhaus posted guards and headed for his secondary target, the north end of the fort, where additional turret blocs were located, or so it seemed.

Team 6, led by Oberjäger Siegfried Harlos, and Team 7, led by Oberjäger Fritz Heinemann, were tasked with attacking the two northernmost turret blocs, 'Objectives 14 and 16', which appeared to be twin 120mm guns like the centre bloc. After landing, the teams cut through the barbed wire with Bangalore torpedoes and headed for the two blocs. It didn't take long for Harlos and Heinemann to discover that the armoured turrets in the northern angle of the fort were actually light metal decoys. A third decoy was uncovered in the southern sector of the fort. The Belgian ruse had worked, but had no effect on the overall result.

Glider Team 4's 'Objective 19' was Mi-Nord. The EBEN 2 observation post was located on top of the bloc. The glider landed 80m from the target. During his approach, Oberfeldwebel Helmut Wenzel, the team commander, noticed that the gun embrasures were still shuttered. Only a few of the

Looking down on the Bloc Mi-Nord at Eben-Emael. The embrasures in the facade were destroyed and a shaped charge placed on the cloche. The insert shows the damage to the facade soon after the attack. (Fortif.BE collection and NARA (insert))

bloc's crew were present, having gone to the lower level of the bloc on their own initiative. The rest were still helping out with the evacuation of the external barracks. The observation cloche was manned by Privates Vossen and Bataille, who spotted the Germans approaching the bloc. There was a small opening in the top of the observation cloche for the periscope which was retracted when the Germans were spotted, so Wenzel, now on top of the bloc, dropped a small 1kg charge with a short fuse into the hole and it exploded, killing Vossen and Bataille. A 50kg shaped charge was then placed on top, completing the destruction of the cloche. A 12.5kg charge blew up the south-facing MG embrasure, followed by a 50kg charge to enlarge the hole made in it. Wenzel and some of his men moved inside. The block was full of smoke and the MG crew was dead. The searchlight was destroyed. At this point the phone inside the bloc rang and Wenzel picked up the receiver – why not? A voice on the other end spoke French, which Wenzel did not, but he succeeded in notifying the caller that the bloc was now occupied by Germans. The attackers then placed a signal flag on top of the captured bloc to let overflying German pilots know that the bloc was in German hands. They then set about securing the bloc from counter-attack. Mi-Nord, with an excellent view of the rest of the fort, became the German command post.

Leutnant Witzig commanded Glider Team 11 and, as we already know, the team did not make it to Eben-Emael with the task force. When the rest of *Granit* learned that Witzig had not arrived (several men were looking for him but couldn't find him), Feldwebel Wenzel took command of the operation. He established radio contact with Koch's command post at Vroenhoven Bridge and, after visiting some of the other blocs, gave his report to the *Sturmabteilung* commander.

Glider Team 2, led by Oberjäger Max Maier, also did not make it to Eben-Emael. Partway into the flight, the Ju 52's signal light flashed prematurely, indicating it was time to drop the tow line. The pilot of the DFS 230 did so, according to procedure but too far away to reach the fort. The glider landed in Holland and Team 2 joined 4th Panzer Division's advance to the west. Team 2's objective was to be the 120mm turret – 'Objective 23'. Inside the turret Sergeant René Cremer watched through the gun sight as the gliders landed. He requested permission to fire case shot and, after a short delay, was given permission but the munitions hoists malfunctioned. The heavy shells then had to be carried up to the turret by hand. Finally, just after the shells were delivered, the counterweight jammed and the turret was completely out of action without firing a shot. Visé 1 was also a target of Team 2. However, Team 10, led by Oberjäger Willie Hübel, in reserve, decided to attack it on their way to the Mi-Nord command post.

By 0435hrs, 10 minutes after the first glider landed, the fort was for all intents and purposes blinded and its weapons neutralized. Only Visé 2 and *Cupola Sud* could still fire. Around 0500hrs Major Jottrand finally got a clear picture of what was happening on the surface. He ordered a sortie to go out from Blocs 1 and 2 but the counter-attack was driven back by recently-arrived Stukas. Heinkel He 111s also dropped bombs on the men working between the barracks and Bloc 1. Jottrand telephoned the *Régiment de Forteresse de Liège* (RFL) and requested support from the adjacent forts. In a short while Forts Pontisse and Barchon began shelling the top of Eben-Emael.

Witzig's glider finally landed near Mi-Nord around 0800hrs. Wenzel met up with his commander and gave him the current situation. The men of *Granit* now needed to maintain control of the surface until the arrival of reinforcements, originally scheduled for 1000hrs but now running behind because of the destruction of the bridges over the Meuse at Maastricht. Until reinforcements arrived, *Granit* was responsible for making sure the Belgian guns were not repaired, and to repulse any Belgian counter-attacks. It would be a tough day for the Germans but the Belgian garrison, with no infantrymen, was ill-equipped to launch effective counter-attacks and were also in a state of shock at the suddenness and violence of the German attack.

In the afternoon Jottrand finally called 7th Infantry Division to request infantry troops for a counter-attack against the Germans. All they could spare was a small forty-man platoon from 2nd Grenadiers. The counter-attack was a debacle. A skirmish with a German patrol took place in the wooded embankment and the Grenadiers suffered some casualties. Another group of 100 to 125 men from the fort split up into three squads, led by Captain Hotermans and Lieutenants Levaque and Quintin, was sent out late in the afternoon by Major Jottrand. Levaque ordered his squad to head to Ma-1 but only seven men agreed to follow him. The small patrol was greeted with heavy German fire and retreated back down the side of the ridge to the fort. Jottrand ordered a new counter-attack to retake Ma-1 but the Stukas were now in command of the surface, and strafed Bloc 1, preventing any Belgian troops from leaving the fort. The time was 1830hrs.

Meanwhile, below Vi-1, which had been attacked earlier by Team 10, the Belgians blocked the airlock with steel beams and sandbags. Around 1000hrs Commandant Van der Auwera ordered Lieutenant Desloover, Maréchal des Logis Delcourt and two other men to retake the surface part of the bloc. The men removed the temporary barricades and ascended the stairwell only to find the casemate empty of German troops. Two of the 75mm guns were still functioning and the Belgians opened fire on the surface of the fort until 1700hrs. The guns were finally silenced when the Germans dropped 1kg charges into each barrel. The explosion drove the crew back to the lower level once and for all, where they remained behind the airlock barricades.

At some point, Oberjäger Arent of Team 3 had re-entered Ma-1 to escape the effects of Stuka bombs. He didn't hear any sounds coming from the lower level and decided to descend the stairs to see what was going on. Arent and two other men moved cautiously down to the intermediate level. The Belgians had removed some of the staircase landings to move equipment up and down the stairwell and this slowed the German descent. At the bottom they reached the blocked airlock doors and unable to proceed further, the men moved back up to the surface. Later that evening Arent went back down with one other man and set a 50kg shaped charge against the airlock door. The fuse was lit and the Germans raced back to the top. The explosion was devastating. It was successful in blowing away the first door, the sandbags and steel beams, plus the second door. The blast wave travelled down the tunnels, knocking over Belgian troops and containers of chlorine-based cleaning fluids, sending the odour of the caustic substance throughout the tunnels. The Belgians smelled the chlorine and, fearing they were under a poison gas attack, put on their gas masks. The blast also went in the opposite direction towards the surface, destroying the munitions elevator and the

The doorway at the base of Maastricht-1 at Eben-Emael blown apart by the 50kg shaped charge placed by Feldwebel Arent on 10 May. (Bunkerfreaks Antwerpen)

metal staircase. The lower level was no longer accessible from Ma-1, but the attack succeeded in sowing panic down below.

* * *

At 0420hrs, the ten gliders of Operation *Stahl* landed near Veldwezelt, four near the canal, one on the east bank and five along the Hasselt road. The Belgians quickly headed for cover in Bunker N and tried to contact Giddelo, but the line was dead. Four kilometres to the north, the Lanaken barracks were under Stuka attack and Giddelo had been killed. Cornée decided to go ahead and blow up the bridge on his own initiative but he was unable to carry out the action because, suddenly, German soldiers appeared. The bunker was sprayed by a flamethrower, the door was blown out and grenades and demolition charges were tossed in. Only one Belgian survived the attack. Bunker C, at the foot of Veldwezelt Bridge, was also breached using a shaped charge. Sixteen men inside, commanded by Sergeant Lemoine, were quickly captured. Most of the men were badly wounded. Veldwezelt Bridge was in German hands.

At 0415hrs, nine of the eleven Vroenhoven gliders of Operation *Beton* reached their target, coming under heavy AA and MG fire. Three landed on the east bank and one near the main Tongeren road. Sergeant Crauwels attempted to contact Lanaken barracks but failed. He called Eben-Emael but learned that they too were under attack. He took it upon himself to blow the bridge, despite protests from the other Belgians. He set the fuse and headed for the ladder to the lower level, but just at that moment the Germans blew open the door with a shaped charge, killing Crauwels and two other Belgians. The Germans stopped the detonation and Vroenhoven was in German hands.

There were no ideal landing spots close to the Canne Bridge. The men of Operation *Eisen* would have to land at a distance and head as quickly as possible to the bridge on foot. The gliders arrived at 0435hrs, behind schedule. One was hit by Belgian fire upon approach, one landed in the barbed wire, but that didn't matter because, while the gliders were still airborne the Belgians succeeded in blowing up the bridge.

Efforts to prevent demolition of the Meuse River bridges in Maastricht failed, causing the delay of forward elements of the ground attack from reaching the Albert Canal. The action to seize the bridges by the 100th Special Purpose Battalion commenced on time but the commandos were recognized as Germans and arrested at Borgharen and Heer. The bridges of the Meuse were blown by the Dutch around 0700hrs within sight of German troops.

At 1300hrs elements of 151st Infantry Regiment (IR) came in contact with the men of *Sturmabteilung* Koch at Veldwezelt and took over for the *Stahl* and *Beton* task forces by 2000hrs. *Kampfgruppe* A of 151 IR, consisting of 51st Pioneer Battalion and 2nd/151 IR, was tasked with crossing the Canne Bridge and relieving Eben-Emael. The task force arrived at the canal across from Canne in the evening. The glider troops still held the Belgian side of the collapsed bridge despite strong attacks from the 2nd Grenadiers on the heights above the canal. A couple of the *Eisen* glider teams were on the Belgian side of the bridge but were pinned down by the Belgians. It was still possible to cross the canal on the remains of the bridge but not in force. Oberstleutnant Hans Mikosch, commander of *Kampfgruppe* A, reviewing the situation from the Dutch side, decided to send 2nd Company of the Pioneers across the remains of the bridge to rendezvous with the *Eisen* team and enlarge the bridgehead. 1st and 3rd Companies would then proceed to Fort Eben-Emael. Mikosch ordered a small squad, led by Oberfeldwebel Portsteffen to paddle across the canal but the boats were hit by the guns from Canal Nord and forced back to the east bank. Witzig, waiting on top of the fort and witnessing the crossing attempt, sent a squad led by Feldwebel Harlos to lower explosives in front of the embrasures to block the viewing ports. This was partially successful, diminishing the intensity of fire coming from the bloc but no further attempts would be made that night to cross the canal.

* * *

Inside Fort Eben-Emael, the atmosphere was described as 'very strange.' The crew of Visé 2 tried sleeping on the cold floor of the bloc. They heard the ventilators and an occasional siren going off below. One of the men ventured down to the barracks. He spotted one of the officers, face white as a ghost with fear. The only sound was from the generator. The tunnels were completely deserted; no signs of life. Documents were being burned by the head cook in the kitchen. None of this was at all encouraging.

On 11 May, having failed to cross the canal the previous night, Mikosch divided his assault into three groups, each consisting of an infantry company and a pioneer company. They were tasked with crossing the canal in rubber rafts beginning at 0400hrs. The operation was a success and the three groups reached the other side of the canal. With the fire from Canal Nord reduced, Portsteffen's group, consisting of 5th Infantry Company and 1st Pioneer Company, moved along the moat on the west side of the fort. Portsteffen and the pioneers headed for Bloc 2 while 5th Company, with anti-tank guns, headed for Blocs 1 and 6. The Pioneers attacked Bloc 2's embrasures with flamethrowers, followed by a 50kg charge. Bloc 2 was silenced. Portsteffen and his men headed up on top of the fort and met up with Witzig. 5th Company silenced the other western blocs and the fort was now wide open to a full attack.

Around 1030hrs, aware of the arrival of additional German forces, Jottrand called together the Council of Defence. The decision was made to surrender. All functioning weapons and machinery were destroyed. Shells were loaded into both barrels of the *Cupola Sud* 75s, the turret was lowered and the firing levers activated from below. The shells blasted into the side of the turret housing, destroying the guns. A hundred dead and wounded men lay among the ruins of the steel and concrete fort. At 1250hrs a Belgian parliamentarian appeared outside the fort with a white flag. A thousand men were taken into captivity. German losses from Operation *Granit* amounted to six dead and twenty injured. An inconceivable victory had been won by four small German pioneer units against over 1,000 Belgian troops fighting inside a powerful, supposedly impregnable fortress.

Fort Eben-Emael had fallen. This was comparable to, and even more joyous news for Germany, than the announcement in August 1914 of the 'Surrender of Liège', and its capture by Ludendorff. But just like that day in 1914, there was much more fighting to be done before the remaining eleven forts of Liège and seven forts of Namur were also silenced and that is what the rest of this account is about.

Leutnant Witzig, commander of Sturmgruppe Granit, *the attack on Eben-Emael.* (Digital History Archive, 'Bunkers of the Blitzkrieg')

Chapter 2

The Defences of Belgium

The defences of Belgium seemed formidable on paper, and they were – on paper, that is. Defensive strategy changed over the years after the Great War from one of stopping the Germans at the border, to falling back to a semi-fortified line in the centre of the country. The trouble was that the strongest line of permanent defences near the border had no infantry troops to support it, and the powerful Allied armies that gathered in the centre on the Dyle did not have any strong permanent defences to

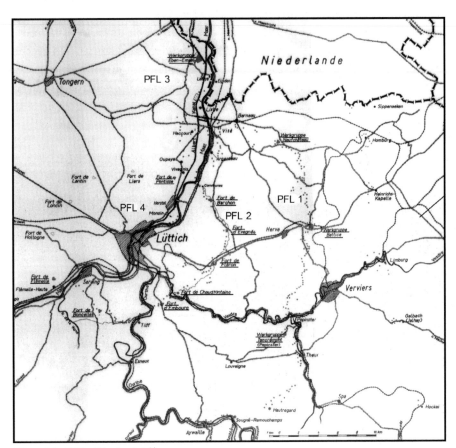

Plan of the PFL. (Denkschrift)

support them. The Germans, however, did not take the permanent defences lightly. They expected the march from the border to the fortress line to be a tough one – heavily defended by bunkers and long-range artillery. The Belgians expected the Germans to launch a direct attack towards Liège, as they had done in 1914. They were not prepared for the speed of the motorized units that bypassed Liège to the north and south, while pioneer squads, heavy artillery and the very powerful Luftwaffe handled the forts left in their wake.

The eastern frontier of Belgium and the approaches to the Meuse at Liège were defended by the *Position Fortifiée de Liège* (PFL). A line of AT and MG bunkers guarded the length of the Albert Canal from Liège to Antwerp. The Konigshookt-Wavre (KW) Line of infantry bunkers stretched along the tiny Dyle River from north of Namur to Antwerp, anchored to the south by the refurbished *Position Fortifiée de Namur* (PFN) and to the north by Antwerp's ring of forts. The Ghent bridgehead fall-back position waited beyond. Permanent defences stretched all across Belgium, but the most significant and noteworthy attacks against the fortifications took place at Liège and Namur.

The PFL was composed of five lines of defence. The first line was a forward screen, the *Position Avancée* (Advanced Position) that consisted of sixty-six 'light' MG bunkers that ran along the German border. The purpose of this line was to slow the enemy advance and cover the retreat of Belgian units guarding the border. However, in the early morning of 10 May the position, never fully manned in the first place, was completely evacuated before the Germans made contact.

The first solid line was identified as PFL 1, built along a 50km arc 18km east of Liège. PFL 1 was anchored by three modern forts – Aubin-Neufchâteau, Battice and Tancrémont. One hundred and seventy-eight bunkers in various configurations were built between the forts. These included a small number of artillery *Posts d'Observations* (PO) located on the highest points and directly subordinate to the adjacent forts, plus infantry and anti-tank bunkers to protect the roads and intervals between the forts. The latter were left unmanned simply because III Corps did not have enough troops.

The next lines were PFL 2 and PFL 3. PFL 3 included forty-three bunkers on the east bank of the Meuse between the Dutch border and the Belgian town of Argenteau. The position was anchored by Fort Eben-Emael, although technically the fort was not officially a part of the PFL. PFL 2 began where PFL 3 ended and ran along a 35km arc about 8km out from the city of Liège. PFL 2's main strength was the refurbished Brialmont forts – Barchon, Evegnée, Fléron, Chaudfontaine, Embourg and Boncelles. The line was reinforced by sixty-two bunkers, including thirteen POs subordinate to the forts.

PFL 4 followed the west bank of the Meuse. It included forty bunkers (many built into the piers of the bridges that spanned the river). Forts Pontisse and Flémalle protected the north and south flanks of the line, Pontisse to the north and Flémalle to the south.

The forts played a central role for the PFL. They anchored the successive lines and were designed to interdict access to specific zones. They also provided artillery support to Belgian troops deployed along the successive lines of defence and the intervals between the forts in ways conventional artillery could not. Sadly the Belgian army did not launch any sorties against the advancing Germans, nor did the forts support interval troops because, shortly after the invasion, there weren't any troops left in the intervals to support.

The forts of Liège, old and new, fell under the RFL, commanded by Colonel Maurice Modard, which in turn fell under III Corps. Modard, born in 1885, three years before construction began on the forts of Liège, served at Fort de Loncin and was wounded when the fort exploded on 15 August 1914. It has been said of him that he knew how to pass the heroic breath of 1914 into the soul of the fortress gunners of 1940. Modard's RFL was broken up into five sub-groups, each with its own commander. Each fort also had a commander. In the structure of the RFL the forts were identified as 'batteries.' In the case of Groups 1 and 5, Forts Eben-Emael (Group 1) and Battice (Group 5) were further broken up into two separately-commanded batteries. This command structure will be followed throughout this book, but to avoid confusion, the batteries will simply be referred to as 'forts'.

The forts of Liège and Namur were a combination of new and old. Four new forts, including Eben-Emael, were built in the 1930s. The Brialmont forts, built between 1888 and 1891 and captured by the Germans in a terrible two-week siege in August 1914, were modified by the Germans during the occupation and then by the Belgians after the German defeat in 1918. The delineation between what was done by the Germans and the Belgians is not completely clear. Documentation during the war and after is scarce. However, certain conclusions have been made. The Germans rearmed the forts in case they were needed to repel an Allied attack at some point in the future. Many of the old gun turrets survived and were repaired and later used by the Belgians in their own modifications to the older forts.

Discussions regarding the role of fortifications began in earnest in 1926. It was agreed that Belgium's existing fortifications, after additional modifications, could still provide good service. The old forts had good features and bad. They were capable of resisting shells up to 210mm and with some modifications, this could be improved. Based on the post-war reports of the 1914 commanders, the 57mm turrets had performed very well and could be put to further use. The FRC was commissioned to study the feasibility of replacing the 57mm guns with a 75mm howitzer with a range of 5km. They would provide flanking protection and could be used in short-range support of adjacent forts or to stop close proximity attacks with shells configured to fire '*boîtes-à-balles*', a version of what could best be described as case shot ammunition that scattered lethal steel pellets at close range on attacking troops.

A modified tunnel inside Fort Boncelles. Note the sheet metal used to strengthen the ceiling. (Bunkerfreaks Antwerpen)

In 1914, the large artillery turrets (120mm, 150mm and 210mm) installed in the forts were already outdated, but they were still quite effective and accurate. With modifications they could continue to serve as the forts' primary weapons and protect Belgian territory from a fast-moving enemy attack with long-range, rapid-fire artillery pieces. To fulfil the long-range mission, the army was in possession of a large quantity of 150mm and 105mm German pieces; the spoils of war. The range of the 150mm L/40 (40-calibre) was 18km. It was a heavy gun, difficult to transport and therefore of little interest to the field army. The army was also in possession of 105mm guns and a large number of projectiles for both guns.

Since it would be too expensive to design and build new turrets for the old forts, the engineers would have to make do with whatever leftover components they could find. The large-calibre turrets of Forts Barchon, Evegnée, Fléron, Chaudfontaine and Flémalle still existed and the FRC concluded they could be rearmed; the old 210mm howitzer turrets with 150mm L/40 guns, the 150mm turrets with the 105mm L/45 (longer range of 14km) or a combination MG/grenade launcher (*lance grenades*, LG);

and the 120mm turrets with the 105mm L/35 with a range of 12km. The 150mm guns were capable of reaching the German border. They could also reach Visé and flank the Meuse almost as far as Maastricht.

The commission decided to reuse all six forts on the east bank of the Meuse and Forts Pontisse and Flémalle on the west bank to guard the Meuse valley upstream and downstream. Seven of the nine forts at Namur were to be refurbished. The rest of the older forts of Liège and Namur, with the exception of Fort Loncin which was considered a monument and a tomb for soldiers killed there in 1914, served as depots for supplies and ammunition to restock the forts.

The Refurbished Forts

General features
Postern Entry. The postern in the escarp kept its basic vaulted shape. The old wooden rolling bridge was incorporated into the defences, as was the iron gate that enclosed the entryway. The original forts had two chambers flanking both sides of the postern entry that looked out on the access

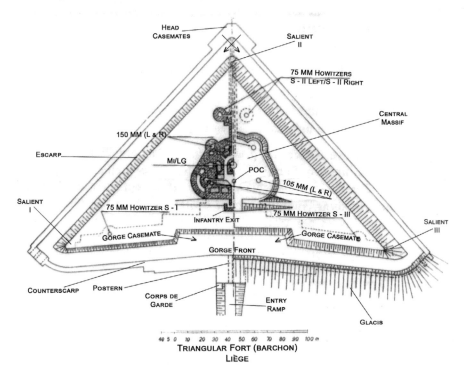

Plan of a triangular fort, in this case Fort Barchon, showing the components and weapons. (Denkschrift)

ramp. One room was modified and served as the wartime *Corps de Garde* (guardhouse). The old iron-barred window looking towards the ramp was sealed up with concrete and small embrasures were added to defend the ramp with machine guns. *Chevaux-de-frise* and anti-tank rails defended the access ramp and a movable gate (Cointet) slid across the ramp and anchored with steel cables to concrete posts (*bornes d'ammarage*) embedded into the concrete on either side of the ramp. The entry to the central part of the fort located in the escarp on the other side of the gorge front ditch was completely altered. The vaulted entry, a copy of the outer entry leading to the ramp, was sealed up, and a smaller entryway added. A decontamination room was added just inside the new entrance.

Ditch Casemates. All casemates that defended the ditches were equipped with MG 08/15 machine guns. Two of these guns were mounted on a single, reversible carriage one above the other so the guns could be swapped over if one gun barrel overheated. An additional embrasure was added to hold an electric searchlight to illuminate the ditch at night.

Quadrilateral. Here is where the forts begin to change quite dramatically. In 1914 the crews inside the forts suffered terribly from bombardment, facing thousands of medium to heavy calibre shells including those fired by the 420mm heavy mortar. Pinned down inside the enormous concrete central massif, they felt the shaking of every shell that hit the concrete, causing dust, rubble and sometimes the entire ceiling to come down on their heads while the tunnels filled with smoke and fumes. The thick concrete of the central massif provided their only protection, despite the fact that, because all of the guns were concentrated there, it was the main target for the German guns. The French found a solution to their own similar problem. During and after the Battle of Verdun, the French began to dig deep tunnels beneath the existing forts. The work later became more sophisticated and defined. At Fort Vachereauville, west of Verdun, tunnels were dug towards entrances far to the rear of the fort, a concept that influenced the design of the Maginot Line. At Liège, where memories still lingered of the destruction of Fort Loncin and the burial of almost 300 men in a single explosion, and at Namur, the Belgians added a new, two-level tunnel system under the old forts that became known as the 'quadrilateral' and the *Galeries de Grande Profondeur* (Tunnels of Great Depth).

The quadrilateral was in the shape of a square, hence the term, with tunnels leading to the base of the gun turrets on the surface accessed via narrow shafts equipped with metal ladders. Small lifts built into a second shaft were used to transfer shells from storage locations in the quad tunnels up to the turrets. The tunnels were 1.5m to 2m in width, much reduced from their ancestors above and therefore better able to stand up to shells and bombs. The quadrilateral tunnel system was accessed via a sloping corridor at the foot of the staircase that led up to the former troop assembly room of 1888. The quad was on the same level as the old capital (central) gallery that led to the casemate at the head of the fort. The old rooms encased in the central massif were completely modified. The only combat components that remained were the circular gun turret shafts. Most of the rooms were sealed off and others were used to hold the earth that was removed to create the new tunnel systems.

The *Galeries de Grande Profondeur* – Tunnels of Great Depth – was a second network of tunnels built below the quadrilateral. A staircase in the quad led down to this lower level. The tunnels here were 1.7m high by 0.7m wide and

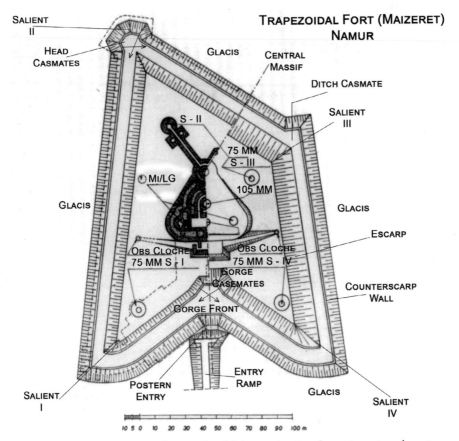

Plan of a trapezoidal fort; in this case Fort Maizeret, showing the components and weapons.
(Denkschrift)

served several purposes, one of which was to serve as a ventilation conduit to bring fresh air into the fort from inlets located outside the perimeter of the fort, some as far away as 1,400m. The ventilation tunnel changed direction in one or two locations, depending on the length, and a small blockhouse was located at the turn to defend against enemy infiltration. It was equipped with an FM and a slot to drop grenades into the tunnel at advancing enemy troops. Another section of this tunnel system was called the *Galerie de Bombardment*, a place for the troops to seek shelter. The tunnels were used to store additional ammunition which could be sent to the upper level of the quad on munitions lifts. Small chambers were located off of the tunnel for the storage of fuses, detonators and grenades. A smaller side tunnel contained water reservoirs. A secondary radio (*Télégraphie sans fil* – TSF) post was located here, plus a room for the officers to rest, the *Bureau de Détente*, that included bunks and a washroom and a ladder that led directly up to the artillery command post, the *Bureau de Coordination de Tir*. Each fort had a different configuration and not all of the forts had the same features. The quadrilateral and lower tunnel vaults were reinforced with corrugated galvanized steel plates.

The Air Intake Bunker/Tower. During the Battle of Liège in August 1914, the main cause of the fall of the majority of the forts was the imminent threat of asphyxiation of the garrison. The old forts had no artificial ventilation system, with the exception of Fort Loncin, which was equipped with experimental equipment. Only the gun turrets were provided with hand ventilators for the evacuation of gasses created when the shells were fired. The rest of the fort relied on air flow, which didn't work very well when the windows were sealed up. The rearmed forts were equipped with external air intakes, some resembling concrete water towers, located at an average distance of up to 200m from the fort, or bunkers with no tower. The air outlets and towers varied in height depending on the terrain and were connected to the main part of the fort by the air tunnel leading to the fort, described above. On the fort side of the tunnel a suction fan drew fresh air to the various rooms and galleries inside the fort. Each ventilation outlet, with or without a tower, also served as a secondary exit for patrols and an emergency exit for the garrison. The exit was defended by an armoured door guarded by an internal blockhouse equipped with an FM. The flow of air into the fort was controlled by a large double sheet metal door in the side of the tower that could be opened or closed by controls in the upper chamber of the tower. The amount of air was regulated by the opening and closing of the doors. The upper chamber of the tower served multiple purposes. It was

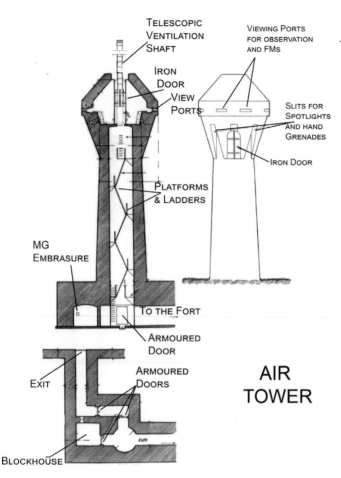

TELESCOPIC VENTILATION SHAFT

VIEWING PORTS FOR OBSERVATION AND FMs

IRON DOOR

VIEW PORTS

SLITS FOR SPOTLIGHTS AND HAND GRENADES

IRON DOOR

PLATFORMS & LADDERS

MG EMBRASURE

TO THE FORT

ARMOURED DOOR

ARMOURED DOORS

EXIT

AIR TOWER

Plan of the air tower found in some of the refurbished forts of the PFL and PFN. (Denkschrift)

zum

BLOCKHOUSE

equipped with six chutes to drop grenades on the base of the tower. Portable searchlights above each chute lit up the base of the tower. It was also an observation post with six observation embrasures around the perimeter to allow viewing in all directions. FMs mounted in each of the six embrasures defended against enemy infantry attack. It was also a primary target for German artillery, especially the 88mm Flak guns.

The air towers and bunkers had different configurations. At Liège, Forts Embourg and Pontisse did not have towers. Their air intake tunnels connected to a small bunker on the hillside of a very steep valley. In Namur's Fort Dave, two outdoor shelters (Troonois and La Relève) were connected to the air intake corridor that led to a cliff face south of the fort, and the emergency exit was through La Relève. Fort Maizeret's tunnel also led to a cliff face to the north. As for Fort Saint-Héribert, it did not have any system of air intake outside the fort, the air passing through armoured shafts on top of the massif.

Communications. Each turret, *Post d'Observation Cuirassée* (POC) (armoured observation post built into the former searchlight turrets at Liège), *Corps de Garde*, ditch casemate, *Bureau de Détente*, air tower and the TSF room was equipped with a telephone connected to a switchboard in the *Bureau de Coordination de Tir*. Eight simultaneous conversations could be had at one time. In addition, each fort, PO and external bunker was interconnected via underground telephone lines that passed through a series of junction boxes. The phone cable passed into the fort via the air tunnel. If the telephone system failed, communication switched to TSF.

Armament

The gun turrets of the rearmed forts of Liège and Namur were a combination of pieces from the older forts and new components manufactured by the FRC. The turrets of the original Brialmont forts included a single or twin 120mm gun, a twin 150mm, a single 120mm howitzer, and a single 57mm quick-firing gun. The rearmed forts used the original steel turret cylinder and cap but in different configurations. At Liège, the 120mm guns were replaced with 105mm; the 150mm were replaced with a combination MG/grenade launcher (Mi/LG); and the 210mm howitzer was replaced by the German 150mm gun. The 57mm gun was replaced by a 75mm howitzer. At Namur the 150mm double gun turret was replaced by two 75mm GP guns. At Fort Maizeret, the 150s were placed by 105s. The 120mm guns were replaced by reversible-carriage twin MGs (one or two pairs depending on the number of embrasures). In other 120mm turrets, the one or two guns were replaced by two or four grenade launchers.

The gun turrets resembled an automobile piston. In the lower level a steel beam with a counterweight at one end was attached to a central shaft that was in turn attached to the floor of a cylindrical chamber containing the guns. This top floor was the gun chamber. The controls to raise and lower and turn the turret were located in the middle level below the gun chamber. The guns were mounted on specially-made carriages. The guns were raised and lowered with controls located inside the gun chamber. Shells were sent up to the gun chamber on special hoists and the guns were loaded and fired by gunners inside the gun chamber. The turret was installed in a cylindrical concrete shaft protected by an outer ring of steel armour. Only the 75mm guns were retractable, i.e., they could be fully raised and lowered. They were raised into the battery position to fire, and retracted below the surface of the outer ring of armour to protect the gun embrasures. The 150mm in the old 210mm turrets had to be raised a few centimetres in order to rotate but the gun barrel protruded from the turret cap at all times. The 75mm howitzer was raised/lowered and rotated manually; the 105mm was rotated manually (the interior of the turret had electric lighting); the 150mm L/40 was rotated electrically with a manual backup.

75mm L/11 howitzer (in retractable turret). This howitzer, used for close defence, fired steel shells that exploded on impact or were provided with a fuse to regulate the timing of the explosion. It also fired '*boîtes-à-balles*', not to be confused with shrapnel. The shell can be compared more closely to case shot, used for close-range defence, such as the presence of the enemy on the glacis. The maximum range of the Model 1929 explosive shell was 5,200m; *boîtes-à-balles* was 250m.

The rearmed forts of Liège used only the 75mm L/11 howitzer. In the rearmed forts of Namur the same was used in the former 57mm turrets and a 75mm GP model was placed in the 150mm turrets, with the exception of Fort Maizeret, where two 105mm GP were installed.

105mm L/35. This gun was installed in the former 120mm turrets. These old turrets had either one or two gun embrasures and were reconfigured accordingly. The gun barrels protruded from the embrasure so the gun was not retractable. The turret had to be turned away from the direction of enemy fire to protect the barrels – not much good if shells were coming from all directions. The gun fired the explosive shell model 1915. The range of the gun was a robust 13,000m. Rate of fire was anything from 3rpm to 1rpm, depending on the length of time the guns fired continuously.

150mm L/40. These were mounted in the old *Grusonwerk* 210mm turrets. They could fire one round every 30 seconds. The gun fired two types of explosive shells, each with a range of 18,000m.

Mitrailleuse/Lance Grenade (Mi/LG) Turret. In the Liège forts, the former 150mm turret in the centre of the massif was rearmed with a combination MG/grenade-launcher mount. At Namur, the 120mm Brialmont turrets were modified to receive either MGs or grenade launchers. The turret was used for close-range defence. The Maxim light machine guns were installed on a reversible carriage. Belgium received a large number of light and heavy MGs from the Germans as spoils of war. The heavy version was the 08/15 model. It was water-cooled with a range of 2,000m with a practical rate of fire of 50 to 100rpm. The gun used the Belgian 7.65mm ammunition. The MG turret guns were provided with 20,000 rounds, in belts of 250 cartridges. The field of fire was 60°.

The grenade launcher for the Mi/LG was specially developed for installation in the 150mm or 120mm turrets. It fired finned steel grenades. The azimuth followed the rotation of the turret. The range was about 320m at an angle of 55°. The grenade weighed 1.8kg and held 265g of explosive. Charges could be set for variable distances of 100m to 320m. It could land as close as the glacis. At a 35° angle the range was a bit further. The rotation of the turret was slow, taking 1,150 turns of the hand crank and 20 minutes to make a complete revolution. The turret configuration varied between one or two pairs of MGs and from two to four LGs. The most common was one carriage for the MG and two LGs. Examples:

- Barchon: two Mi and two LG.
- Chaudfontaine: two Mi and four LG.
- Evegnée: one Mi and three LG.
- Flémalle: one Mi and four LG.
- Fléron: two Mi and two LG.

The Maxim 08 heavy machine gun was used in the MG casemates. It was manufactured by the Spandau Arsenal, *Deutsche Waffen und Munitions Fabrike*, Berlin. Calibre was 7.92mm. Its rate of fire was 100rpm and effective range 650m (maximum range 3,000m).

Fusil-mitrailleur 1930 (FM 30) Light Machine Gun. This weapon was built by *Fabrique Nationale*, Herstal, Belgium. The calibre was 7.65mm, with 20-round magazines. Its rate of fire was 600rpm and effective range 55m. The gun was based on the American Browning Automatic Rifle. It was used in various locations throughout the forts.

Post d'Observation Cuirassée – POC. While it did not contain any weapons, the former retractable armoured searchlight turret from the Brialmont era was transformed into an observation post. The hole for the searchlight was sealed up with steel plates and four viewing ports were cut into the thin metal wall. Two periscopes fitted into slots in the roof and could be raised and lowered. The armour was only 10cm thick and therefore quite vulnerable.

The forts were equipped with a number of FM cloches that also served as observation posts. Additional observation posts made of concrete were installed along the parapets in the escarp or counterscarp.

The New Forts

Construction

The new forts were very strongly built. Fort Eben-Emael was built to resist 280mm shells; Battice, due to its close proximity to the border, 520mm; Aubin-Neufchâteau and Tancrémont, 420mm. With the exception of the escarp and counterscarp walls, which were not reinforced, the combat blocs were constructed of reinforced concrete, 450kg/m³. The steel reinforcing rods were from 15mm to 20mm in diameter and were wired every 15cm. The surface blocs were surrounded by an envelope of stone 5m thick and 10–15m deep. The artillery bloc walls of Tancrémont, Aubin-Neufchâteau

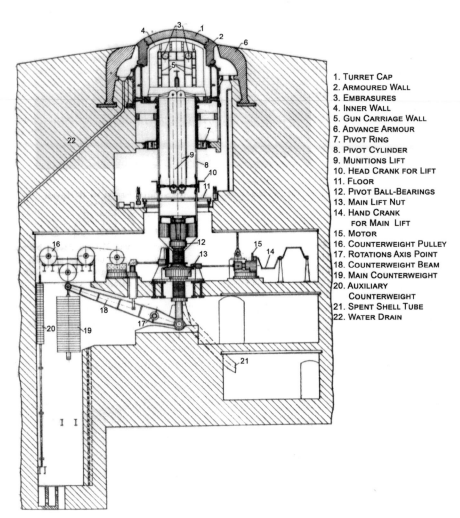

1. Turret Cap
2. Armoured Wall
3. Embrasures
4. Inner Wall
5. Gun Carriage Wall
6. Advance Armour
7. Pivot Ring
8. Pivot Cylinder
9. Munitions Lift
10. Head Crank for Lift
11. Floor
12. Pivot Ball-Bearings
13. Main Lift Nut
14. Hand Crank
    for Main Lift
15. Motor
16. Counterweight Pulley
17. Rotations Axis Point
18. Counterweight Beam
19. Main Counterweight
20. Auxiliary
    Counterweight
21. Spent Shell Tube
22. Water Drain

Schematic of a 75mm turret bloc in one of the new forts of the PFL. (Denkschrift)

and Battice were 3.5m thick and the roof 4.5m. The defensive blocs were 2.8m thick for the least exposed to 3.5m for the more exposed walls and roof. Eben-Emael's artillery casemate walls were 2.25m thick; the 75mm and 120mm turrets were surrounded by 3m of reinforced concrete. The other walls were from 2.25m to 2.75m thick, depending on their degree of exposure.

Armament
75mm GP gun in casemate:

- Based on the 75mm *Tir Rapide* (TR) Model 1905 (Krupp). Only twelve of these guns existed in four casemates at Eben-Emael, three guns per bloc.
- Range: 11,000m.
- Field of fire: 70°.
- Elevation: -5° to +37°.
- Rate of fire: 13rpm.
- Fired explosive and case shot rounds.

Retractable turret with twin 75mm FRC Model 1934 guns:

- Based on the 75mm Bofors Model 1934, used by the *Chasseurs Ardennais*. These turrets, with twin guns, were used only in the new forts: two at Eben-Emael, two at Aubin-Neufchâteau, three at Battice and two at Tancrémont.
- Range: 10,100m.
- Field of fire: 360°.
- Elevation: -8° to +38°.
- Rate of fire: 13 to 24rpm.
- The gun was used for long-range interdiction fire but could also provide close-range defence with *boîtes-a-balles* shells. The armour came in different strengths, based on its placement location – light, medium and heavy. The movable part of the turret weighed 120 tons (for the heavy type). The turret was raised 53cm from its resting position to fire. Movement was done electrically.

Non-retractable turret with twin 120mm Long FRC Model 1931 guns:

- With a range of 14,000 to 17,000m, its primary mission was to hit targets at the frontier. It also provided counterbattery fire, interdiction fire and mutual support of neighbouring forts. Only three examples were installed: two at Fort Battice and one at Eben-Emael. It fired two types of explosive shells. The turret had a diameter of 5.75m. The movable section weighed 210 tons. The cap of the turret was 5.9cm thick.

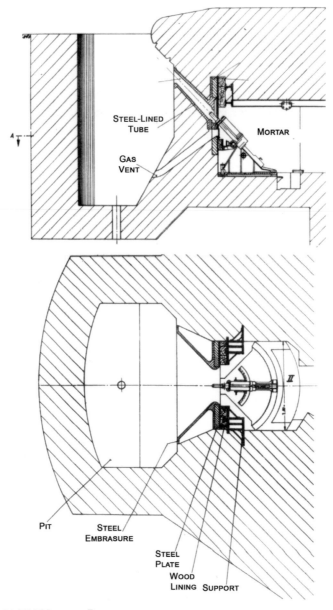

81 MM MORTAR BLOC

Plan of Mortar Blocs at Aubin-Neufchâteau and Tancrémont. (Denkschrift)

81mm Model 1932 mortar:

- This was the same French model 81mm mortar used in the Maginot Line, built by the *Ateliers de Tarbes*. Its mission was to reach the valleys and deep slopes on the Plateau de Herve. Unlike the French version, which could be mounted in a twin 81mm turret, the Belgian mortars were only installed in casemates. The tubes were at a fixed angle of 45°. The range was regulated by the amount of gas in the two tubes located on top of the barrel. Maximum range was 3,600m. Its horizontal field of fire was 90°. The mortar embrasures were built at the top of a shaft built into the sides of the bloc, invisible from view at the ground level and, except for the slim chance of a very lucky shot, invulnerable to enemy shelling and bombardment. A 'Mortar Bloc' was equipped with three mortar casemates that covered a field of 270°. Mortar Blocs were only installed at Forts Aubin-Neufchâteau and Tancrémont.

60mm FRC Model 1936 AT gun for casemate:

- One of the most powerful AT guns in the world at the time, the 60mm was installed in all of the flanking casemates of Eben-Emael, and in Blocs 1 and 2 at Battice. The gun fired high explosive (HE) and armour-piercing (AP) rounds (*Obus de Rupture*). The range of the gun was 3,000m. It was manufactured by the FRC in Herstal, Belgium.

47mm FRC Model 1936 anti-tank gun for casemate:

- This gun was also built by the FRC. Muzzle velocity was 675m/sec (AP) and 450m/sec (HE). Effective range was 2,000m. This gun was the predecessor to the 60mm and fired the same type of shells. The gun was installed in the counterscarp casemates of Forts Tancrémont and Aubin-Neufchâteau as well as in several cloches at Aubin-Neufchâteau.

Cloches:

- There were several types of cloches that included: observation cloche (*cloche de guet*) with four viewing ports and a shutter on the top that could be opened to fire a flare gun; cloche FM with six embrasures that came in four models, one with a periscope through the top; artillery observation cloche with periscope (Eben-Emael and Battice); searchlight cloche (Aubin-Neufchâteau); twin MG cloche (Tancrémont, Battice, Aubin-Neufchâteau); 47mm anti-tank cloche – only two were installed at Aubin-Neufchâteau.

Armament in the new forts also included the twin Maxim 08 and the FM Model 1930. Willocq-Bottin searchlights placed in the casemates illuminated the forts at night.

The configuration of individual forts will be discussed in the next chapter. The exception is Fort Eben-Emael, which has been previously described.

Chapter 3

Friday, 10 May 1940:
Opening Action at Liège

The German Sixth Army[1] moved out from Aachen in the early morning hours of 10 May in the direction of Maastricht. The mission of its XXVII Corps was to protect the left wing of Sixth Army from enemy action coming from the PFL, in particular Fort Aubin-Neufchâteau. The corps was to then move north and north-east, cross the Meuse at Visé and reach the west bank of the river to surround and attack the fortress of Liège.

XXVII Corps, consisting of 253rd and 269th Infantry Divisions (ID), and 4th Panzer Division plus 251 ID from V Corps, expected the advance to be difficult. The route was exposed to the direct fire of the fortress artillery, in addition to the presence of obstacles, minefields and demolitions. The corps brought with it a large contingent of artillery pieces to oppose the Belgian guns and to destroy the concrete installations. This included several *Schwere Artillerie-Abteilung*: 427 – three batteries of 100mm guns; 536 – 150mm field howitzers; 736 – three motorized batteries of 305mm Czech howitzers; 815 – four batteries of 305mm howitzers; II/66 Artillery Regiment (AR) – three horse-drawn batteries of 150mm Rheinmetall field howitzers; II/59 AR – three batteries of Krupp and Rheinmetall 150mm heavy field howitzers (15.6km range); and 607 – one battery of 150mm guns and two batteries of 210mm mortars. *Stuka-Geschwader* 77 provided air support throughout the campaign.

253 ID was commanded by Generalleutnant Fritz Kühne. Its original mission was to neutralize the forts of Aubin-Neufchâteau, Barchon and Evegnée and the division's 453 IR was tasked with the seizure of Fort Aubin-Neufchâteau. But due to a change of plan by Sixth Army, this mission was handed over to 223 ID although the initial attacks were carried out by 253 ID. On 10 May, the 253rd advanced along the Belgian-Dutch border and wheeled south. Upon reaching the Meuse, the division came under intense artillery fire from Fort Pontisse. On the evening of 10 May, 453 IR surrounded Fort Aubin-Neufchâteau and was prepared the following morning to carry out the first attack on the fort with 2nd Battalion.

Generalleutnant Paul-Willi Körner commanded the 223 ID, composed of 344, 385 and 425 IR, each with three battalions, 223 AR, 223rd *Panzerjäger* Battalion, 223rd Reconnaissance Battalion, and 223rd Pioneer Battalion (Pi. Bn.). 223 ID was a Third Wave unit made available to Sixth Army.[2]

251 ID was commanded by Generalleutnant Hans Kratzert. It fell under *Heeresgruppe* A, Fourth Army, V Corps, but it would be used to attack the forts south of Liège. The division consisted of 451, 459 and 471 IR, each with three battalions, and four light artillery batteries from 251 AR.

The 3rd Squadron of the Luftwaffe's 13th Reconnaissance Group – 3 (H) 13 – flew reconnaissance missions in Henschel Hs 126s for V Corps. The two-man crews consisted of a pilot and observer. The squadron patrolled the Herve Plateau to the Ardennes and to the west of Liège. On 10 May, the following observations from 3 (H) 13 were reported to V Corps:

- 0642hrs: No enemy movements; no enemy anti-aircraft defence; normal street traffic; no bridges destroyed.
- 0700hrs: field fortifications 1.5km SE Galbach (Jalhay, probably at Charneux); Map point 598 on Galbach-Malmedy Strasse and crossroad 1km N destroyed; field fortification at Hockai but no troops observed; N and E Meiz light field reinforcement; Point 543 S Francorchamps no infantry observed; battery position W Francorchamps appears occupied (horses observed); battery position point 570 Malchamps probably not occupied; no troop movements on the Francorchamps-Sart-Verviers and Verviers-Theux-Spa-Francorchamps roads; fortification line Pepinster-Theux-La Reid-Remouchamps no troops, no hostile air activity, no anti-aircraft defence; Spa airport (Hippodrome) no airplanes, no flights.
- 0714hrs: *Eisenbahnbrucke* [Railway Bridge over the Vesdre] Limbourg-Verviers blown up. Road east Limburg broken up in places.
- 0721hrs: Road blown up 500m south of the Route de Hèvremont (S of Limbourg). Enemy column presumably retreating on the Gulpen–Verviers road.
- 0726hrs: No enemy troops were found at any point. All recognized movements are backwards.
- 0825hrs: No [air] defence over Liège. Ourthe and Amblève bridges undamaged.

Two hours later:

- 1038hrs: Railway bridge north of Trois Ponts (outskirts of Trois-Ponts where it crosses the Ambleve River) blown up. All other bridges ahead of Trois Points to Remouchamps OK.

- 1107hrs: Entrance to Tancrémont thick clouds of smoke;[3] the railway bridge at Trois-Ponts blown up. Detonation observed in Gegene 2km SE Stoumont whether road or rail, not recognizable. Own [German] troops observed around 1025hrs in the Weismes-Ondenval line.

It appeared that not much had been done in the early morning between the border and the PFL to slow the German invasion. Field fortifications were unoccupied and the small number of troops observed were retreating. Belgian demolition teams started working on the roads and bridges sometime after 0700hrs. Hardly an Allied air mission was flown. The Belgians started blowing the railway bridges around 1030hrs. All the attention was further to the north at Maastricht and the Albert Canal, where the defences were supposed to be the strongest, but where they were actually turning into a huge hole in the dike.

The following is a summary of action that took place in the forts on 10 May 1940.

RFL Group 1

Fort Eben-Emael was addressed and its story completed in the previous chapter.

RFL Group 2 – Fort Pontisse – Fort Barchon – Fort Aubin-Neufchâteau: Group Commander Major F. Simon

Fort Pontisse was commanded by Captain Fernand Pire. It was a large quadrangular fort located north of Liège on the west bank of the Meuse, with the mission to guard the roads and bridges along the Meuse valley to the north. Its armament included twin 105mm guns installed in a 120mm turret taken from Fort Flémalle, and four single 75mm howitzer turrets, one in each of the four salients, or angles, of the fort. The 105mm turret's shells could reach Fort Eben-Emael. The fort did not have an air tower. Instead, the air intake, a bunker with its own entrance, was located outside the perimeter of the fort in a ravine about 40m north of Salient II.

Fort Pontisse received an alert message from the RFL at 0040hrs. The radio message included the code execution word 'Alfred'. The duty officer opened the safe and unsealed an envelope kept inside. The authentication document matched 'Alfred'. Belgium was at war. All turrets were quickly manned and ready to fire, and the defensive blocs were ready to repel enemy attacks on the fort. Around 0430hrs, Captain Pire was notified by Major

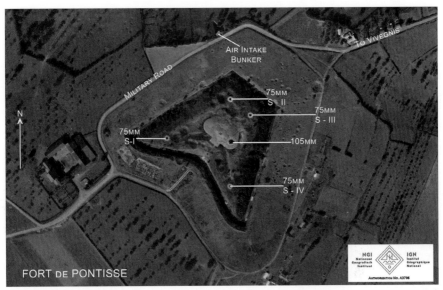

Aerial image from 1947 showing Fort de Pontisse. (© – NGI – authorization A3796 – www.ngi.be)

Jottrand of the landings on top of Fort Eben-Emael, and was asked to fire on top of the fort to dislodge the 'paratroopers'. The 105mm turret was chosen for this assignment and fired a salvo of 100 shots, the first combat action of Fort Pontisse since the morning of 13 August 1914. This fire mission was repeated several times throughout the course of the day. The shots initially targeted Eben-Emael's 120mm turret, followed by Visé 2 at 0745hrs, the western slope at 1045hrs and the north end at 1330hrs.

At 1200hrs, 1645hrs and 1730hrs, Pontisse fired the 105mm guns on German boats from 269 ID attempting to cross the Meuse at Eysden. The boats were destroyed or capsized and the Germans abandoned this attempt to cross the river for the day. Captain Pire ordered increased vigilance towards the skies overhead.

61st Company of 3rd Battalion of the Belgian Frontier Cyclists was tasked with blowing up the *Pont de Chemin-de-Fer de Visé*. This railway line ran from Aachen through Montzen, Belgium, crossed the Meuse and the Canal 800m north of Visé, and continued on to Tongeren, a strategic point 17km west of Visé. On a map the roads leading to and from Tongeren look like the hands of a clock, reaching in all directions. The railway bridge was an objective of extreme importance, to say the least. Around 0615hrs the order was given to complete the destruction but the engineers only had partial success. After a second failed attempt, Lieutenant Parent, commander of 61st Company, asked Fort Pontisse to shell and destroy the bridge. The fort fired dozens of shots at the railway bridge but failed to destroy its steel and concrete. However, by 1400hrs the bridge was damaged enough to be unusable. The company also destroyed the road bridge of Visé at around 1000hrs.

On the right bank of the Meuse, one of the German *Brücken-Bau* (bridge building) battalions[4] failed in two attempts to lay a pontoon bridge over the river at Lanaye, south-east of Eben-Emael, in support of 269 ID's crossings. Around noon they attempted to erect another bridge further south of Lanaye but Fort Pontisse's 105s and Eben-Emael's Bloc Visé 2, plus two artillery batteries assigned to 7th Division, bombarded the bridge, which was destroyed around 1240hrs. Due to heavy losses 269 ID made no further attempts to cross the river that day.

Fort Barchon was commanded by Captain-Commandant[5] Aimé Pourbaix. The fort was located about 8km north-east of Liège near the major mining operation of Blegny. It was a large triangular fort that guarded the roads along the Meuse valley and the main roads leading to Liège from the east. With two 150s, four 105s, four 75mm howitzers and a Mi/LG turret, it was one of the best-armed artillery strongholds of Liège. Barchon was equipped with an air tower located about 200m due west of Salient I. In 1936 five rows of anti-tank rails, ranging in height from 80cm to 1.20m, were put in place between Forts Barchon and Evegnée.

At 0045hrs, Fort Barchon was notified by HQ RFL that Germany had violated Belgian territory and to order all the men to their combat posts. One of the fort's crew, Joseph Lecane, stated that around 0100hrs he and the men reported to the fort from the outside barracks, laughing and joking as always. They gathered around the commander, Captain Pourbaix who told the men that: 'I have just received the communication to put all the men immediately at their combat stations because our territory is threatened.' The men were no longer laughing. Orders were then shouted and the men rushed to their stations.[6]

Around 0415hrs, Pourbaix learned of the glider attack on Eben-Emael from Captain Pire at Fort Pontisse and at 0435hrs was ordered by RFL to open fire on the top of the fort with Barchon's two 150mm turrets. It took 30 minutes to prep the two turrets and train them in the proper direction. The process to move the shells up to the gun chambers from the quadrilateral began, but the shell storage box lids were so tightly wedged shut that they could not be opened by the loaders in the lower level. A new tool had to be forged to open the boxes and the shells started moving up the hoist to the turrets. Finally at 0455hrs, 150mm shells were heard leaving the turrets on their 12km journey to Eben-Emael. Pourbaix ordered the burning of the outside barracks to clear the turret sight lines and remove potential cover for German troops. At times throughout the day the two 150mm and four 105mm guns fired simultaneously. It was very impressive. With each shot the fort trembled on its foundations.

As the second war of the century broke out, Belgian civilians began their own long journey to unknown destinations. The fortress troops watched as long columns of women, children and the elderly dragged themselves and their scant belongings towards the west along the Wandre road. The men from Barchon, and in all of the forts of Liège, wondered where their own wives and parents were at that time.

In the afternoon, German troops appeared in the Remersdaal region (3.5km north-east of Aubel) and the train station of Montzen, located on a branch of the Aachen–Liège line about 18km north-east of the fort. Montzen station was on the limit of the 150s' range. Fort Barchon was ordered to fire on these two locations. At 1740hrs Fort Aubin-Neufchâteau called to notify Pourbaix that a large German force was infiltrating the Bois de Loé (2.8km from Fort Aubin-Neufchâteau) and more troops had been spotted on the roads approaching Aubin-Neufchâteau. Barchon's 150mm guns drove the Germans back from both locations but it was not enough to stem the tide. An hour later Aubin-Neufchâteau called again to say there was a large concentration of troops in the vicinity of Trois Cheminées, less than 500m east of the fort, and the guns were trained and fired in that direction. The guns continued to fire at the railway station of Montzen as evening arrived.

Each fort's garrison consisted of two teams – A and B. While one team was at the fort, the other was in the rest barracks. At 1915 Team A left Barchon for the rest barracks at Wandre and Team B arrived for duty. Unbeknownst to the men of Team B, the fort would soon be cut off and they would not be relieved for the remainder of the battle. As the 150mm turret crew of Team A debriefed the relief crew, the news was not good. The team reported that the ventilation inside the turret did not function properly and the men were feeling the effects of the fumes – a very bad sign since this is what contributed in large part to the surrender of the forts in 1914. Also, the electric motor that moved the 150mm turret had broken down so the turret had to be traversed by hand.

The 150mm L/40 was the least efficient gun of the rearmed forts. It was a naval model mounted in the turret. It had no recoil or braking mechanism to counter the shock of firing. The recoilless 210mm gun used in 1914 had worked fine and it fitted well into the turret, but a more powerful gun such as the 150mm did not work as well. The gun needed to be placed at an angle of 35° in order to be reloaded and this proved to be a very tight squeeze. Traversing the turret was tough and therefore it was done by electric motor.

The controllers used to adjust the level of electric current were made of cast iron. Since cast iron is not very ductile, these controls would break, leaking oil and making the floor slippery. The different layers of the turret cap were assembled with rivets, bolts and blind screws. Due to the shock while firing, these components sheared and flew into the heads of the soldiers. Also the turret had to be raised several centimetres in order to turn it to the firing position. These additional operations were difficult for the crew to carry out.

Fort Aubin-Neufchâteau, commanded by Captain Oscar d'Ardenne, was located about 20km north-east of Liège and in range of the guns of Forts Eben-Emael, Battice and Barchon. Its mission was to protect the main roads and the railway line running between Visé and Aachen and to interdict the major crossroads in the Val Dieu region to the south-east. Construction of the fort began in 1936 and was completed just prior to the start of the war. The fort was relatively small, about 30 hectares, and triangular in shape, each lateral 300m long. The superstructure was surrounded by a dry anti-tank ditch 16m wide with walls 6m high. Casemates equipped with AT guns and MGs guarded the ditch. Blocs P and O (see below) lay outside the perimeter of the fort and protected the air intakes for the ventilation system. Bloc P was also the wartime entrance to the fort.

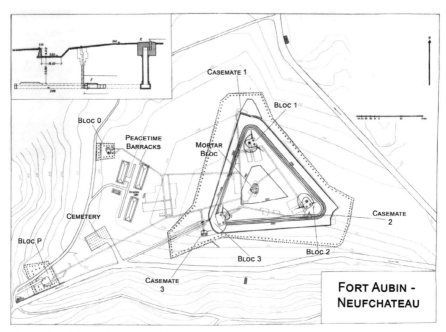

Plan of Fort Aubin-Neufchâteau. (Denkschrift)

Fort Aubin-Neufchâteau's armament included two twin 75mm FRC Model 34 turrets, three 81mm mortars, three 47mm AT guns, seven MG cloches to defend the glacis, two 47mm AT cloches and four FM cloches for close-range defence. The combat blocs included:

- **Bloc 1**: artillery bloc located in the northern salient with one twin 75mm turret and two MG cloches.
- **Bloc 2**: artillery bloc identical to Bloc 1, located in the south-east salient.
- **Bloc 3**: the main entry to the underground part of the fort. The postern entrance to Bloc 3 was protected by an iron gate and a retractable bridge, guarded by an internal FM blockhouse. Three machine gun cloches on top of the bloc covered the glacis. A twin MG and a searchlight guarded the access ramp that led from outside the fort into the ditch.
- **Bloc M (Mortar Bloc)**: located in the centre of the triangle, it was equipped with three 81mm Model 32 mortars, developed for the Maginot Line by the *Ateliers de Tarbes*. An observation cloche on top of the bloc was equipped with an FM to defend the approaches.

The ditches surrounding the central part of the fort were defended by casemates identified as follows:

- **Casemate 1**: between Blocs 1 and 3. Equipped with a 47mm AT gun, a twin MG, a searchlight and an FM. The guns fired in the direction of Bloc 3.
- **Casemate 2**: A double casemate that defended the ditch in the direction of Blocs 1 and 3. Equipped with two 47mm AT guns, two twin MGs and two searchlights. Two FMs defended the dead angles.
- **Casemate 3**: built on the glacis of the fort just outside the perimeter, it guarded the Chemin de Neufchâteau with its two 47mm AT cloches. This was a unique configuration where the cloches, already modified to hold MGs, were further modified to hold the AT guns. A third cloche held the searchlight.
- **Bloc O**: located outside the perimeter about 300m to the north-west of Bloc 3. This bloc contained a telescopic ventilation tube that could be raised above the surface of the bloc. An observation cloche with an FM guarded the western approaches.
- **Bloc P**: located outside the perimeter of the triangle, 600m south-west of Bloc 3. Bloc P served as the secondary entrance to the fort with its own small access ramp defended by an FM. The entrance

door was defended by an FM in a small interior blockhouse. The bloc contained a second telescopic ventilation tube plus an observation cloche with an FM.

The anti-aircraft defence position, equipped with six tripod-mounted Maxim 08/15 MGs, was located on a rise in the centre of an imaginary triangle formed by Blocs O, P and Casemate 3.

The fort's external observation posts were located in bunkers MN 11 (600m south of Route de Loé), MN 18 (600m north of St. Jean-Sart), NV 2 (900m north-west of the fort), and NV 5 (900m south-west of Warsage). Additional posts were set up at Fouron-Saint-Martin and La Heydt.

Fort Aubin-Neufchâteau's terrible ordeal – the fort would suffer nearly continuous infantry attacks until it capitulated – began like the rest of the forts with the receipt at 0050hrs of the RFL alert message. The duty officer telephoned Forts Fléron and Eben-Emael to confirm they had received the same message. It was confirmed. Two minutes later the alarm was sounded and the garrison awakened. The crews of the observation posts attached to the fort were put on high alert. The peacetime barracks situated adjacent to the fort was evacuated and the men and equipment moved inside the fort. At 0232hrs the radio room received a call from Colonel Modard ordering the gun crews to man their stations. At 0400hrs enemy aircraft formations were seen flying over Dutch airspace. Tracer fire and searchlights from the Dutch AA batteries lit up the night sky. The fort's AA guns, under the command of Lieutenant Evérard de Harzir, opened fire. The sound of heavy fighting was heard near Maastricht and red flares were seen over Eben-Emael. A few minutes later dozens of German aircraft crossed into Belgian airspace.

At 0531hrs, one of the gun turrets was ordered to fire on German troops of XXVII Corps near the village of Beusdael, a short distance away on the Belgian side of the Dutch border, and to fire on and destroy the Teuven bridge.[7] At 0630hrs enemy columns were moving on the road from 's-Gravenvoeren (about 1km south-west of the Dutch border) to Moelingen, west of Lixhe. The area around Moelingen was repeatedly shelled by the fort's guns. The POs also reported what appeared to be a fire blazing at Fort Eben-Emael. German troops at Hombourg, less than 10km from the fort, were targeted by fifty rounds from one of the 75mm turrets.

Shortly after 0900hrs the Germans captured the village of Aubel and closed in on Fort Aubin-Neufchâteau. Belgian troops blew up the bridge over the Berwinne River outside Val Dieu. At 1000hrs the civilian electricity grid failed and the fort switched to emergency backup power. Observers at MN 11 spotted Germans digging in at the Aubel marketplace; twenty-five shrapnel rounds were fired. A patrol spotted the Germans attempting to set up an observation post near the Ferme Snowenberg.[8] The 75mm turret fired twenty-five rounds. The mortar block dropped fifty 81mm shells on the Fouron post office. At 1634hrs the fort opened fire on a German artillery battery being set up near the Dutch border and a direct hit destroyed the German guns. The fort continued to carry out its fire missions throughout the day as the enemy continued to advance towards Liège.

Aubin-Neufchâteau's first fatality was Brigadier Lescrenier, a crewmember at the Fouron-Saint-Martin PO that looked directly over the railway. The Germans moved in on the observatory and around noon Lescrenier was killed by MG fire. Two of his comrades, Privates Bastin and Halleux, were captured. Sergeant Gosset, the chief of the post, and Privates Beckers and Longton escaped as the Germans seized the bunker. Gosset arrived some time afterwards at the PO of La Heydt, 2.5km south. That post was also evacuated at 1730hrs and at 1837hrs the crew arrived at the fort.

Fifteen minutes later German troops from 453 IR were spotted 200m away, crawling towards the fort. Bloc 2 opened fire with 75mm *boîtes-à-balles* rounds and the bloc's MG cloche also opened fire along with that of Bloc P. A request was quickly sent to Barchon to fire around the perimeter of the fort. At 2018hrs more Germans appeared in the Neufchâteau cemetery, 60m from Bloc P and 250m from the main fort. The Germans were now coming from all directions. A minute later some *boîtes-à-balles* rounds were fired on Germans at the Trois Cheminées crossroads, 200m from the fort. The Mortar Bloc and the 75s silenced an MG targeting Bloc 1. Similar action continued late into the night.

At 2100hrs an unfortunate but all-too-familiar incident occurred at the wartime entrance of Block P. A three-man reconnaissance patrol tried to reach the entrance door but they were not recognized by the sentry who opened fire, killing Private Louys and seriously wounding Private Van Ingelgom. Due to an increasingly heavy German presence, other patrols in the Voeren region were forced to retreat towards Liège. On only the first day, with the loss of its patrols and the Fouron-Saint-Martin post, Aubin-Neufchâteau's observation capabilities had been seriously depleted.

RFL Group 3 – Fort Evegnée – Fort Fléron: Group Commander Major V. Herbillon

The triangular Fort Evegnée was commanded by Captain-Commandant Laurent Vanderhaegen. Although it was small in size, its armament included one 150mm gun turret, two turrets each with a single 105mm, one Mi/LG turret and three 75mm howitzer turrets. The fort was 3,400m from Fort Barchon. The air tower was located 200m slightly south-west of the tip of Salient III, along the Rue de Thier. Evegnée was supported by the external observatories FE 5 (interval Fléron–Evegnée) and EB 2 (interval Evegnée–Barchon), plus a post inside the Café Bellevue on the Battice–Visé road.

The message – 'Alert – Territory Threatened – First Name Alfred' – was sent by radio to Fort Evegnée at 0105hrs and the message was passed on to Commandant Vanderhaegen. At 0145hrs the men of the garrison in the outer barracks returned to the fort and headed to their combat posts. Commandant Vanderhaegen remarked in his post-war journal that the men were mostly calm.[9]

By 0125hrs, the three long-range turrets were ready to open fire. At 0230hrs, all of the fort's weapons were ready. The Belgian infantry from 12th and 1st Line Regiments were in their assigned positions in the trenches to the left and right of the fort. Dawn broke around 0430hrs. A large number of German aircraft flew over the region of Tongeren–Maastricht–Eben-Emael. At 0500hrs German aircraft flew over the fort and the AA guns went into action. Less than half an hour later the fort fired twenty shots in the direction of Eben-Emael.

Around 0600hrs Evegnée was ordered to fire the 150mm at Eben-Emael. On the left, Barchon and Pontisse also participated in this action. The scene must have been incredible to an observer sitting on top of the fort, to hear the sound of the guns booming and shells flying by the dozen to the north. Around 0730hrs, the 150mm turret resumed its normal interdiction mission, this time on the main crossroads at Henri-Chapelle. At 0900hrs, Vanderhaegen sent Sub-Lieutenant Dinant and an engineer detachment to set fire to the wooden barracks and to demolish the nearby farms of Hosay and Gitken and the Café Mawet with explosives so they could not be used as cover by the enemy. The destruction was completed and the old buildings were flattened. At 1100hrs Vanderhaegen received a message from Major Herbillon, the commander of Group III, asking him to cover the retreat of the Frontier Cyclists occupying a position east of Fort Battice. As the Belgians moved out the Germans moved in. Battice itself was now in danger of being surrounded.

The 105mm turrets began their mission of interdiction and harassment, targeting the Berwinne and Vlamerie bridges. Observers in the forward PO located in a first-floor room of the Café de Bellevue, on the Battice–Visé road, watched the shells fly overhead. They were rapid and accurate and the two turrets took turns firing throughout the day. The 105s were remarkable.

In the evening, the last of the defences designed to block the approach to the fort were put in place. Anti-tank mines were dug into the road, and previously prepared *chevaux-de-frise* were set up to block the access ramp. From now on, the fort had only one avenue of escape to the outside: through the air tower. As night descended, everything seemed calm around the fort, but it was the calm before the storm. Nearby, the Belgian infantry, unseen and silent, occupied the adjacent trenches and for the second time in 26 years, the people of Liège Province fled to the west, while tens of thousands of German troops moved closer and closer as each minute crept by.

Fort de Fléron was commanded by Captain A. Glinne and situated along the main road between Aachen and Liège. It was a large triangular work like Barchon. During the 1930s the fort served as the local training battery for the fortress troops of Liège and all of its armour was replaced. The fort was equipped with two 150mm turrets, two twin 105mm turrets, one Mi/LG turret and four 75mm howitzer turrets. The air tower, also a secondary entrance to the fort, was located 250m due north of Salient I, along the Rue de Retinne. The fort was 3,500m from Evegnée and 4,600m from Fort Chaudfontaine.

Fort Fléron received the alert at 0100hrs. Lieutenant Henry, the adjutant, was the first to arrive at the fort. The garrison spent the early hours getting the fort ready for combat. Orders arrived from Major Herbillon the group commander to begin interdiction fire. The guns opened up for the first time on predetermined targets at Nasproue, Bilstain and Aubel and continued throughout the day. In the distance, German aircraft were seen flying over The Netherlands. Nothing took place around the fort for the remainder of the day.

RFL Group 4 – Fort de Chaudfontaine – Fort d'Embourg – Fort de Boncelles – Fort de Tancrémont – Fort de Flémalle: Group Commander Major Parmentier

On 10 May the group commander Major Parmentier moved his command post from the Citadelle to Fort Chaudfontaine.

Chaudfontaine was commanded by Captain-Commandant Raymond Clobert. The fort dominated the Vesdre valley from a height of 220m. It was a trapezoidal work that covered the Verviers–Liège road and the Aachen–Liège railway. Fort Chaudfontaine was armed with one 150mm gun, two 105mm guns, one Mi/LG turret and four 75mm howitzer turrets. The fort's air tower overlooked the Vesdre valley from the woods 140m north-west of Salient IV. There are no significant details of the action at Fort Chaudfontaine on 10 May.

Fort Embourg was commanded by Captain-Commandant Marie François Jaco. Fort Embourg dominated the Vesdre and Ourthe valleys and covered the Spa–Liège road and Aachen–Liège railway line. The fort was trapezoidal in shape. It was equipped with four 75mm howitzer turrets, its only guns. Embourg had no air tower. Instead, it possessed an air intake in a bunker built into the side of the hill. In addition to the armoured observation post in the former searchlight turret, the *Post d'Observation de l'Eperon*, an external post, was accessible via the air tunnel. This post was equipped with a FM cloche and two FM embrasures.

When the alert message was received by Commandant Jaco, who was present at the fort, the officers, non-commissioned officers and soldiers staying in their nearby homes were recalled to the fort. Team A was on duty on 10 May. Team B was also present and were involved in the evacuation of the barracks and setting up obstacles around the fort. Anti-tank mines were laid on the road to the Ferme Ancre (Chemin de l'Ancre, west of the fort), near the air intake, and along the path to the bottom of the Fond de Cris. The access ramp, the only one that led uphill to the fort was blocked by *chevaux-de-frises* and a Cointet barrier put in place at the base of the ramp. By 0130hrs the fort was in a state of defence.

The Belgian 1st Lancer Regiment had not yet passed by so the road destructions in the vicinity of Embourg, the responsibility of the fort, could not yet be started. Around 0130hrs Lieutenant Poswick of the Lancers arrived at the fort on a motorcycle. He asked to use the radio to report the current situation to III Corps. He told Embourg's command post staff that the Germans were being slowed down by the destructions. He stated that there were no more Belgian units behind him. Poswick left, wishing the men of the fort good luck. The local roads were eventually blown up, but the blasting charges were poorly placed and also damaged the telephone lines leading to the fort and to the observation posts of Beaufays, Bois-les-Dames and Avister. The lines to the fort were repaired during the night, but the observation posts remained cut off.

As dawn broke German aircraft were spotted heading north. A cannonade was heard in the distance and around 0900hrs a glow could be seen in the direction of Chaudfontaine, followed by an explosion. It was the 150mm turret going into action. At Embourg everything was running very smoothly.

In the afternoon the driver of a food delivery truck returning from the military bakery brought news of the dire situation at Eben-Emael. Bottles of milk, beer, etc., were delivered and stored at the postern. A German aircraft flew over the fort and the AA guns opened fire. Later another aircraft flew over without shooting and a French Air Force identification symbol was spotted. It was the only Allied plane the Belgians would see. In the afternoon Team B left the fort its barracks. It would not return. The afternoon was mostly calm. A parade of civilians headed to the west. In the distance the boom of the 150mm guns could be heard, sending their shells towards the Albert Canal. As night fell over Fort Embourg, artillery fire lit up the sky to the north. That same night the 28th Line Regiment quietly left the interval positions between the forts. The infantry around Fort Boncelles had also pulled out during the day and the forts were now on their own.

Twelve kilometres to the south-east the command post of the 6th Company of cyclists was set up at Cornesse, near Bunker VM 3. From 0730hrs to 1130hrs the company skirmished with small German units at Pepinster. Bunkers VM 2 and VM 4 were temporarily manned by the Frontier Cyclists. At 1130hrs the company was ordered to withdraw to Liège. Prior to departing they completed the prepared destructions in Rue Massau at Pepinster and in the Jaminon quarry. Once the destruction was completed, the company left for Liège via the Vesdre Valley. The Casemate BV Vesdre (BV = Becco-Vesdre), equipped with a 47mm gun, an MG and an FM, blocked the road through the valley and defended the anti-tank barrage that ran across the valley. The company made a brief stop there to help the crew of the casemate close the Cointet barriers to block the road.

Internal blockhouse in the tunnel leading to the air tower. (Bunkerfreaks Antwerpen)

Fort Boncelles was commanded by Captain-Commandant Charlier, a First World War veteran. Boncelles was a triangular fort built on a ridge between the Meuse and the Ourthe. Together with Fort Embourg, it was the least heavily armed of all the forts of the PFL, with only four 75mm howitzer turrets. With a range of 5,200m the guns were unable to support either neighbour, Flémalle or Embourg. The main task of the fort was limited to providing fire support to the 6th Line Regiment between Seraing and Boncelles and to the 28th Line Regiment between Boncelles and the Ourthe. The fort was equipped with an air tower 200m north-west of Salient III. Due to the geology of the location on which the fort was built, there was no deep-level gallery, therefore the configuration of the chambers in the quadrilateral were modified as necessary. There are no details of the action at Fort de Boncelles on 10 May.

Fort Flémalle's commander was Captain-Commandant Barbieux. Flémalle was a large quadrangular fort (like Pontisse) located on a plateau south of Liège overlooking the heavily industrialized Meuse valley. Its mission was to guard the passage of the Meuse to the south of Liège and the Liège-Namur railway. The fort's armament consisted of a 150mm turret, one turret for two 105mm guns, a Mi/LG turret and four 75mm howitzer turrets. The fort's observation post was in the form of a cloche like that of the new forts of Liège. The fort was connected to an air tower 200m north-east of Salient IV east of Rue Profondval.

Just after midnight Fort Flémalle moved to the highest level of alert. By 0700hrs the reserve crew had moved to the cantonment in Jemeppe-sur-Meuse. A truck arrived with engineers tasked with clearing the fields of fire in the immediate vicinity of the fort. Two small houses were destroyed with explosives and the wooden barracks on the glacis of the fort was set on fire. Commandant Barbieux arrived at the fort around 1030hrs. During the day the fort was sporadically fired on by German aircraft.

Group V: Fort de Battice: Captain-Commandant Guéry

- 1st Battery – artillery turrets (Captain-Commandant Fichefet).
- 2nd Battery – defensive blocs (Captain Vanderkam).

Fort Battice was located east of the village of Battice and interdicted traffic along the Aachen–Liège railway further to the south, the Aubel–Battice road, and the Aachen–Battice–Liège Road. The railway line running across the northern perimeter of the fort, and defended by Blocs 1 and 2, was the Liège–Verviers Line 38. Fort Battice also protected the intervals to Aubin-

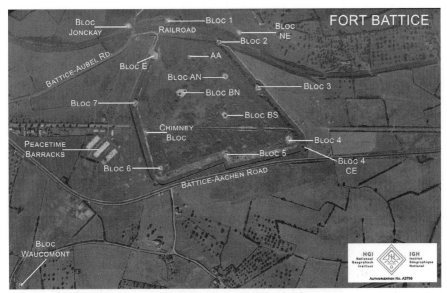

Aerial image from 1947 showing Fort de Battice. (© – NGI – authorization A3796 – www. ngi.be)

Neufchâteau to its north (Aubel, St Jean-Sart and Henri-Chapelle) and Tancrémont to its south (Petit Rechain, Grand Rechain and Wegimont).

The superstructure of this large fort was five-sided and surrounded on four sides by an anti-tank ditch 5m deep and 15m wide with a counterscarp wall 1m thick and a sloped earthen escarp. The railway cut served as the ditch for the north flank and a concrete wall was built along the fort side of the cut. The fort had two entrances, the peacetime entrance in Bloc E and the wartime entrance at Bloc Waucomont.

Its armament included two twin 120mm gun turrets, three twin 75mm Model 34 gun turrets, four 60mm AT guns, eleven twin Maxim MG cloches to defend the glacis, two FM cloches to defend the approaches to the ventilation shafts and eight MG cloches to flank the glacis.

Combat blocs:

- **Bloc 1**: defended the railway and the Aubel–Battice road, and protected the Bloc Jonckay, the entry bloc and crossed fire with Bloc 7. Bloc 1 had an infantry patrol exit. Armament included two 60mm AT guns, one twin MG, one FM to defend the entry and one searchlight.
- **Bloc 2**: a caponier located on the north flank of the fort, alongside the railway, with weapons facing east and west. The bloc interdicted

enemy infiltration of the railway cut. Armament included two 60mm AT guns, two twin MGs, two searchlights and one artillery observation cloche with a periscope.

- **Bloc 3**: a caponier located along the ditch on the north-east flank, between Blocs 2 and 4. Armament included two twin MGs, three cloches equipped with twin MGs and two searchlights.
- **Bloc 4**: mounted both artillery and infantry weapons. It defended the glacis with two MG cloches. Artillery included one twin 75mm Model 34 turret.
- **Bloc 4 Counterscarp**: located across the ditch from Bloc 4, built into the counterscarp wall, a small bloc with a twin MG that defended the south flank of the ditch.
- **Bloc 5**: an impressive caponier located at a bend in the ditch in the centre of the southern flank of the fort. Its mission was to serve as an artillery observation post from a cloche on the top of the bloc, defend the glacis and the ditch with MGs. It included an infantry exit. Armament included one twin MG embrasure, one twin MG cloche, one FM to defend the exit, one searchlight and one artillery observation cloche with a periscope.
- **Bloc 6**: artillery bloc located in the south-west salient, armed with a 75mm Model 34 turret.
- **Chimney bloc**: no combat role; used to protect three ventilation exhaust shafts for the motors.
- **Bloc 7**: caponier similar to Bloc 3. The bloc defended the ditch in the direction of Bloc 6 and Bloc E and the glacis with three MG cloches. Armaments included two twin MGs to flank the ditch, three MG cloches to defend the glacis and two searchlights.
- **Bloc E (Entry Bloc)**: the main entry to the fort. The postern was defended by an iron gate, a rolling bridge that exposed a 3m deep ditch, and an internal blockhouse for FM.

Three artillery blocs were located in the centre of the fort, laid out in a triangle:

- **Turret A North**: armed with a twin 75mm FRC Model 34 turret.
- **Turret B North**: armed with a twin 120mm FRC Model 31 turret.
- **Turret B South**: armed with a twin 120mm FRC model 31 turret.

The fort's external blocs were:

- **Bloc Jonckay**: located on the opposite side of the Battice–Aubel road north-east of and outside the perimeter of the fort. The bloc contained two telescopic cylindrical air ducts, plus an FM cloche with a periscope.

- **Bloc North-east**: built on the north side of the railway line to cover a dead angle in the Stockis ravine. Armed with an MG cloche.
- **Bloc Waucomont**: located 1km south-west of the fort (present-day Rue du Bê Pâkî in Herve), Bloc Waucomont was the wartime entry to the fort. It also contained two additional telescopic air ducts, an observation cloche with FM and periscope, and a twin MG cloche to defend the valley in the direction of Chaineux. The access ramp was defended by an FM.

The fort had two AA positions. One with two Maxim 08/15 MGs on tripods was located between Bloc 2 and Bloc E; the other, with four guns, was located near Bloc Waucomont. The fort also had four external armoured observation posts – VM 23, MM 305, MM 12 and MN 29.

The reversible carriage for twin machine guns. The carriage could be spun around to switch over the guns if one became overheated. (Bunkerfreaks Antwerpen)

Adjutant Duvivier was on duty in the command post of Fort Battice when the alarm message was received at 0035hrs. Only a few officers were present in the fort at the time, among them Commandant Fichefet, Lieutenants Tiquet, Leclercq and Renaux and Adjutants Duvivier and Doultrepont. Major Bovy, the commander of the fort, was being treated in the military hospital of Liège for heart problems. He arrived at the fort at 0430hrs. The rest, including the second-in-command, Commandant Guéry, were at the shooting range of Helchteren, about 20km north-west of Maastricht. Commandant Fichefet took command of the fort until Major Bovy's arrival. The alarm sirens blared throughout the fort and by 0100hrs the crews had moved to their combat blocs and all the gun positions were manned, turrets ready to fire. At the same time, the first detachments of the 1st Battalion of Frontier Cyclists moved past the fort towards Liège.

Around 0500hrs, when German ground forces crossed the border, the fort opened fire for the first time with the 120mm guns towards the border. This interdiction fire was intended to prevent German engineers from repairing Belgian demolition work. At the same time the RFL ordered the execution of the prepared demolitions in the vicinity of Battice, including the wooden barracks. Around 0600hrs a terrible thing happened. Major Bovy suffered a heart attack and died in the command post of the fort. Fichefet again took command of the fort until Commandant Guéry returned to the fort.

At 0700hrs the 75mm guns opened fire towards Welkenraedt. From then on Battice, supported by Fort Fléron, fired continuously on predetermined interdiction targets and those identified by the forward observers. At 0800hrs patrols were sent out to set fire to Ferme Donéa and several houses in the immediate vicinity of the fort.

The fort was provided with a unique system to allow troops staying in the outside barracks to quickly gain access to the underground part of the fort in an emergency. The toboggan, as it was called, was a double sliding board about 20m long that ended at a short tunnel. From there the men climbed down two sets of stairs to the lower tunnels. There is no record that the toboggan was ever used. At 0900hrs the entrance to the toboggan was blown up by Belgian engineers. The partially-destroyed tube was filled with rubble and a wall of concrete was poured to cover the entrance.

During the day the 75mm turrets encountered assorted problems, and specialists from the FRC in Liège were called in to fix them. Shortly after 1700hrs the coverage order of the 1st Border Cyclist Regiment was completed and Major Hermand, commander of the 2nd Battalion of Frontier Cyclists, notified the fort that his command post was moving to the west bank of the Meuse. During the night the fort was directly attacked for the first time.

The ditch between Bloc E (entry) and Bloc 7, which can be seen on the far left. (Bunkerfreaks Antwerpen)

The turret of Bloc 4 came under fire from a small-calibre AT gun, probably a *Panzer Abwehr Kanone* (PAK) 36, from the area of Chaineux. The gun was located and hit by the 75s.

At 0600hrs the Depot and Supply Battery at Fort Hollogne was bombed by Stukas. Moments later, some of the students from the *Batterie d'École* took up position at three AA machine guns installed earlier on top of the fort and kept a watch out for additional German aircraft. The *Batterie d'Ecole* at Fléron had only a limited number of students present on 10 May and during the morning the students were divided up amongst the forts.

At 0300hrs Observation Post MN 29, subordinate to Fort Battice, received the alarm notification. At that moment the post commander Sergeant Servais and Private Mertens were in the bunker. The rest of the men, Privates Burton, Schene and Canon, were in the nearby Ferme Brouwers. The observation team reacted lukewarmly to yet another alarm, but took steps to organize the PO for defence. Their attitude changed quickly when, around dawn, they spotted a large number of German aircraft flying overhead. Around 0500hrs the first refugees passed by the post, among them one of the Frontier Cyclists who informed the team that German infantry had crossed the border. Shortly after noon MN 29 reported German troops at the intersection of Rue de Merckhof and the N608. The Germans were immediately shelled by the guns of Fort Battice. For the rest of the day they continued to report German troop movements. Observation post MM 12, a few hundred metres north of Fort Battice, started the day quietly, but late that night enemy infantry fired at the viewing ports of the observation cloche from the burned-down Ferme Donéa. Battice then shelled and flattened what was left of the farm.

Now we go back a few hours to find out what happened to the men from Fort Battice on range duty at Helchteren. At 0020hrs the men were informed of the alarm. Commandant Guéry ordered them to load the transport vehicles and at 0230hrs they began the trip back to the fort. At 0330hrs the column stopped by Fort Eben-Emael to drop off transmission equipment that had been taken from the fort for the target practice in Helchteren. The column then crossed the Meuse at Visé, but when they tried to leave the village in the direction of Julémont, a roadblock prevented them from moving forward. Guéry contacted the RFL by telephone to ask how he could get to Battice. He was told by Lieutenant Walbers that he must go to the RFL command post in Liège to receive his orders there. When the convoy tried to go back over the bridge at Visé, it was already closed off with Cointet barricades so they followed the east bank of the Meuse for a couple of kilometres and crossed over on the Hermalle-sous-Argenteau Bridge which was fortunately still intact. At the Citadel, Guéry was informed of the current strategic situation and of the recent attack on Fort Eben-Emael. He was also instructed to get as close as possible to Fort Battice with the trucks but if necessary to complete the last part on foot. The column set out again in the direction of Battice along the Bois-de-Breux, Beyne-Heusay and Fléron roads. They finally arrived at a barricade blocking access to Battice. At 0625hrs access to the fort was granted and the road cleared. Guéry was met by a motorcyclist who drove him to the fort. He was informed that Major Bovy had just died and that he was now in command of Fort Battice. Around 0700hrs the last vehicle of the detachment arrived back at Fort Battice.

During the early morning, ominous and shocking news came from the zone of the First Army Corps north of Liège that the Germans were already on the west side of the Albert Canal near Vroenhoven and Veldwezelt, expanding their bridgehead and opening the road to Tongeren. Eben-Emael had been attacked in an airborne operation that may have silenced the fort. Towards evening, the Germans were threatening 7th Infantry Division across the entire width of the sector. If and when the Germans crossed and opened up the Tongeren Road, the PFL was in danger of encirclement from the north-west. On the evening of 10 May the Belgian High Command decided that the infantry positions in the trenches along the PFL 2 east of the city could no longer be held by III Corps. The Army did not want to take the risk of an encirclement of the field troops and at 2000hrs ordered the evacuation of the interval troops from the east bank of the Meuse, with the exception of the fort garrisons.

At 2130hrs Colonel Modard travelled with the commanders of 2nd and 3rd Infantry Divisions to III Army Corps headquarters where he received the message from Lieutenant General de Krahe that the interval troops were being pulled out during the night. The men in the forts were to remain behind to slow the German advance as much as possible. There is no record of his reaction to the news but it must have come as a great shock to him that one of the major pillars of the defence of the PFL was being taken away so soon after the war had begun. Modard decided that the School Battery students, the Battery and Supply Depot troops, surplus staff members and the reserve crews of the forts were to be withdrawn to Mechelen the next day. He ordered these troops to assemble by 0600 on the 11th at Fort Liers. The forts of Liège now stood alone.

Message: HQ German Sixth Army, 10 May 1940 2040hrs

Army order for continuation of attack (excerpts)

Holland and Belgium are resisting the German invasion and have asked for immediate help from the Western powers. Until now, a penetration of English or French forces has not been established. On the army front, the enemy, alerted very quickly, tried to escape, often without a fight, behind the Meuse and into the line of the forts of Liège; to this end, he carried out numerous destructions and placement of obstacles. In spite of this, our troops, by rapid movement, have succeeded in drawing the enemy into a fight, seizing important bridgeheads, and capturing prisoners.

At the Albert Canal, there were counter-attacks on the Veldwezelt-Vroenhoven bridgehead. It is possible that on 11 May there will be more intense enemy artillery and aviation action there.

In the course of the afternoon the following units arrived:[10]

> XXVII CA: Bridgehead west of Eysden, Fouron-Saint-Pierre, Henri-Chapelle, Limburg. Airborne troops have landed on the fort of Eben-Emael. All the bridges between Venlo and Maastricht are destroyed.

> XXVII CA penetrated deeply on the left flank, has begun to cross the Meuse at Visé, covering the left flank of IV Corp against a sortie from Liège.

It is important to bring as quickly as possible the main forces to the Albert Canal, to cross and enlarge the bridgeheads west of Maastricht so as to permit the deployment of mobile forces in the general direction of Gembloux. The rapid achievement of the construction of auxiliary bridges at Maastricht is of paramount importance.

Army Group Reserves
223 DI: from its arrival at the debarkment location it will be placed under the orders of the army and will concentrate on the morning of 12 May in the vicinity of Slanake–Hagelstein–Henri-Chapelle–Hergenrath–Raeren (Division HQ: Hombourg).

VIII Air Corps will provide support to IV Corps and in particular to the right wing of XXVII Corps after direct consultation with the corps commanders.

Army Command Post as of noon on 11 May: Sittard.

The Commander-in-Chief,
(s) von Reichenau[11]

Report of Belgian GHQ on the Strategic Situation of the Armies on 10 May

On the 10th of May, at 0400, without ultimatum or declaration of war, the German air force attacked aerodromes, army posts, and communication centres. The Belgian air force was caught on the ground and lost half of its aircraft.

On the front Eben-Emael–Vroenhoven–Veldwezelt, in the salient of the Albert Canal, German glider-born troops and parachutists landed behind the bridges and on the superstructure of the fort, surprising and exterminating the detachments on guard, dislocating and damaging the armament and casemate control sections of the fort of Eben-Emael, by means of high explosives; the bridges of Vroenhoven and Veldwezelt are in their hands; the fort of Eben-Emael was partially neutralized. In the region of Canne, the bridge was blown up. During this time, the German air force ceaselessly bombed troops in the entire sector of the 7th Infantry Division. Detachments of German troops crossed the river Meuse at Maastricht in boats and gradually reinforced the airborne troops. A detachment of German sappers forced a crossing of the canal near Canne, and will, on the morning of the 11th, support the besiegers of Eben-Emael.

Blockhouse overlooking the damaged Kanne Bridge. Remnants of the bridge allowed German troops to cross on foot. (Digital History Archive, 'Bunkers of the Blitzkrieg')

In the provinces of Liège and Luxembourg, forward troops fought until the evening against powerful armoured German detachments; in spite of the presence of parachutists in their rear, the 1st Division of Chasseurs Ardennais performed wonders. At nightfall the Chasseurs fell back as ordered towards the Ourthe; the 1st Cyclist Regiment, the 2nd Guards Regiment and the 1st Regiment of *Chasseurs à Cheval* have fallen back from the junction of the Meuse-Escaut and Albert Canal; the 1st Regiment of Frontier Cyclists and the 1st Lancer Regiment have fallen back on the Liège stronghold during the course of the day.[12]

Chapter 4

The Fortified Position of Namur from 10 to 14 May 1940

The *Position Fortifiée de Namur* (PFN – Fortified Position of Namur), the western component of General Henri Alexis Brialmont's *Forts de la Meuse*, was built during the years 1888 to 1892. It encircled the city of Namur with a belt of nine forts and suffered the pounding of the heavy German guns in 1914 during a short siege. The Germans made

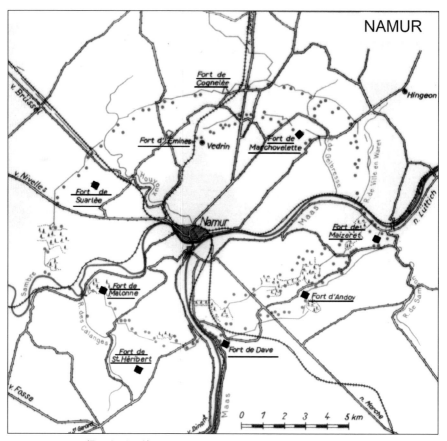

Plan of the PFN. (Denkschrift)

modifications to the forts during the occupation, as they had done at Liège, and after the war the forts were abandoned. Then, in line with the new Belgian strategy, the forts of Namur were refurbished in the 1930s. No new forts were built. In 1940 the fortress consisted of the nine old forts with bunkers and a complete chain of anti-tank and anti-personnel defences in the intervals. Two of the forts, Cognolée and Émines, were used as depots.

The fortress of Namur was traversed by the Meuse and the Sambre Rivers. The terrain forms a plateau covered with flat ridges and crests, the height of which gradually decreases to the north. The Meuse and Sambre valleys are deeply cut, with winding valleys that could only be covered by gunfire for a short distance. The right bank of the Meuse is higher than the left, which is why the Germans attacked in the north in 1914. Numerous streams crossed the plateau in mostly steep-edged and deeply cut gorges. Extensive forests obstructed the view of observers, especially south of Namur. Numerous small villages dotted the countryside. According to a pre-war German study, 'The ground was good. The soil was rock and clay, hard in dry weather and suitable for gun transport. In wet weather fields and meadows were soft and not sustainable everywhere. Hedges and numerous wire fences, however, often complicated troop movements outside the roads.'[1]

The northern front of the fortress stretched from the Meuse to the Sambre, and consisted of a dense belt of field fortifications with obstacles at a depth of about 1km, reinforced by numerous new MG and AT gun positions. In front of it ran an anti-tank ditch, triangular in section and about 7–8m wide, which was completed in its entire length and used the streams of the Waret and the Ruisseau de St. Lambert. Only in the villages were there gaps in the ditch. A second line, which was not continuous, ran from 2km to the south of Fort Marchovelette–village of Cognelée–Védrin–Fort Émines to Fort Suarlée. It consisted of field fortifications of low density and depth, reinforced by a number of observation bunkers. An anti-tank ditch was located between the Brussels–Namur road and the village of Suarlée. Anti-aircraft positions could be found in both lines. Most of the field fortifications and interval bunkers were not manned in May 1940.

The garrisons of the Namur forts fell under the command of the *Régiment de Forteresse de Namur* (RFN – Fortress Regiment of Namur) commanded by Colonel Adolphe Drion. It included two groups:

Group 1: Major Edward Pinchard:

- Fort Marchovelette – Captain Georges De Lombaerdt.
- Fort Maizeret – Captain Léon Hambenne.

- Fort Andoy – Captain Auguste Degehet.
- Fort Dave – Captain Fernand Noel.

Group 2: Major Jules Decoux:

- Fort Saint-Héribert – Captain Leon L'Entrée.
- Fort Malonne – Captain Edgard Demaret.
- Fort Suarlée – Captain Fernand Tislair.

Forts of Group 1

The mission of Fort Marchovelette was to cover the Gelbressée–Hingeon–Bierwaert road, the Namur–Hanret road and the Tillier–Sclayn road, as well as the Meuse valley. These points could only be taken under indirect fire. The fort's field of fire was limited by woods and heights up to 1,500m. The valley of the Ruisseau de Gelbressée on the east side of the fort was also difficult to see. The Chaussée Gelbressée-Namur was partly visible, but not the north part. Fort Marchovelette was at an altitude of 195m. Armament included one turret for twin 75mm GP in the former 150mm turret, three retractable turrets for single 75mm howitzers in the former 57mm turrets, and two grenade-launcher turrets in the former 120mm turrets. The ditch-defence casemates and the wartime *Corps de Garde* were equipped with MGs. The air tower was located to the rear of the fort.

Fort Maizeret was located on a steep hill at an altitude of 190m that sloped away to the north, east and south. It had good views to the north-east to the Meuse Valley and the railway and road to Sclayn that ran along the Meuse. To the north-west was the confluence of the gorges at Hannut and Marche les Dames. Visible in the north was the height of Bellaire. The view to the east extended to 4,000m, but in the south-east it was limited to 1,200–1,800m by the mountains above the Samson Valley. The valley was hidden from sight and the direct fire of the fort. In the south, the landscape rose to 1,200m. Armament included one turret for two 105mm guns, four turrets for single 75mm howitzers and two grenade-launcher turrets. The entry ramp and the ditches were defended by MGs. There was no air tower, instead, the ventilation outlet was located in the side of a cliff that looked out on the Meuse Valley.

From Fort Andoy the view was good, although the forested areas immediately in front of the fort were thick and enemy infantry could find good cover in the ravine-rich terrain. The road to Marche could be seen up to the Bois d'Ausse. Fort Andoy was equipped with one turret for twin 75mm GP guns (non-retractable) in the former 150mm turret in the centre of the fort, four 75mm howitzer turrets, one in Salient I, one in Salient III and two in Salient II, one turret for twin MGs in the former 120mm turret on the Salient I side of the massif, and one turret with two grenade launchers in the former 120mm turret on the Salient II side of the massif. Casemates equipped with MGs defended the ditches: the gorge front casemates protected the Salient I to III lateral in both directions while the head casemate defended Salient I to II lateral and Salient II to III lateral. The air tower, built in the same configuration as those at Liège, was located 1,400m to the rear of the fort and was equipped with FMs.

Fort Dave dominated the Meuse Valley both upstream and downstream to a distance of about 4,000m. The immediate vicinity of the fort was heavily wooded. To the east, the field of fire was only good to the north of Naninne. To the south, the view extended 1,000m to the Bois de Dave. The ravine climbing from the village of Dave could be seen about 100m forward of the fort. To the west, the view was good. The ridge, fortified by the works of Maizeret, Andoy and Dave, dominated the foothills and was a very good defensive position. Armament included one turret for twin 75mm GP guns, three turrets for 75mm howitzers, one turret for a twin MG and one turret for a grenade launcher. The air intake opened along the cliff face to the south-west of the fort, overlooking the Meuse Valley.

Forts of Group 2

Fort Saint-Héribert dominated the Meuse Valley (but only indirectly), the Wépion–Lesves road and the roads leading through the Bois de la Haute Marlagne from Burnot to Floreffe and the road from Sart-Saint-Laurent to Floreffe. The field of fire to the north-east, east and south was good and sometimes reached 3,000m, but was crisscrossed by unseen gorges. To the south-west and west the view was limited to 1,500m approaching Bois de la Haute Marlagne. The altitude of the fort was 250m. Armament included: one turret for twin 75mm GP guns, four turrets for single 75mm howitzers and two turrets for twin MGs. The fort had no air tower, instead the outlets were located on top of it.

Fort Malonne dominated the Sambre Valley and by indirect fire the roads of Namur–Floreffe, Fosse, Namur–Temploux and Floreffe–Burnot (on the Meuse). The area was heavily wooded and only the immediate vicinity of the fort had been cleared in May 1940. Numerous obstacles significantly limited the view of the gunners. Observation was also limited by numerous blind spots and the steep-edged ravines. Altitude was 200m. Armament included one turret for twin 75mm GP guns, four turrets for single 75mm howitzers and two double grenade-launcher turrets.

Fort Suarlée was located on a small hilltop where it dominated the Namur–Beuzet and Namur–Temploux–Mazy roads as well as the railway to Brussels. The railway station of Rhisnes was not visible from the fort but was in range. To the front, the view was good, but the valley of the Ruisseau St. Lambert, which led from the village of Émines to Rhisnes, and the Fond du Maréchal (near Rhisnes) could only be seen in some places. In the south-west, the view was limited by the village of Suarlée and the forest. Armament included one turret for twin 75mm GP guns, four 75mm howitzer turrets and two twin MG turrets. It was the only fort at Namur with a *Galérie de Bombardment* in the lower tunnels.

*   *   *

Here are the events that took place at Namur from 10 to 14 May. Since very little action took place here during the first four days, they have been condensed.

The RFN received the general alarm from Army HQ shortly after midnight on 10 May. The staff of the RFN moved into its command post in the Citadelle of Namur. Commanders of the Namur forts recalled their garrisons. Like the other Belgian forts, most of the men were in barracks in the vicinity of the forts. Around 0200hrs the crews left the barracks and headed to the forts which reported as ready for action by 0400hrs. The reserve garrisons remained in the barracks. At daylight the Luftwaffe appeared and attacked some of the forts. Otherwise it remained relatively quiet in the vicinity of Namur.

Espionage efforts against Namur had begun early, possibly years before the war. The Germans came into possession of classified maps of the PFN that included all of the existing military structures and their organization. At some point before the war started, Lieutenant Fisette, deputy commander of Fort Saint-Héribert, while passing by a house not far from the fort overheard a conversation in German. He went to the army headquarters at Namur to report this information but they thought he was crazy. He also told Commandant L'Entree, who related in his diary that the day after the first bombing of the fort, they had spotted a red rocket in the sky. They looked at the map and realized it was over the house that had so intrigued Fisette earlier. Shortly after that, several other rockets rose from suspicious houses and the bombing of the forts began.

The men of Fort Marchovelette spent the initial hours putting the fort into combat readiness. The fort's AA emplacements were set up and frequently strafed by German aircraft. As the Germans moved in on Namur a few days after the war began, some of the outer bunkers were abandoned and the crews evacuated to the forts. Marchovelette was equipped with two generators in case power from the civilian grid was cut. One of the generators broke down and the fort was left with only one.

During the morning of 10 May the peacetime barracks located just outside the fort was destroyed with dynamite to clear the field of fire in that direction. The fort also received supplies for the last time and the reserve crew arrived at the fort via the ventilation tower. Apart from sporadic bombing by the Luftwaffe, Fort Marchovelette's first few days of war were quiet.

Fort Maizeret was alerted at 0114hrs. The garrison occupied the fort and was ready for action by 0210hrs. The first combat action came from the 105mm turret that fired several shots towards the north-east at German troops approaching from north of the Meuse. The 75s also fired counterbattery missions. It would remain relatively quiet at the fort for the next few days.

Fort Andoy deployed its AA guns and fired at German aircraft without much success. Similar scenes took place at the other forts. The Luftwaffe caused limited damage but their primary mission at this stage was reconnaissance and disruption. Early in the morning of 10 May the garrison of Fort Dave was assembled in the gorge ditch and the officers took charge of placing the men in their combat posts. The PO teams headed out in trucks to man their posts. Dave had four such positions:

- A factory near the Naninne railway station.
- Cemetery of Naninne.
- Néviau station.
- Near Covis Chapel in Lustin.

The Lustin post overlooked the Meuse and covered one of Fort Saint-Héribert's blind spots. Private Widar was taken to his position at Lustin where he was connected by telephone, via the civilian network, to what was referred to as '*Maison Mere*' (the 'Mother House') – Fort Dave. Widar's partner, Private Lustinois went to find food in the nearby village and upon his return, he said that everyone in the village confirmed that '*C'est la guerre!*' Widar thought that the sounds of explosions he had been hearing were coming from workers in the local quarry using dynamite.[2]

In addition to the main fort, the Dave garrison was also responsible for manning the *Abris* Troonois, located on a hill overlooking the Meuse River and connected to the fort's ventilation tunnel. Troonois was equipped with a 60mm AT gun and a pair of MGs for defence in the direction of Wépion.

At first, the Germans left the fort alone and only showed interest after they crossed the Meuse between Namur and Dinant, when it became clear that Dave still had the potential to slow their advance. Nevertheless, there were five air strikes on the first day and the AA guns of the fort took action.

The first hours of the war passed by, full of news (or lack thereof) and rumours. The guns of the fort came into action for the first time on 10 May against German motorized reconnaissance units, an incredible demonstration of how quickly the Germans penetrated into Belgium on the first day. At 0645hrs the 75mm GP guns fired on armoured vehicles near Godinne. The 75mm howitzers also opened fire around 1000hrs. The Germans moved into Godinne, about 10km south of Fort Dave, in the afternoon. Two POs at Naninne, about 2km east of the fort, were evacuated at the end of the day and the observers returned to the fort.

On 11 May German aircraft flew over the fort and targeted the access ramp and the external barracks. This increased nervousness and caused several friendly-fire incidents against Belgian patrols. On 13 May Dave executed its first shots on the Courrière-Maillen sector. However, French artillery, which had moved into the area over the past couple of days, also opened fire in the direction of the Belgian PO of Lustin, believing firmly that all activity on the far side of the Meuse was hostile. The French were warned but refused to cease fire. This forced the observers in the post to retreat to the fort.

Dave and the other forts continued to be supplied from the Aubelais depot but on 14 May the last food supplies were delivered. The forts would also no longer be supplied with munitions. On the evening of 14 May the ammunition delivery truck attempted to reach the Cognelée depot but after a long trip, could only bring back a small load.

Captain Leon L'Entree, commander of Fort Saint-Héribert, was awakened sometime around 0115hrs on 10 May by Brigadier Mignolet with the message: *'Commandant, l'etat-major telephone: Alerte generale.'* L'Entree made his way to the command post, opened the safe, retrieved an envelope, and confirmed that the alert was authentic. The time was 0124hrs. L'Entree thought to himself: The guns had been quiet for more than a quarter of a century. Were they once again going to be heard echoing along the hillsides of the Meuse?[3]

All tasks prescribed in the *Dossier de Défense* were prioritized. At 0138hrs the *Bureau de Tir* (Artillery Fire Control Post) was fully operational, the turrets were manned and the AA crew left to take up positions in the Bois Triangulaire, adjacent to the fort. Observation crews headed out to the following posts:

- Post 1 on the Renier farm.
- Post 2 on the Laquisse farm.
- Post 3 near the Route d'Insperé.
- Post 4 at the Régina intersection.

Advance artillery POs were located as follows:

- Post G 6 at Lannoy Castle in Annevoie.
- Post G 7 near Al Parapette in Bioul.
- Post G 8 at Montigny farm in Arbre.
- Post G 9 on the Libenne farm in St-Gérard.

For the rest of the day the crew was busy at work around the fort. The turrets were fully stocked with ammunition, and minefields and barbed wire installed along the approaches to the rear of the fort. At 1230hrs POs G 8 and G 9 reported the arrival of the first French troops in the Meuse Valley. Late in the evening Casemate Wépion phoned to say that a French officer staying in the Chateau de Fooz-Wépion asked to set up a liaison with the

75mm GP turret at Namur. (Digital History Archive, 'Bunkers of the Blitzkrieg')

fort the following morning. Lieutenant Fisette drove over to the chateau the next morning but was unable to locate the French officer.

Work inside the fort continued on 11 May. A shelter was built at the new location of the AA guns near the Gesnot crossroads. At 1030hrs a German aircraft strafed the position with MG fire. German aircraft patrols increased. The AA guns fired on the Germans who responded with strafing and dropping small bombs that were more effective in lowering morale than any destruction they caused.

Fort Malonne's observers put out a message that paratroops had landed between the water tower of Bois-de-Villers and the fort, as well as the Bois de Haute-Marlagne. Two patrols sent out by Saint-Héribert found nothing. At 1230hrs, Fort Saint-Héribert received its first fire command for the 75mm guns against a German observation post in the Saint-Roch chapel.

Posts G 8 and G 9 continued to report French columns moving into the region. Finally at 1600hrs a French artillery officer, Lieutenant Tordeur, showed up at the fort. French artillery was now in place at Ferme Bournonville. In the evening Casemate Wépion reported a French battalion encamped on the left bank of the river from La Pairelle to a point south of the Ile de Dave. At 2200hrs the railway station of Ronet was bombed by the Germans.

During the second half of the night of 11/12 May, the wooden barracks were set on fire by order of the RFN. Pungent smoke filled the air and the structure's slow collapse sounded like guns going off. From that date the crew stayed continuously in the fort. Lieutenant Blavier left for Verdin at 0900hrs to collect 130 land mines to plant near the bunkers in the vicinity of the fort. Throughout the day, one air raid alarm followed another. The observation team at Saint-Hubert reported that two German armoured vehicles were spotted near the Covis chapel. At Fort Saint-Héribert, damage to the barbed wire at the entrance ramp was repaired. The enemy presence still remained only in the sky. The men manning the AA guns were the most exposed and on 12 May, three of them, Privates Basseille, Grignard and Rousseau, were slightly injured.

May 13th was a day of abandonment and retreat. Maréchal des Logis Simon, manning one of the roadblocks in the vicinity of the fort, reported seeing a continuous line of civilian refugees and army stragglers. He also found an abandoned truck full of military supplies and was ordered to bring back machine guns and ammunition to his post. Another patrol returning to the fort found boxes and papers dumped in the ditch along the Saint-Gerard road. Lieutenant Delvigne of 1st Battalion of Frontier Cyclists, was ordered to go to the location and burn the documents. Throughout the day

German aircraft flew over the fort. The AA guns were busy. The French units which had crossed to the right bank of the river were ordered to pull back. At 2000hrs POs G 7, G 8, and G 9 were abandoned and the crews pulled back to the fort. Worse, the spearhead of the German Blitzkrieg, the Panzer divisions, were about to cross the Meuse to the south.

On 14 May French artillery batteries were set up at Fontaine-Meurette, Aux Vivis and west of the Bois-de-Villers church near Six Bras and Profondeville. Lieutenant Fils was sent to make contact with the French. The group commander's command post was in the Bois-de-Villers. The regiment command post was at the Chateau d'Arbre. As Fils arrived the French opened fire. The command post at Saint-Héribert made contact with a French officer at the PO Pruniers and the following conversation took place:

Saint-Héribert: 'What are you shooting at?'
French officer: 'On the right bank of the Meuse.'
Saint-Héribert: 'On which objective, precisely?'
French officer: 'On any target that presents itself.'
Saint-Héribert: 'Aren't there [still] friendly units on the right bank?'
French officer: 'In principle, everything on the right bank is enemy.'

Communications were then cut off. The French fire continued as caisson after caisson was emptied, firing at nothing. Now out of ammunition, the French batteries pulled back. Lieutenant Fils went to find what was going on but was unable to find anyone. French observers showed up at several Belgian posts but with their talk of retreat, ended up demoralizing the Belgians, resulting in desertions. Soon the POs of St. Hubert and Manoir did not respond to calls. At Pruniers only Private Pinchart was left. Two volunteers, Dandoy and Poisseroux were sent from the fort to join Pinchart. Eight men were sent to a field battery at the church of Lives to replace deserters.

At 0645hrs on 10 May 1940, about 150km to the east, the commander of the German 211 ID received the following message: 'The attack has started – 0900 to all divisions: Alarm command – 1300: divisional command No. 1 – to advance.' Crowds of German civilians lined the streets of Liblar and Lechenich, about 60km east of Aachen, and in all places in which the path led to the border and cheered on the regiments of 211 ID as they began their long march to the west – to Namur.[4]

On the night of 11 May, the division marched into the area of Merzenich–Düren–Nideggen–Vollersheim–Vettweiss–Hochkirchen. The division command post was moved to Nideggen.

On 12 May the division crossed the border into Belgium. After passing the mountainous terrain at Schleiden, 317th Infantry Regiment passed the border at Wahlerscheid and reached the Elsenborn camp. The division followed Fourth Army in reserve towards Flanders.

On 13 May the 211th reached Kalterherberg–Elsenborn–Schleiden. Division staff was in Schleiden, and on 14 May Born Meyrode–Honefeld–Mürringen. They were 100km from Namur.

Chapter 5

Saturday, 11 May 1940

Report from General Alfred Wäger, XXVII Corps – 11 May 1940
The second day of the attack was very hard for the corps, which had to cross, fighting, the northern half of the fortified region of Liège. Following the withdrawal of enemy [Belgian] troops in front of the Sixth army, the resistance of the fortress troops remained tough along the Meuse and the Albert Canal. The fire from the forts of Neufchâteau, Battice and untraceable batteries installed near the Meuse south-west of Eysden was particularly deadly. To this must be added the violent action of machine guns hidden in the banks of the Meuse and the Albert Canal that were difficult to locate. Thus the attack launched with great courage on the morning of May 11 by the 269th Infantry Division from Eysden was initially doomed to failure, although some smaller units managed to cross the canal. Subsequent attempts failed because all means of transportation were destroyed by artillery and machine gun fire; in fact, almost everyone visible and the rafts were hit. Likewise, the troops between the canal and the Meuse suffered terribly under the fire of an enemy who, despite the use of all means of observation, remained untraceable. I personally realized, on the front line, that the continuation of the attack at this location was not justified and I had it stopped.

Expecting that, under the pressure of IV Corps which had attacked at 1000, the enemy would also retreat, I ordered the continuation of the attack further north. At 1440, 489th Infantry Regiment, under the orders of Major Berend, successfully crossed the Meuse and the canal and occupied hill 119.[1] It was a glorious action.

While parts of 269th Infantry Division remained blocked near Eysden under the unchanged action of the enemy, the crossing operations could take place east of hill 119. The bridge over the canal was temporarily repaired. The 269th received the mission to reach the Saint-Trond–Liège route. 253 ID, after working through the bunkers around Berneau,[2] took Visé at 1600. The enemy still resisted in the fortified positions. Aubin-Neufchâteau was surrounded. It was now clear that from an operational point of view the main enemy forces had abandoned the fortified position of Liège; it only held on by its forts. The intermediate ground was no longer or only very lightly occupied. Now, the mission of the corps was no longer the encirclement of the fortress, but the pursuit on the left wing of the Sixth Army.

So the question arose: was it possible to pass with the corps next to the line of forts without attacking them, despite the fact that they still made an effective shot? I realized that it would be difficult. But, given the need to continue the pursuit, losses had to be accepted. Another problem was the lack of bridge engineers. The corps had to be content with its own resources, which were quite limited. In addition, until the forts were neutralized, all the crossing points remained under heavy artillery fire.

Nevertheless, thanks to the courage of the troops and in particular the engineers building the crossings it was possible to move a great quantity of troops throughout the day of 11 May. They were mainly mobile units intended for pursuit of Sixth Army to the west. The bridge near Maastricht did not become available for certain motorized units until 12 May at noon.

/s/ Wäger[3]

The message above contains a wealth of information on the Belgian resistance to the attempted crossings of the Meuse on 10 and 11 May, and supports the Belgian accounts. The main resistance was coming not only from the forts but also the 2nd Frontier Cyclists Regiment, which guarded this sector of the river. General Wäger's report mentions 'machine guns hidden in the banks of the Meuse and the Albert Canal'. These were most likely small MG and AT bunkers occupied by the Cyclists. A line of bunkers was built along the left bank of the Meuse, and in this case the ones between Jupille to Maastricht defended the Visé and Lixhe gaps. About twenty shelters were built in the Pontisse-Lixhe sector in two groups: the first between the Meuse and Albert Canal and the second built on the right bank on the heights of Haccourt. The shelters were designated as 'PL' for Pontisse-Lixhe, and the sector began at the Chertal factory. PL b and PL c were equipped with MGs and FMs. PL 5 and PL 6 were located at Basse-Hermalle (PL 1 to 4 were not built.). PL 7 guarded the Visé Bridge. PL 8 and 9bis (PL 9 was not built) were built on the bank of the Meuse to discourage any crossing there by the enemy. They were backed up by a series of field works, trenches, MG nests, fortified houses and the soldiers of the 2nd Cyclist Regiment. The stand by the 2nd Cyclists on 11 May has been compared to the same stand against the German crossings at Visé made by the 12th Line Regiment in August 1914.

PL 10, 10ter, and 10bis were constructed where the land between the Albert Canal and the Meuse was at its narrowest (750m). PL 10 flanked the Meuse; PL 10ter, with a 47mm gun, guarded the Lanaye road and PL 10bis, also with a 47mm, flanked the canal. These blocs, together with Cointet barricades blocking the Lanaye road, formed a very powerful anti-tank position. The remaining eleven bunkers were placed in a second echelon from Oupeye to Haccourt to defend the roads coming out of Visé and Lixhe. A narrative written by a veteran of the Frontier Cyclists[4] states that there were some so-called 'Abri Contre-Irruption' (IR), 8.5m x 6.65m with two gun embrasures and an observation cloche. In Visé there were four IR bunkers, designated Vi 2, 6, 7 and 11. Vi 2 blocked the Dalhem–Visé road and was located above Visé along the Dalhem road. Vi 6 was in the Visé barracks to defend access to the Rue de Berneau and the second behind the barracks to guard the Rue de Mons. Vi 11 was near the railway bridge and guarded the Mouland road. Their main purpose was to watch for motorized columns and for this they were equipped with a 47mm gun plus an MG for infantry.

V Corps Message Traffic: 11.5.40 at 1750 (VIII *Fliègerkorps*, 3rd Squadron, 13th Reconnaissance Group)[5]

Air reconnaissance report:

- Pilot: Oberleutnant Glitz.
- Observer: Oberleutnant Schaefer.
- Flight time: from 1620 – 1720hrs.

Reconnaissance results:

1. All roads and railway bridges over the Amblève from Remouchamps to the mouth of the Amblève into the Ourthe are destroyed (see point 4).
2. All railways and road bridges over the Ourthe from Esneux to Hamoir are destroyed. A small branch line railway bridge 1km W Poulseur not destroyed.
3. Big train station near Deux Flamme,[6] N of Comblain-au-Pont with about 500 carriages. No locomotives detected under steam.
4. Railway bridge 3km W Aywaille not destroyed.
5. Own troops detected in Hautregard and 500m E Vert Buisson at 1630hrs.
6. Combat actions did not take place in the line La Reid–Hautregard–Remouchamps. Enemy artillery was not observed.

Just after midnight, Major Simon, commander of RFL Group 2, was informed that Belgian army troops in the PFL were to be evacuated beginning on 11 May, but that the crews in the forts would be left behind. Colonel Modard had then decided that the reserve crews of the forts would join the regular army and evacuate to the west. All the reserve crews were ordered to assemble at Fort Liers by 0600hrs to be evacuated to Mechelen near Antwerp. Major Simon and his staff moved to Fort Pontisse at dawn.

Around 0130hrs Fort Pontisse received the order to fire on a German artillery battery near Saint-Rémy. Half an hour later the reserve garrison left the fort to join the field army. Pontisse continued to fire on the attempted crossings over the Meuse and the Albert Canal. At 0430hrs a German observation post in Grand-Lanaye was shot at, along with some twenty landing boats on the banks of the Meuse, putting a temporary halt to the German crossing attempt. Bombardment of the Mouland road viaduct followed 90 minutes later.

German troops appeared on the heights of Berneau north of the railway tracks and in the railway cut. A very violent fight ensued with the 3rd Battalion of the 2nd Border Cyclists along the battalion front. The Germans made no attempt at this time to cross the river, but were pounded by the defenders on the left bank and Fort Pontisse. The fighting lasted until 1500hrs and the Germans withdrew. 253 ID attempted to advance along the right bank of the Meuse but made no progress. At 2015hrs 3rd Battalion of the 2nd Border Cyclists was given the order to withdraw. 51st Company made up the rearguard and their last duty was to blow up the Haccourt Bridge over the Albert Canal. At 0700hrs Fort Eben-Emael came under fire from Fort Pontisse for the last time. Around 1100hrs communications with the fort were cut off.

Pontisse had an observation post in interval bunker PL 13 on the road to Oupeye. The observers were under fire by German artillery in Dalhem, but remained in place for the time being. The Germans had set up their own observation post at Villa Joassart in Argenteau. The 75mm turret of Salient III fired on the post. Reports on enemy troop activity continued throughout the evening. Scouts were spotted near the bridge of Vivegnis. Salient III's 75s bombarded the bridge and after the sixth shot it collapsed. The 105mm turret along with the guns of Barchon shelled the railway tunnel in Dalhem. After darkness the bridges of Hermalle and Haccourt were blown up by Belgian engineers.

Just after midnight Commandant Pourbaix, commander of Fort Barchon, was notified that the Belgian infantry had pulled back across the Meuse and the fort was now isolated; now a *'Fort d'Arrêt'*. Fort Barchon carried out two fire missions on the village centre of Fouron-le-Comte,[7] a few kilometres south of the Dutch border. Barchon's six heavy guns opened fire, causing serious damage to the small village. The 105mm guns of Barchon and Pontisse concentrated their fire on a German gun battery to the north. The shelling lasted three minutes and the German artillery limbered up and moved out of range. All throughout the early morning hours Barchon's guns kept German troops from moving towards Eben-Emael and the Albert Canal to relieve the paratroopers there. At first light, Sergeant Van Michel sent out a party to survey the outside of the fort. It would have been found in good condition at this point since German bombardment had not begun in earnest. They might also have noticed glaringly empty interval troop trenches on both sides of the fort.

During the morning, the 150mm turret fired sixty rounds on the top of Eben-Emael to try to dislodge the German glider troops, but the fate of the large fort had already been sealed. Throughout the day, Barchon's guns focused on the road junctions north-east of Liège, in particular the crossroads at Trois Cheminées near Fort Aubin-Neufchâteau. The railway tunnel in Dalhem, where 200 to 300 Germans were spotted, and the coal mine of Trembleur were also struck. German troops were targeted at Roclenge-sur-Geer, an indication they were now moving west of Fort Eben-Emael. The three 75mm turrets fired on the Bois de Trembleur, between Visé and Barchon, where observers at Leval reported seeing German troops. In the evening shelling continued against the coal mine of Trembleur and on the village of Supexhe near Blegny continued.

The fort started to experience a variety of mechanical difficulties. The electric lights inside the right 150mm turret went out and the electrical current to the munitions hoist failed. The high rate of fire of the guns led to a number of mechanical breakdowns. The left 75mm gun of the Salient II turret overheated, causing the premature explosion of a shell. Four men were injured including Brigadier Léon Schoofs who suffered a broken arm, fractured skull and burns on the face and hands; Brigadier Darchambeau was burned on the hands and face; and Private Dethier had burns to the face. The ammunition lift of the right 150mm turret was jammed and unrepairable. From then on the shells had to be carried by hand up to the guns. This was a significant problem because the shells were stored in the quadrilateral tunnels of the fort and the men had to climb a ladder to reach the surface, an extremely difficult feat when carrying a 75mm or 150mm shell. In the Salient II turret the recoil brake of the right 75mm gun jammed and took several hours to repair.

The AA battery on top of the fort was hit by the Germans. One aircraft flying at low altitude was shot at and hit, and made a forced landing in the open countryside.[8] Two of the gunners, Brigadier Jules Braham and Private Westphal, were injured by German gunfire and Captain Pourbaix ordered the crew inside the fort. The fort also lost the use of several POs. The observers in one post no longer answered their phone and were considered lost. The elevator shaft in the Hasard coal mine in Cheratte used as PO 206 was evacuated when Belgian engineers came to destroy the shaft with explosives. An observer at the Trembleur coal mine, Maréchal des Logis Defauw, was shot and killed at his post. Around 2230hrs observation bunker AC 1 on the Rue des Crêtes in Aux Communes was hit by artillery fire. Brigadier Miessen's face was badly burned by the explosion. Doctor Wiener from Fort Barchon headed out to tend to the injured man. The turrets continued to fire as night fell. At 2000hrs Pourbaix received a message from Colonel Modard congratulating the gunners at Fort Barchon for their excellent job in supporting the defence of Eben-Emael.

Overnight, German troops from 269 ID surrounded Fort Aubin-Neufchâteau. At 0130hrs on 11 May a Belgian patrol returned to the fort. The corporal leading the patrol had been killed. The remaining members reported artillery batteries being set up between the villages of Bombaye and Fouron and that the fort was slowly but surely being surrounded and it was getting difficult to get through the enemy lines. They brought back enemy weapons and equipment to show they had had to fight their way back through.

At 0100hrs a sentry in Bloc 3 saw lights moving on the glacis at the edge of the ditch and heard tapping sounds on the outer wall. An order was sent to Casemate 2 and the gun turret of Bloc 2 to open fire with machine guns, anti-tank guns, and shrapnel rounds. After this the tapping sounds ceased. A German MG located near Bloc P was firing at the gun turrets. It was silenced by the MG cloche in Bloc 3 and FMs from the observation cloches. Around 0430hrs one of the two MG cloches of Bloc 1 was hit in the viewing scope, possibly by a sniper, and put out of action. At 0507hrs Stukas made their first attack on the fort. The gun turrets were retracted to protect them from the bombs. The explosions could be felt inside the blocs.

At 0605hrs Bloc P signalled the presence of enemy troops moving along the wall separating the bloc from the road. The order was given to the Mortar Bloc to fire fifteen rounds on Bloc P and Casemate 3 to fire ten 47mm rounds. The German troops were driven off. At 0715hrs enemy infantry was spotted moving towards Bloc O. They were hit by the 75mm guns and Bloc 3's MGs. Forty-five minutes later the fort was hit by heavy-calibre shells and the turrets were retracted. The German battery doing the damage was spotted and Commandant d'Ardenne called Fort Battice to request supporting fire against the battery. A moment later rounds from Battice rained down on the German battery. One gun was destroyed and the rest abandoned by the fleeing Germans.

A German artillery unit with 88mm and 37mm guns approached from the direction of Warsage. Both guns would cause devastating damage to the cloches. The German guns were set up at the top of the road near Trois Cheminées. At 0900hrs Bloc 3 was hit by 37mm shells. The bloc fired twenty rounds and the gun was silenced but the 37mm gun got off a final round, destroying the aiming scope of the bloc's gun. From that point on the crew had to aim down the barrel.

At 0930hrs the fort was attacked by 2nd Battalion of 453rd Infantry Regiment but the attack was repulsed. In the afternoon, the fort was attacked by a large formation, and requested supporting fire from Fort Battice. This second attack was also neutralized. 2/453 IR was trying to make quick work of the fort. At the end of the day, the fort repelled about twenty platoon-strength attacks. The optical equipment of several of the observation cloches was damaged, seriously effecting the fort's infantry observation capability.

At 0950hrs Bloc 1 fired fifty shells in the direction of one of the heavy batteries. The gun accidentally fired while the turret was being raised into the battery position, damaging both guns. The engineers worked to repair the guns and the barrels were shortened to remove the damaged parts. One gun was operational by evening and the other the following morning. At 1000hrs the Germans opened fire from the Trois Cheminées crossroads on Blocs 1, 2, and 3 with 37mm and 88mm guns. At the same time German infantry launched another assault on the fort. The Mortar Bloc opened fire and the assault was repelled. Battice fired on and silenced the batteries at Trois Cheminées.

There follows a fascinating, detailed synopsis of the attacks that took place throughout the day against Aubin-Neufchâteau by 453 ID and its support batteries. It reveals the intensity of the attacks designed to eliminate the threat posed by the fort against movement of German troops towards the Meuse on 11 May. It was the most significant attack against a fort of the PFL with the exception of Fort Eben-Emael.

1115hrs: The Mortar Bloc reported enemy MGs at La Heydt. Bloc 2 engaged them with fifty 75mm rounds.

1230hrs: An enemy gun firing at Bloc 1 was spotted near the Goffart farm. The target was neutralized by the guns of Fort Barchon.

1245hrs: Bloc 2 engaged an enemy battery at Berneau with 100 shells from the 75. The enemy retreated, leaving several dead men and horses and damaged equipment behind. Bloc 1 and 3 under heavy enemy fire and shelling.

Information reached the fort from RFL that, thanks to its action and the action of the other forts of the region, German convoys were avoiding driving on roads as it was deemed too dangerous.

1330hrs: One of the remaining two interval shelters was attacked by enemy infantry and twenty-five rounds from the 75mm turret were fired in support. Bloc 2's 75mm gun turret engaged enemy guns near La Heydt with fifty rounds. One of the MG cloches on Bloc 2 was hit by a German 88mm anti-tank round. The aim was perfect and it hit the embrasure, totally destroying the guns and the mount. The enemy shell passed between the men manning the MG and became embedded in the metal. Fortunately no one was hurt. The embrasure was repaired with steel beams and the gun crew used an FM from that point on. An MG cloche at Bloc 1 suffered the same fate.

1400hrs: Battice was asked to target the Goffart farm.[9] At 1430hrs Battice fired on the Bois Canelle, and the crew of a German battery there abandoned their guns and retreated. They attempted to return to save their guns, but again came under fire from Battice and decided to retreat for good. They were then engaged by Aubin's MGs.

1510hrs: Casemate 1 signalled that the outer wall in front of Bloc O was being heavily shelled. A German aircraft was spotted flying over the fort to help fine tune enemy artillery fire. The AA gun crews had to seek shelter inside the fort as enemy shelling made their position outside Bloc P too dangerous.

1534hrs: A new enemy gun crew appeared at Bois Canelle and another at Goffart farm. A call for support fire was sent to Fort Battice to engage Bois Canelle and to Barchon to engage Goffart farm.

1551hrs: The Germans launched another infantry assault on the fort in the direction of Blocs O and P and toward the fort itself from both the east and the west. Barchon fired shrapnel shells over Blocs O and P while Aubin-Neufchâteau engaged the other assault groups with its MGs.

1600hrs: Counterbattery fire from Battice drove the Germans from Bois Canelle. Blocs 1 and 3 were under heavy fire. Thirty to forty Germans were spotted near Goffart farm and engaged with MGs.

1621hrs: Both MG cloches of Bloc 1 were hit. They were patched up but the crew had to use FMs as both MG mounts were damaged.

1630hrs: Very heavy shelling.

1700hrs: The Mortar Bloc observation cloche received a direct hit from an AT gun, probably a PAK 36. One of the embrasures was damaged. There were no casualties.

1730hrs: The Germans launched a new assault on the fort toward Bloc 1 and 3. Bloc 2 fired shrapnel, the Mortar Bloc fired fifty bombs and Bloc 3 engaged the enemy with the MG cloche.

1745hrs: Casemate 2 reported a direct hit on its 47mm gun.

1800hrs: Casemate 1 reported a direct hit on its FM embrasure.

1807hrs: The turret of Bloc 2 was jammed in the battery position. Numerous glancing blows on the turret created grooves along the flanks that prevented it from being lowered. The crew finally managed to lower it manually. The engineers got to work smoothing away the grooves with blowtorches.

1811hrs: The Germans launched a new infantry assault on the fort at the time both gun turrets were out of order. A call for support was sent to Battice.

1845hrs: One of the two guns inside the Bloc 2 turret suffered a direct hit. It could not be repaired, as the whole assembly was broken. The gun embrasure was then sealed shut with armour plates and sandbags. This turret would now be required to continue operation with only one gun.

(To sum up the day, two of the turret guns in Bloc 1 were damaged and fired to a shorter range and with a slower rate of fire; the gun turret of Bloc 2 had only one gun remaining in service.)

1928hrs: Battice called to say they had spotted and neutralized an enemy battery. HQ called and announced that Aubin-Neufchâteau was being cited in today's dispatches for its stubborn resistance (twenty enemy infantry assaults were repulsed that day).

2135hrs: Calm returned. HQ was informed about the damage to the gun turrets. New guns were requested to replace the damaged ones. In the current situation it was an impossible request to fulfil.

2345hrs: The Mortar Bloc was ordered to fire randomly on all three sides of the fort during the night to deter enemy assaults.

The 3rd Infantry Division occupying the PFL 2 line from Visé to Chaudfontaine abandoned its positions during the early morning of 11 May. As of 1000hrs the intervals between the forts of Barchon, Evegnée, Fléron and Chaudfontaine were void of troops. From now on the forts were dependent on themselves.

Around 0100hrs Group 3 commander, Major Herbillon, arrived at Fort Evegnée through the air tower. Herbillon briefed Captain Vanderhaegen of the current situation:

The enemy opened a large gap in the line of the Albert Canal. To avoid encirclement, the troops of III Corps evacuated the line of rearmed forts and retreated behind the Meuse. Their withdrawal [is] to be completed before dawn. By order of the commander of III Corps, the rearmed forts will have to fulfil a new mission: that of *Forts d'arrêt*. Colonel Modard and the group commanders were now each located in one of the forts where they would coordinate the defence [Colonel Modard was in Fort Flémalle].[10]

In the morning Vanderhaegen informed the garrison of the situation and the change in the mission. The men accepted the news, not without some surprise, but with the 'calm and courage of good soldiers'.[11]

The retreat of III Corps, which was carried out quickly under cover of darkness, caused two serious consequences for the defence of Fort Evegnée. Both the crews of the AA guns and external observation posts were part of the army and left along with the rest of the infantry. At dawn, Vanderhaegen sent out patrols to the positions evacuated by the infantry to recover equipment, ammunition and food that had been abandoned and that could be useful for the continued defence of the fort. There was no enemy opposition. The patrols were frequently overflown by enemy reconnaissance aircraft which followed, at low altitude, the general route of the abandoned trenches. The patrols recovered four AA guns and 33,000 cartridges from the AA position. These guns were installed on the central massif on either side of the infantry sortie. Crates full of infantry ammunition – charged cartridge belts for machine guns, loaders for the FMs, 47mm rounds, flares, signal flares, etc. – lay in the empty trenches, in shelters and in roadside ditches. Because of the discoveries the allocation of ammunition for each of the six air tower FMs went from 12,000 to 30,000 rounds; grenades were increased from 48 to 120 per launching position. The patrol also killed and butchered a cow which provided extra fresh meat to the garrison.

The upper platform of Evegnée's air tower was designated as a permanent observatory. This position provided a fairly good view of the intervals, especially towards the rear to the left bank of the Meuse from Fort Pontisse to the Citadel of Liège. It provided a great overhead view of the fort and its glacis. The tower was commanded by Sous-Lieutenant Dinant.

At 2200hrs, Colonel Modard ordered the 150mm turret to fire on the village of Wonck to support the retreat of Belgian infantry being pursued by a German motorized column that had crossed the Albert Canal near Eben-Emael. The garrison learned of the fall of Fort Eben-Emael. Despite the depressing news their morale remained excellent, at least according to Commandant Vanderhaegen. It is hard to believe that morale was excellent knowing that the Goliath to the north had been the first to fall. The men had worked hard for two days and hardly had time to think or discuss these events among themselves. More than anything they needed rest.

As night fell observers could see, to the east, searchlights from German AA positions watching for Allied aircraft, and the beams of the searchlights of Fort Battice. Flares fired by the Germans lit up the sky like summer fireflies a short distance ahead of the line of the rearmed forts. The long-range turret guns of all the forts spit orange flames into the night, continuing to wreak maximum havoc on the Germans who, despite the resistance, continued to pour into Belgium from the east.

Overnight the crew of the Café Bellevue post moved into a field adjacent to it to escape German fire. At 0400hrs Sergeant Horion decided to return to the café because more could be seen from there than from the field. The crews manning posts FE 5 and EB 2 left when the infantry pulled out and headed back inside the safe walls of the fort. Fort Evegnée thus lost its two permanent POs, leaving only Horion's Café and the observation cloches on top of the fort. At 1000hrs Horion was ordered to send a patrol to Charneux. Privates Verdines and Tenaille 'volunteered' and discovered German artillery pieces set up along the Les Fawes road north of Charneux. The coordinates were passed on to the artillery command post. At 1800hrs German patrols passed by in front of the PO and some of the men entered the café. However, observation continued discreetly.

At some unknown point in time, the electricity at Fort Fléron failed. All operations now had to be carried out manually, including delivering ammunition to the turrets and raising, lowering and aiming the guns. The

150 and 105s fired on interdiction objectives as well as a column of German armoured vehicles at Biomont, 5km south-west of Battice. While firing its very first shots, the barrel of the 75mm of Salient I exploded on the second shot and three of the crew were injured. Pieces of the projectile were found among the debris. The cause was either the fuse going off early or the shell becoming jammed in the barrel.

During road demolition work by the engineers the underground telephone cable at Romsée was cut and Fort Chaudfontaine lost its connection with Fort Fléron. The communications staff established an alternative connection between Chaudfontaine and Fléron via bunkers MG 1, the PO for Chaudfontaine and MG 4, the PO for Fléron located in Magnée. At 0200hrs the commander of Group 4, Major Parmentier, arrived at the fort. A short while later a man wearing civilian clothes was spotted in the steeple of a church in Cornesse, and suspected of being a German observer. Chaudfontaine's 150 fired on the location. The fate of the man is unknown.

Embourg followed the day's events at a distance. No direct contact was made with the Germans that day and the crews used the time to pack the gun turret magazines with ammunition. At dawn, the interval trenches were deserted. Shelter EC 1bis and EB 8 called to report the departure of the infantry. This resulted in a brief moment of panic for all the men, but it quickly passed. Along the front, the German 253 ID approached the Amblève River. In the afternoon, observers reported a massive bombardment coming from the north-west of Liège. The rail station of Liers, where the reserve troops assembled for their journey to Mechelen, was heavily bombed causing many Belgian casualties.

The garrison of Fort Boncelles took advantage of the relative calm to stock up on its supplies of ammunition, food and weapons left behind by the 6th and 28th Line Regiments. Nothing further of any note took place.

Belgian refugees continued to move west along the edge of Fort Tancrémont. At 1400hrs a German column was spotted on the Desnié–Haut-Regard–Route de La Reid road. The fort came into action for the first time and fired on the column. During the afternoon news of the surrender of Eben-Emael reached Tancrémont. Volunteers were sought to leave the fort and join the field army. The younger recruits were advised to leave due to their age and brief time in the service. Yet many of the men wanted to stay. The command staff of the fort decided who would join the volunteers and they left in the middle of the night to their destiny. Around 0100hrs on the 11th, a patrol of five men went out to visit the abandoned shops at Pepinster, and brought back eggs, cigarettes, liqueurs, bacon and cakes.

Some of the men made a quick visit to their homes and their friends and were each given a bottle of rum.

Fort Flémalle was spared the worst violence during the first days of war. Around 0700hrs the destruction of the Meuse bridges of Val-St-Lambert and Ivoz was heard in the distance. The reserve team joined the evacuation to Flanders. Observers witnessed the heavy air raid on the Belgian troops during their passage through Liers.

At 1730hrs Flémalle was ordered to open fire with its 150mm gun on the roads in the vicinity of Tongeren – thirty interdictory shots per hour. Calculations for range and direction were made and the shots were under way at 1745hrs. Everything went well in the beginning but as the night wore on, several mechanical and electrical problems occurred – failure of the munitions lift, oil leaks, broken coupling on the steering motor, loose nuts, bent firing pin. The steering motor coupling was irreparable. The firing pin was replaced. During the first night the specialists were constantly at work repairing one piece or another. Now that the lift was no longer working the shells had to be moved by hand from the quadrilateral up to the guns. Furthermore, the ventilation system was found to be inefficient and it was very noisy in the gun chamber. These problems indicated that the crews were in for a difficult ride in the days to come.

During the night of 10/11 May, the Germans approached Fort Battice, firing continually on the fort's cloche observation ports. In the morning post MM 305 reported a large concentration of German troops assembling in the centre of Chaineux. All of the 75mm turret guns opened fire on the town and the roads leading into it, scattering the German troops. Around noon the fort was hit by small-calibre artillery. The 120mm Bloc Nord and Bloc 2 in particular were targeted. When a large concentration of enemy troops was observed in Aubel, Commandant Guéry called for support from Evegnée and Fléron. All in all, 200 shells were fired at Aubel by the three forts. Captain d'Ardenne requested fire on an enemy battery positioned on the edge of a wooded area along the Rue de Merckhof (outskirts of Aubel). Fort Battice reacted immediately with counterbattery fire from the 120mm turret. One enemy artillery piece was damaged and the crew fled into the forest.

German patrols passing along the Stockis road north of the fort were shelled by the 150mm gun of Fléron. The shots fell near the Sainte-Odile chapel at the intersection of Stockis and Rue Margensault. Priority was now given to observed targets and no longer to the execution of random suppression and destruction fire on predetermined coordinates. Despite the ongoing neutralization of enemy artillery batteries, new batteries continued to appear. At the end of the day one of the 120mm guns from the south bloc was damaged and could no longer fire. The other one could only be loaded by hand.

At dawn, German reconnaissance and bomber aircraft flew over the fort. The AA section between Bloc 2 and Bloc E fired 6,000 shots and remained active until around 1300hrs when they came under heavy enemy fire. While being bombarded by enemy artillery, they were pinned to their position by MG fire coming from two directions. Some time later they were able to evacuate the position, taking their weapons and ammunition with them.

At daybreak the crew of MN 29, the *Observatoire d'artillerie de la Croix de Charneux*, did not know if the Germans were in the vicinity of the bunker. The chief of the bunker sent out three soldiers to explore the immediate surroundings. At first the coast appeared to be clear, but when the patrol was on their way back to the bunker, German infantry appeared and the bunker's guns opened fire to provide cover. The Germans responded immediately with MGs and grenades and the bunker was attacked on all sides. The patrol rushed inside and locked the armoured door behind them. MN 29 requested support and a few seconds later a shower of friendly shells hit the bunker. The Germans immediately broke off the attack.

The ammunition depot at Fort Hollogne received the order to bring all its arms and ammunition to Flémalle and to evacuate the depot. At 1900hrs a crew loaded the equipment on a truck and left for Flémalle. After the delivery they headed out in the direction of Huy.

On the evening of 11 May the garrison of Fort Eben-Emael was sent through Maastricht to Fallingbostel, Germany, location of POW Camp Stalag XIB. The transfer to Germany was kept quiet and the prisoners were secluded in order to prevent details about the way the fort was overpowered from leaking out. 1st Group of the RFL had ceased to exist.

Strategic Situation in Belgium at the End of 11 May 1940

On 11 May, German engineers set up temporary bridges over the River Meuse at Maastricht, and armoured detachments joined in the battle for the Albert Canal. Crossing the bridge of Veldwezelt, tank formations deployed on either side of the road, and penetrated deeper into the Belgian lines, followed by powerful infantry units which enlarged the breakthrough, supported all the time by the Luftwaffe. Fort Eben-Emael surrendered at 1230hrs.

In spite of stiff resistance, 7th Infantry Division was overwhelmed; the neighbouring 4th Infantry Division pivoted on its left flank. The presence of the 1st Cavalry Division brought up from the south was not enough to stabilize the situation.

In the province of Luxembourg, light French forces and *Chasseurs Ardennais* on the line Ourthe–Saint-Hubert–Étalle, were strongly engaging the enemy. In Holland, the Peel sector was overrun, and German armour reached Willemsvaart.

The Allies advanced towards the main defence position; the French Seventh Army reached the Dendermonde-Tilburg line; the vanguard of the British Expeditionary Force (BEF) reached the Dyle, while the French First Army took up position on the railway line Brussels–Gembloux–Namur and sent out advanced elements along the River Gete; Ninth Army reached the Meuse.

Towards evening the Belgian commander decided to withdraw troops from the Albert Canal to the line Antwerp–Namur, screened by a rearguard established first at Tongeren, then on the Gete.

1st Division of the *Chasseurs Ardennais* withdrew to Suarlée. 2nd Division of the *Chasseurs Ardennais* took up a sector of the PFN. 6th Infantry Division marched off to occupy a sector on the Antwerp-Namur position, south of Lier,[12] leaving a rearguard on the Albert Canal and junction canal.

Chapter 6

Sunday, 12 May 1940

Report from General Alfred Wäger, XXVII Corps – 12 May
On the third day of the attack, the gunfire from the forts of Neufchâteau [*sic*], Battice, Fléron, Evegnée and Barchon directed at Visé and the crossing points was felt very strongly; the enemy still resisted on the Meuse facing Visé. Despite this, 253 ID succeeded in securing the Meuse crossings. The vanguard units did not allow themselves to be stopped by the fire coming from all sides, because the ground between the forts was not occupied. Already in the morning, an advanced unit of 269 ID occupied the Citadel of Liège and other units of the same division seized the forts of Lantin and Loncin in the afternoon. Notwithstanding the shooting [by] the forts in its flank and rear, the division continued to move forward unshakably and forward units were already attacking *en masse* in the Huy sector. Because of the staggered crossing conditions, 253 ID followed 269 ID on its left.

In order to clarify the situation, I considered it necessary to put an end to the troublesome forts and I instructed 253 ID to reduce the forts of Pontisse and Flémalle; 223 ID was to do the same with the forts of Battice, Barchon, Fléron and Evegnée. German artillery fire[1] and Stuka attacks had no effect. It was obvious that only the work of pioneers[2] with shaped charges could lead to a result. However, an order from Sixth Army relieved the corps of this mission which, from May 14th, was entrusted to the 223 ID, which was placed under the direct orders of the army command.

/s/ Wäger[3]

A Luftwaffe reconnaissance mission took off from the airfield at Sourbrodt at 1030hrs on 12 May. Its assignment was to observe the condition of bridges along the Ourthe and Meuse, to see if there were any troops or artillery in the Chaudfontaine–Boncelles–Chatqueue–Sauheid area, to check the situation at Fort Tancrémont, and check the roads in the Poulseur–Engis–Liège area. The flight reported that the Meuse bridges were all blown from Huy to Liège; the Ourthe bridges between Poulseur and Tilff were blown up and the Tilff Bridge damaged. The Engis

Bridge in Liège was still intact. No enemy troops or artillery were observed south of Liège. Fort Tancrémont was undamaged and there was no activity around the fort. No enemy aircraft or Flak was noted.

223 ID was at Hombourg, 12km south of Aachen. They were to maintain their advance towards Maastricht and would be reinforced with 385 IR and 223rd Pioneer Battalion. 344 IR was in the second echelon.

Around 1400hrs Colonel Modard ordered the rate of artillery fire to be lowered in all of the forts. Because of the retreat from Liège, the staff feared that the forts would fall because they would run out of ammunition.

Various patrols were sent out from Fort Pontisse during the night. In the meantime, the 105mm turret continued to shell intersections and bridges, including Withuis (part of Eysden on the Belgian-Dutch border), Wonck and Bassenge. Shortly after 0415hrs Barchon reported the presence of enemy infantrymen near the fort. Pontisse's four 75mm turrets opened fire on the zone between the southern edge of Housse and the entrance to Fort Barchon.

German pioneers from 253 ID moved closer and closer to Pontisse. During the morning, patrols were sent to the valley of the Geer, Milmort, Hermée and Grand'Aaz and the Lanaye sector to follow the German progress. The scouts called in targets for the 105mm turrets. At 1130hrs observers in bunker PL 13, the observation post for Fort Pontisse, reported a German motorized column heading along the road from Haccourt to Oupeye. The four 75mm turrets of Pontisse drove them off. At 1300hrs a column of infantry moving on the same road was driven off by the 75s. The Germans escaped the shelling by taking shelter in nearby houses. PL 13 provided the coordinates of each house and they were reduced to rubble. The Germans then fled into the countryside. PL 13 had become a thorn in the Germans' side that needed to be removed. Fort Pontisse came under artillery fire for the first time around 2000hrs by a German battery near the Chapelle de la Lorette in Visé. The 105mm turret provided counterbattery fire. German artillery action gradually slowed down and stopped at nightfall.

Throughout the night of 11/12 May German troops, also from 253 ID, had infiltrated to the immediate vicinity of Fort Barchon. They had reached the anti-tank rails and barbed-wire entanglements. German pioneers cutting through the barbed wire could be heard by the fort's sentries. Within a one-hour period two companies (about fifty soldiers each) were driven away from the anti-tank rails near the glacis and on the road leading to the fort by shrapnel shells from the 75mm turret of Salient II. However, a malfunction caused the turret to become jammed in the closed position. Mechanics immediately set to work fixing the problem. German troops appeared in the vicinity of Bacsay, a little over 1km north-east of the fort. Pontisse also shelled the top of Fort Barchon. Despite the heavy defensive fire of the 75s and MGs, the Germans continued to surround the fort, their numbers growing throughout the night.

A German artillery battery was set up between Barchon and Heuseux. Fort Barchon fired to the north-west on Riemst, Roclenge-sur-Geer and Wonck. During the afternoon German troops in Zichen-Zussen-Bolder, 3.5km west of Eben-Emael in the Flanders region of Belgium, and in Riemst were targeted by the 150mm guns. The 75mm guns intervened against the infantry attacks on Pontisse. Targets were hit at the request of Fort Aubin-Neufchâteau. In the early evening forward observers in bunker AC 1 at Aux Communes indicated the presence of enemy troop concentrations near the Monami farm near Chertal, located between the Meuse and the canal across from Argenteau, prompting the fort to fire a salvo of 120 75mm shells. At 1145hrs, while shelling Roclenge and Wonck, the sighting scope of the 105mm right turret was damaged and had to be repaired. Forts Barchon and Pontisse provided support to eliminate a German battery firing on Aubin-Neufchâteau. At 1810hrs a patrol was dispatched to locate the large battery firing on Pontisse. It was discovered at Lorette, south of Vise, and coordinates were passed on to Pontisse.

To the east, Fort Aubin-Neufchâteau was now surrounded by German troops while the bulk of the German army passed by to the north, heading for the Meuse crossings, and to the south along the Meuse Valley. The following is taken from entries in Captain-Commandant d'Ardenne's logbook for 12 May.

0115hrs: A noise was heard above Casemate 1. Bloc 1 fired shrapnel rounds in that direction.

0536hrs: The mortar blocs fired on the main crossroads of Fouron. One of the gun turrets opened fire on a convoy of vehicles. The lead vehicle was damaged and the convoy blocked and in disarray. The artillery commander ordered a high rate of fire on the objective. Fifty mortar shells were also fired at the Val Dieu crossroads a few minutes later.

0755hrs: A column of German soldiers on bicycles headed toward the town of Warsage. Bloc 1 fired shrapnel rounds on the cyclists and the mortars fired on the La Heydt road that led in the direction of Trois Cheminées. The column panicked and tried to turn around but by doing so they crossed through the field of fire of Bloc 1's MG cupola and the 47mm gun installed in the cloche of Casemate 3.

0845hrs: The gun turret of Bloc 1 fired twenty-five rounds at the entrance to the village of Bombaye, on a column of 100 German soldiers on horseback. A few minutes later a German convoy on the road that led from Aubel through Val Dieu to Warsage was engaged by Casemate 3's 47mm and MG cloche. One of the trucks caught fire and the convoy turned around and headed back towards Aubel.

0904hrs: German soldiers crawling through the tall grass toward the ditch were hit with twenty-five mortar rounds. RFL asked d'Ardenne to send out recon patrols but he explained that the fort was surrounded and he was unable to carry out the order. There were also multiple sightings of German planes, some flying over the fort at low altitude.

0933hrs: Another concentration of German soldiers on horseback appeared in Bombaye. Bloc 1's turret opened fire but one of the already damaged guns jammed. Both guns could only fire low yield, short range charges so a request was sent to Battice and Evegnée to take care of the horsemen. On several occasions throughout the day, German infantry attempted to crawl towards the fort from the direction of Trois Cheminées and were driven off by the mortars.

1107hrs: Germans in the cemetery were hit by twenty-four rounds from the Mortar Bloc.

1227hrs: Infantry approaching the fort from the Trois Cheminées crossroads was engaged by one of the 47mm guns and the MGs from Casemate 3. Bloc 2 opened up a sweeping artillery barrage on the position.

1243hrs: The one gun inside the Bloc 2 turret broke down just as the guns in the Bloc 1 turret were repaired. The engineers moved on to Bloc 2 to make repairs. The gun had a broken firing pin which was repaired and by 1250hrs it was operational again.

1259hrs: Bloc 2 fired twenty rounds on a German convoy approaching Fort Battice.

1330hrs: One of the MG cloches of Bloc 2 was damaged and had to be replaced with an FM. One of the two 47mm guns of Casemate 3 was put out of action and it was also replaced with an FM. The anti-tank gun was repaired by the engineers and back in action by 1950hrs.

1351hrs: Once again a group of men tried to cut through the barbed wire network around the fort and were hit by MG fire. Casemate 3 reported being hit by an anti-tank gun that was out of their field of fire. The Mortar Bloc fired twenty-five shots and neutralized the gun. One of the MGs of Bloc 1 took a direct hit from an 88mm gun, destroying the gun's optics. Engineers were called in to replace them.

1437hrs: Three horse-drawn heavy guns, most likely 150mm *feldhaubitze*, were spotted on the road between Warsage and Berneau, heading toward Fouron. The 75mm turrets fired fifty rounds on the convoy at the maximum rate of fire.

1530hrs: Battice reported a German convoy in Hagelstein, north of Aubel. One of the gun turrets fired fifty rounds in that direction.

1550hrs: Heavy shells started to fall very close to the fort, coming from the heights of Richelle along the Meuse. Fort Evegnée located and engaged the battery. A German mortar team in the Neufchâteau cemetery was hit by rounds from Fort Battice.

1600hrs: Artillery shells began to rain down on the fort, in particular the two turret blocs. The muzzle flash of the German guns was seen between Berneau and Fouron. Bloc 1's turret scored a direct hit on an ammo crate, creating a violent flash that sent black smoke into the air. Fifty more rounds were fired on the battery and then the turret was hit by an 88, forcing it to shut down.

1754hrs: The fort was hit by another round of heavy shelling. This time the muzzle flash originated from the vicinity of the Mortroux-Bombaye road. The Mortar Bloc fired fifty rounds on the battery.

1808hrs: Bloc 1's 75mm fired twenty-five rounds on a column of trucks heading toward Fouron.

1941hrs: Cows appeared on the glacis near the ditch. This indicated the barbed wire surrounding the fort had been cut by pioneers or damaged by the shelling. At the same time a small group of Germans was heading towards an abandoned bunker in the valley below the fort. The 75mm turret of Bloc 2 fired twenty-five rounds on the bunker.

2000hrs: The anti-tank obstacles near Bloc 2 were damaged by German shelling. A repair team closed up the breach as soon as darkness set in. The job was very dangerous since the anti-tank rails were outside the perimeter of the fort.

2023hrs: In light of the German attempts to infiltrate the perimeter of the fort, Commandant d'Ardenne sent an order to all blocs: beginning this night and every night, from dusk till dawn, the Mortar Bloc would fire on all three sides of the fort at a rate of thirty rounds per hour. All MGs were to randomly fire a couple of rounds through their fields of fire every 10 minutes and the gun turrets were ordered to fire shrapnel in random directions. D'Ardenne hoped that these actions would keep the Germans away from the fort at night. It would also use up a lot of ammunition.

2350hrs: Bloc P reported two German teams coordinating their positions by firing flares. The Mortar Bloc fired thirty rounds on both teams and the Germans dispersed. With that the long day came to an end.

On this first Sunday of the war, Chaplain Van Eycken of Fort Evegnée gathered the troops in the main gallery for Mass. Outside the fort, interdiction fire continued. The Germans were moving closer and closer to the fort by the hour. Small squads came within range of the air tower and fired a few MG and rifle rounds on the concrete tower, not causing any damage but hoping the Belgians inside might keep their faces away from the observation ports.

PO Bellevue was directly threatened. German motorcyclists moving along the Battice–Visé road passed directly in front of the café where Horion and his men were hiding. Vanderhaegen ordered them to stay where they were but if they believed they might be seen, to get out and return to the fort. During the day a German patrol entered the building. Horion and his men ran down into the cellar with their equipment and documents. The Germans searched the ground floor and the first floor but neglected to search the cellar. At nightfall, the team left the post without being seen and returned to the fort, entering through the tower. Vanderhaegen congratulated them for their service and for the courage and coolness they demonstrated.

Now that there were no longer any external observation posts, Evegnée's gunners had to rely on their own means of observation. The turret commanders were given permission to fire directly at targets if spotted in their viewing scopes without waiting for orders from the command post. Targets included German infantry digging in close to the fort, and small detachments or vehicles within reach of the 75mm guns. The Germans had also set up gun batteries to target the fort and every time one of the turrets lifted to fire it was hit by German shells. No detailed record of this back-and-forth action was kept but Vanderhaegen noted that he believed the

Belgian guns inflicted losses on the Germans, that the forts were putting up a determined and careful defence, and that the Germans would be punished each time they made the mistake of sticking their heads up. The 75mm howitzer proved to be a sturdy and reliable weapon.[4]

The long-range heavy guns continued to fire, but their rate was slowing down due to electrical equipment failures and repairs to the 150mm. It was also critical to start rationing 105mm ammunition before the stock was depleted. Despite the hits on the turrets and air tower, and the fact that the Germans were closing in on the fort, according to Commandant Vanderhaegen, the morale of the men remained high.[5] Around midnight the commandant retired for the night and the command of the fort was handed over to Lieutenant Decarpentrie.

Not much information is recorded about Fort Fléron on 12 May. The bombardment of the fort by small-calibre guns continued. The fort fired on German troops in Louveigne, and on a column of motorcyclists near Soumagne. The 105mm and 150mm turrets fired interdiction shots. Around 2050hrs the observation posts of Fort Chaudfontaine in Magnée (Mg 1 and Mg 4) were attacked by enemy infantry. Fire support was requested from Fléron and Chaudfontaine to relieve the pressure. Both forts unleashed a heavy barrage on the two POs and the Germans aborted the attack. Fléron also fired on the Bois des Mazures in support of Fort Tancrémont. Late at night Fléron's sentries heard noises in the ditch and spotted shadows on top of the massif. Captain Glinne ordered the 75s to fire *boîtes-à-balles* and the Mi/LG turret to strafe the massif, and the FMs in the flanking casemates to open fire. Chaudfontaine also fired on top of the fort and calm returned. What was on top of the massif? Was it German pioneers, or phantoms, the latter being a quite common occurrence on the Maginot Line at night. Radio Operator Digneffe explained in his journal:

The men were busy since 10 May. Artillerymen and observers were vigilant day and night. I was on duty in the telephone central inside the fort along with the *Officiers de Tir* and the commandant of the fort. At some point I heard the following from the observer: 'The Germans are on the fort.' A general stupor took over – where did they come from? The guard posts had not seen anything. The commandant reacted immediately. He ordered the actions discussed above – for the 75s of S-II and S-III to open fire with *boîtes-à-balles*. The flanking casemates in the postern and ditches were alerted. The FMs opened fire. Grenades were tossed into the ditches. The *Bureau de Tir* asked for information from the POC, which responded, 'The Germans are crawling on the massif.' Firing continued. After a certain time, Lieutenant Henry decided to see what was happening and he went out on the massif by the infantry exit. He returned laughing loudly at what he had seen. The soldiers of the fort had earlier rounded up pigs from the local farms to supply fresh meat for the men. That night the pigs moved up on the massif to eat and the observers thought they were Germans. The next morning a dead pig was found and the rest were still wandering around. This one pig had cost plenty of ammunition.[6]

At 0250hrs observers on top of the massif of Fort Chaudfontaine also believed they had spotted Germans in the ruins of the barracks. A group led by Lieutenant Ledent, commander of the 150mm turret crew, made a sortie to drive them off but it turned out to be a false alarm. Regular patrols were still being sent out. Private Lemperez, on patrol at Chaudfontaine village, reported enemy troops at Ensival. The patrol also destroyed a supply of munitions left behind by friendly troops at Romsée and Henne. Chaudfontaine's long-range turret guns fired on various targets in support of Tancrémont. The 75s also came into action. The electrical motors for the 150mm malfunctioned and the turret then had to be turned by hand. The PO of Calvaire de Trooz reported the approach of German infantry and soon afterwards communications were cut off.

It was a mostly quiet day for the men of Fort Boncelles. No enemy activity was observed in the immediate vicinity of the fort. From dawn the AA crews fired on German aircraft flying over PO Cockerill. German troops were spotted on the right bank of the Ourthe but were out of range of the fort's guns. Embourg intervened instead. In the evening, Boncelles opened fire for the first time on the temporary bridge thrown up over the Ourthe near Tilff.

Around 0200hrs Fort Flémalle was hit for the first time by artillery of the 251 AR, probably 105mm guns. The AA positions were hit by medium-calibre guns. The 150mm turret remained in action until around 1800hrs with interdiction fire on Dolembreux, Mery, Tilff, Cote d'Esneux and then again on Tongres starting at 2130hrs. The rest of the night was calm around the fort. Due to the loss of observation capability after the retreat of the field army, the fort started sending out its own patrols. A dozen soldiers volunteered for long-distance patrols (*Service de Reconnaissance*) to seek out targets for the fort's guns, to obtain information about what was going on further out from the fort, and to observe enemy movements. While out on the long-distance patrols, the volunteers wore civilian clothing and carried false IDs. They travelled up to 20km behind enemy lines in cars or bicycles.

Upon their return to the fort they marked the results of their findings on maps. The men on local patrols wore uniforms and carried weapons.

*   *   *

Fort Tancrémont was the southernmost fort of the PFL, 18km south-east of Liège. Its mission was to interdict the valley of the Vesdre and the road from Theux to Mont, as well as to support the line of interval shelters. The fort's surface area was 30 hectares. The Germans referred to it as 'Pepinster,' the name of the village closest to the fort.

Construction was completed on 8 August 1938 and the quadrangular fort included five combat blocs, three casemates to protect the ditch and two ventilation blocs outside the perimeter. It was surrounded by a 15m-wide and 5m-deep anti-tank ditch with a counterscarp wall. The main firepower of the fort was supplied by Blocs 2 and 4, each equipped with a turret for twin 75mm FRC rapid-fire guns with a range of approximately 11,000m. The defensive firepower included three 81mm mortars located in Bloc M.

The Combat Blocs:

- **Bloc 1**: the main entry to the fort, defended by an internal blockhouse with an FM plus an iron gate and rolling bridge over a deep pit. Armament included a twin MG to defend the access ramp that ran through the counterscarp to the ditch, plus a twin MG cloche and FM.

The entry ramp leading to the ditch of Fort Tancrémont. (Bunkerfreaks Antwerpen)

- **Blocs 2 and 4**: identical artillery blocs equipped with twin 75mm FRC Model 1934 turrets and two MG cloches to defend the glacis.
- **Bloc 3**: originally intended to house a 120mm turret, later scrapped in favour of three MG cloches to defend the glacis.
- **Bloc M**: the Mortar Bloc was equipped with three French 81mm mortars set to fire at 90° vertical and with an embrasure designed to allow for a horizontal firing angle of 270°.
- **Casemate 2**: a simple casemate armed with a 47mm AT gun and one twin MG. Located on the north-west corner of the fort to defend the western flank of the ditch.
- **Casemate 3**: a double casemate with two 47mm AT guns and two twin MGs. Located on the north-east corner of the fort to defend in the direction of Casemate 2 and Casemate 4.
- **Casemate 4**: a simple casemate armed with a 47mm AT gun and one twin MG. Located on the south-east corner of the fort to defend the southern flank of the ditch.
- **Bloc O** (*Prise d'air*): guarded a telescopic air duct, and served as an emergency exit and observation post to guard the approaches to the fort. This bloc was located outside the perimeter to the west of the fort.
- **Bloc P**: the wartime entrance to the fort, located outside the perimeter to the south of the fort. This bloc also contained a telescopic air duct

The ditch and Casemate 2 of Fort Tancrémont. (Bunkerfreaks Antwerpen)

and an FM cloche to guard the approaches. The access ramp to the entry was guarded by an FM blockhouse with a second FM guarding the armoured entry door.

The fort had two AA groups, each with four Maxim 08/15 MGs mounted on tripods. One was located close to Bloc P and the other behind the peacetime barracks. The fort's external observation posts included BV 7, Casemate Mont, Casemate Vesdre, VM 3 and VM 29 ter.

*   *   *

At 1027hrs German artillery struck Fort Tancrémont for the first time, but without causing any damage. Around 1800hrs German infantry, supported by pioneers, launched their first attack on the fort from the direction of Banneux and the Bois des Mazures. Grenades landed around the fort. The ventilation duct in Bloc P was damaged by explosives. The attack was successfully repelled by the 75mm turrets using *boîtes-à-balles* shells.

The attack on Fort Battice continued on 12 May. At 0530hrs heavy 305mm howitzers started firing at the fort. The impact shook the blocs to their foundations, but the crews remained relatively safe. All observation viewing slots and gun embrasures were kept constantly under artillery and MG fire. The fort was surrounded and the Germans attacked the turrets from close range. During the course of the night of 11/12 May, Bloc 7 reported that the trenches of the AA section were being used by the Germans to fire on B Nord. During the morning, the Germans set up a command post in the home of the mayor of Herve. At 1200hrs sixty shots were fired at the house. At 1300hrs a column of German bridging vehicles moving along the road from Henri-Chapelle to Battice was hit by the 75mm turrets. The Germans headed for cover south of the road and then continued on their way to the south-west. Throughout the rest of the day the fort fired on more columns in Froidthier, Merckhof and Clermont.

Strategic Situation in Belgium at the End of 12 May 1940

On 12 May, the German Army continued to advance in the north. The southern flank of Eighteenth Army overran the position of Willemsvaart and one of its spearheads pushed on as far as Dordrecht. Sixth Army began to pursue the withdrawing Belgian divisions, and reached the river Gete. Von Rundstedt's Army Group, with its right wing at Liège and left wing at the forward edge of the Maginot Line, pushed on in the Ardennes. Twelfth

Army, preceded by von Kleist's armoured group, drove on via Neufchâteau-Bertrix towards the Meuse, up and down stream of Givet. In the evening the tanks reached the Meuse. The Cavalry Corps of the Second French Army was thrown back south of the Semois and that of the Ninth withdrew the evening of the 11th, following the failure of the former Cavalry Corps. The bridge at Dinant was blown at 1600hrs. The forts of Liège were holding out. The commander of the stronghold of Liège (Modard) shut himself up in the fort of Flémalle in order to encourage the resistance of the place.

In the afternoon, a conference of Army commanders was held in the Chateau de Casteau, near Mons. The King of Belgium and General Pownall, Chief of Staff of the BEF, agreed to give General Billotte supreme command, in order to assure coordination in the operations of the Allied armies in Belgium and Holland. From that moment, the Belgian Army entered into the general plan of the Allied forces.

Chapter 7

Monday, 13 May 1940

On 13 May, German units involved in the attacks on Liège and Namur were, according to the *Oberkommando des Heeres* (OKH – German Army High Command) *Lagekarten* West Front maps,[1] at the following locations:

- 251 ID – Regiments moving towards the southern forts of Boncelles, Embourg and Chaudfontaine.
- 269 ID – Bypassed Liège along the Meuse – headed towards Namur.
- 253 ID – North-east of Liège. Lifted siege of Aubin-Neufchâteau due to pending arrival of 223 ID; some units had crossed the Meuse and were facing Pontisse.
- 223 ID – Approaching the Herve region near Aubin-Neufchâteau and Battice.
- 211 ID – Near Malmedy – would move south of the Meuse towards Namur.

On 13 May at 0645hrs Captain von Grothe, an adjutant with the German V Corps, sent a message to subordinate units:[2]

1) The course of the night was generally calm;
2) During the night, the retreat of civilians was heavily monitored. Four civilians coming from Liège were detained and sent to corps HQ, as they could make important statements about the present situation there; and
3) Enemy artillery fire from the outskirts of Liège and the *Werkgruppe Tancrémont* stopped during the entire night. Notifications about losses are not yet available.

At 1045hrs, Oberleutnant Sandorfer and his observer, Feldwebel Ruger, took off from the airfield at Spa. The mission was to fly south of Liège to look for Belgian batteries and Flak in the Liège-Engis-Esneux area. The results were as follows:

1. On all roads leading from the Meuse between Liège and Engis to the south, no movements were detected. No enemy defence.

2. No movement detected in Liège.
3. Enemy batteries and enemy Flak not detected.
4. Own troops (vehicles) in the area of Mons and Jemeppe (west of Liège).
5. South-east of Herien (about 15km west) own troops, probably intelligence officers.
6. Battle taking place (heavy artillery strike) north of Bierset (about 8km west of Liège).
7. No troops observed at Forts Embourg and Boncelles. No fire; all quiet.
8. All Meuse bridges destroyed from Huy to Liège.
9. During the entire flight, no enemy air patrols or anti-aircraft defence encountered.

223rd Infantry Division – 13.5.40 – 0100
Orders for May 13th[3]

1) The enemy was pushed back from the front. Up to now no Belgian infantry has been found east of the Meuse. Enemy artillery in Fort Battice is still firing from four turrets at German troops in Aubel, Altena [2km south-west of Aubel], Clermont and Heinrichs-Kapelle [Henri-Chapelle].

2) The division will start the attack on the forts on May 13th at dawn in order to push through to the city of Liège between Barchon and Evegnée.

3) Clarification of the situation in the interval between Barchon and Evegnée continues. The following is to be determined:

- Are the forts of Barchon and Evegnée and the intermediate area between the two forts occupied?
- Is enemy artillery of both forts still firing?
- What is the best way to attack both of the forts?
- If there is no longer any infantry occupation on the east bank of the Meuse, the situation becomes clear and division units will move through the interval[4] and take possession of [the bridge] in Liège before it is destroyed.

4) At dawn IR 344 will advance between Barchon and Evegnée on the city of Lüttich [Liège]. Depending on the situation, the division will decide whether an attack against both Barchon and Evegnée is necessary, or whether one of these two could be taken.

5) One battalion of IR 385 reached the Herve area at night with one company of Pioneer Battalion 223. The regiment moved on

the line of les Triches-Roixleux-Charneux, in order to take Fort Battice from behind. The attack against Fort Battice is to be carried out around 0800 after the fort's artillery has been silenced. Bulk of IR 385 will follow IR 344 at a distance of about 3km.

7a) Divisional artillery of the division to support the attack of IR 344 against the Barchon-Evegnée line includes:

7b) Heavy artillery division 641[5] [305mm] and two 88mm anti-aircraft guns to be used against Fort Battice from around 0500 – 0800. The use of the heavy artillery division 624[6] for the same task has been requested from the [XXVII] Corps.

XXVII Corps command message: 13.5.40 (1400hrs)

1) Of the outer line of forts, only the works of Aubin-Neufchâteau and Battice are still in enemy hands.[7] Of the inner line the enemy is still holding all the works on the eastern front, and particularly lively fire is reported from Evegnée and Barchon. Pontisse and perhaps Liers, Lantin and Loncin are in our hands.[8] The positions between the forts are no longer occupied, or only by weak enemy forces.

2) XXVII AK covers the left flank of the army in the direction of Namur N of the Meuse, the fortress area of Lüttich is to be cleared with partial forces.

[Items 3) to 5) omitted]

6) Orders for the divisions:

b) 253 ID to continue crossing the river and will take Fort de Pontisse and push forward to the NW exit of Liège in the area of Glain.

c) 223 ID to take Battice and approaches to Lüttich.

7) Corps Artillery:

- To support the attack of 253 ID against Fort de Pontisse, AR 614 with *Abteilung* 536 and 736 remains in their previous positions at Mollingen-Grafenvuren. These units will send forward observers to Oupeye to support the attack against Fort de Pontisse and possibly Fort de Liers in observing fire.

- *Lange Mörsergruppe* remains in its position.

- *Abteilung* 783 fires on Aubin-Neufchâteau at dawn with *Artillerie Abteilung* 624, with *Abteilung* 815 (1 bat.). If necessary, two batteries are to be brought into position early from Aubin-Neufchâteau and Battice to be used against Forts Barchon, Evegnée and Fléron.

- *Artillerie Abteilung* 641 is placed under 223 ID for the attack on Battice.[9]

The day had barely dawned over Fort Pontisse when the action in front of the fort resumed. It would last until the evening and reveal the true power of the two northernmost forts. German message traffic had already revealed conflicting facts about Pontisse. It was already in German hands. It might be in German hands. But the fact is that it was not in German hands, nor would it be for several days to come.

The Germans were surprised, especially after the speedy collapse of the much larger and more powerful Fort Eben-Emael, that the older forts guarding the northern crossings could cause so much difficulty to their passing troops and put up such a significant fight. It was perfectly clear that moving troops across the waterways and to the west would remain dangerous as long as Pontisse and Barchon remained in action, and thus the decision was made to take them out of the equation. The previous day, General Wäger, commander of XXVII Corps, made the decision to 'put an end to the troublesome forts', but then his corps was partially relieved of this mission by Sixth Army. The final action would be carried out by 223 ID against Forts Barchon, Evegnée and Fléron, while 251 ID would attack Chaudfontaine, Embourg, Boncelles and Flémalle. 253 ID's Pioneer Battalion would finish the job against Pontisse.

During the night of 12/13 May the Germans set up several gun batteries to target Pontisse. At 1000hrs the commander of the air intake bunker north-east of Pontisse reported that he was being hit by shots from a small-calibre gun firing from the Fond de la Vaux at the foot of the hill below the fort. The 75mm guns and MGs of the fort immediately opened fire on the German positions at La Vaux. It was now apparent that the air intake shelter, with access to the inside of the fort, was a primary target. The guns swept the woods below the slopes of the fort as well as any buildings that could serve as a refuge for the Germans. The enemy then moved out from Vivegnis towards the military road to attack the fort.

The 75mm turrets struck the advancing Germans who, as expected, directed their attack on the air intake. Two German guns in a garden at Fond de la Vaux were spotted and silenced. The battle continued until 1330hrs and the Germans, having gained no positional advantage, retreated. At 1400hrs no more Germans were spotted in the vicinity of the fort with the exception of reconnaissance vehicles on the Oupeye–Hermée road and these were also hit by shots from the fort.

At 1630hrs, a German battery set up at a farm north of Dalhem was targeted by the guns of Forts Barchon and Pontisse. At 1700hrs, German troops took up position on the outskirts of Oupeye and along the Liège–Bassenge tram line that ran past the fort. The 75s opened fire, driving them back to the gun foundry's test field,[10] where they were again dislodged by the howitzers. At 1830hrs, the Germans signalled the start of a new offensive by firing small-calibre guns at the air intake shelter. The fort itself was bombarded with medium-calibre shells to suppress the turrets. Despite this, the howitzers kept up a steady fire on the attackers, but the situation was becoming chaotic and the observers were having difficulty tracking all targets. The Germans were getting dangerously close to the fort, in increasing numbers.

By nightfall, with the help of Barchon, Evegnée, Fléron and even Flémalle, the German attack on Pontisse failed. As darkness fell, the fighting slackened off. A patrol left the fort in the direction of PL 13 to deliver supplies. They returned three hours later, unable to get past Oupeye and Vivegnis and make the delivery, all roads being heavily guarded. It would have been a waste of time and a big risk because, when the chief of PL 13 realized the phone connection with the fort was broken, he left the post with his men under cover of darkness, taking refuge in the cellar of a nearby house where they would spend the next three days.

After midnight, the bombardment of Fort Barchon was heavy and particularly concentrated on the access ramp. Huge shells, possibly from the *Schwere Artillerie Abteilung*'s 305mm howitzers, crashed down on top of the

Aerial photo showing Fort Barchon. (Marc Romanych Collection)

massif. Just before dawn, German pioneers approached the fort but came under fire of *boîtes-à-balles* from the 75mm howitzers. Around 0700hrs, the intensity of the bombardment increased even more. By mid-morning, shells of all calibres were falling on the fort and by early afternoon they were described as 'raining' down. The noise inside the turrets was terrible as the shells ricocheted off the cap and exploded in the distance. Around 1000hrs, the heavy batteries firing on Barchon were finally located near the cemetery of Lorette below Visé and quickly silenced by the 105s. Finally there was a period of calm and the exhausted crews could get some much needed rest, but it didn't last very long.

Meanwhile, Barchon continued to fire on other targets moving across the plateau of Herve towards Liège. The support of Pontisse continued. The 105s dropped shells on top of Pontisse and fired on German troops approaching it from the village of Haccourt. Three of the 75mm turrets fired to the north-east on Werihet.

At 1030hrs there was a terrible explosion in the 75mm turret of Salient II right, causing serious burns to the face and hands of four of the crew, Maréchal des Logis Kreutz and Fraikin and Privates Ernotte and Reuter. The accident was caused by the explosion of a shell in the overheated barrel. The barrel broke in two and fell to the floor of the gun room. Other barrels were becoming noticeably overheated – in some cases glowing red – and the commandant called for a cease fire to let them cool down.

After 1100hrs, firing continued with the 105mm on Fexhe-Slins, far to the west above Hauts-Sarts, on German troops attempting to flank Pontisse. The 150s also fired on the now German-occupied Citadelle of Liège. Around noon the German bombardment again intensified and it was estimated that 1,000 large and medium shells had already fallen on the fort. The shelling continued all afternoon, the Germans hoping to eliminate the threat from Barchon from a distance. At 1850hrs the 305mm shells fell again, giving the impression that the central massif was being lifted off the ground. One shell damaged the right 150mm turret but this was quickly repaired. A barrage intended to mask the movement of troops towards shelter BM 3 began to fall near the air tower. Nevertheless the observers caught sight of the action and FMs in the tower opened fire on the Germans.

German shelling continued into the night and showed no signs of letting up but neither did the mutual support between the forts, even though all of them were under attack. Fort Aubin-Neufchâteau fired on a heavy battery in the vicinity of Bolland-Julemont that was firing on Barchon. Pontisse's observers located another large battery near Lorette at the Ferme du Temple, which had been targeted earlier in the day by Belgian guns. Fire from Barchon's two 105mm turrets silenced the battery.

The attack on Fort Aubin-Neufchâteau by 453 IR continued into 13 May. 253 AR's four batteries fired 105mm and 150mm howitzers throughout the day, moving their mobile batteries from place to place to avoid Belgian counterbattery fire, like a deadly chess game.

At 0120hrs, Bloc 2's 75s fired twenty-five rounds on the Trois Cheminées crossroads. Support was requested and provided by Fort Battice. The bloc also fired shrapnel rounds toward 'La Sablière'. Mortars were fired on a farm located along the road leading from Warsage to the fort. Battice was notified that lights were spotted in the Bois d'Als and St. Gilles near Fourons. The fort's 120mm guns responded. German infantry attempted to approach Bloc P but the Mortar Bloc fired twenty-five rounds and Casemate 3 fired twenty-five 47mm rounds in their direction. At 0430hrs Bloc 2's gun turret fired twenty-five *boîtes-à-balles* rounds to clear the massif of suspected enemy troops. The 47mm guns defending the moat were ordered to fire over the massif by ricochet (aiming at the outer wall, the gunners could bounce a shell against it and send it flying over the massif itself). All three mortars fired a rolling barrage along the outer walls.

At 0450hrs enemy shelling intensified. Ten minutes later Bloc O reported muzzle flashes coming from the ruins of the peacetime barracks. The Mortar Bloc fired twenty-five rounds, assisted by Battice. Over the next hour an ever-increasing barrage of German medium-calibre shells landed on the fort. The vibration of the shells was felt within the fort itself, 35m underground. Commandant d'Ardenne reported to the RFL that the fort had fired close to 5,000 shells of all calibres in the past three days, but was holding out very well.

Throughout the morning, Aubin-Neufchâteau, assisted by Battice, fired on numerous targets where German troops and convoys were spotted. These seemed to be mostly Wave 3 and 4 units attempting to move past Liège to the west. But the fort itself was still being probed by small pioneer squads. Fort Battice was called upon throughout the day to assist in hitting a number of targets, such as the Ferme Cranhez, site of a German battery that was firing on the fort. Bloc 3's observers noted that many of the anti-tank obstacles and barbed-wire entanglements had been destroyed by the German shells but the rate of the shelling was slowing down, which was either good or bad news. An order was sent to all the sentries to be on high alert as there was a serious risk of an enemy infantry assault. The Germans were working to fortify the Ferme Weykmans and fifty mortar and 75mm rounds were fired on the farm. Around 1000hrs a large German convoy appeared on the Mortroux–

Bombaye road. Twenty-five 75mm shells were fired in that direction. The turrets of Blocs 1 and 2 also opened fire again on the Weykmans farm. A couple of hours later another German convoy appeared on the same road heading toward the Netherlands. Blocs 1 and 2 opened fire again.

Throughout the afternoon and early evening more vehicle and troop convoys were hit on the Bombaye–Warsage road by the 75s and mortars. The shelling of the fort also resumed. In the early evening observers in Bloc P could see a massive artillery bombardment accompanied by tons of smoke over Richelle, along the Meuse between Barchon and Pontisse. This was being directed at Fort Pontisse. At 2015hrs German infantry at Chateau Regnoul and the Fouron-St. Martin crossroads was targeted by the mortars. Muzzle flashes were coming from the Remersdaal railway station and 100 75mm rounds were fired.

Enemy shelling damaged the fort's radio antenna. Battice was asked to inform HQ of the situation. Repairs were carried out on the antenna as soon as it was safe to send somebody out on to the massif. At 2200hrs the antenna was repaired by Sergeant Elias, who crawled up to the top of the fort and made the repairs while under enemy fire. HQ RFL requested a status report and d'Ardenne replied that morale among the men was good, the fort's concrete was holding up well to the enemy shelling which was estimated to be 210mm in calibre, and all equipment was in good working condition.

German activity around the fort had been minimal for most of the day. The 453 IR was moving out, being replaced by troops from the 223 ID. Just when things seemed quiet, German MGs opened fire from the cemetery. The AT guns of Casemate 3 fired twenty-five rounds on the cemetery. At 2212hrs the Germans fired a white flare above Bloc 3, signalling a possible infantry attack. The turrets fired *boîtes-à-balles* shells over a 360° arc. The gun turrets and Mortar Bloc opened fire along the perimeter of Bloc P where more German machine-gunners were spotted. All MGs were ordered to fire in a low trajectory over their respective field of fire to drive off any possible German intruders. Machine guns and 47mm guns in the casemates likewise fired on the ditch. The observation cloche on the Mortar Bloc, damaged earlier in the day, was repaired. One of the embrasures had been severely damaged by direct hits from an anti-tank gun, most likely an 88. The engineers placed an armour plate with a small opening over the damaged embrasure. 13 May ended as it had begun. It would be another day before Belgian troops from Fort Aubin-Neufchâteau could venture out to check on the condition of the structure and to look for their wounded.

On 13 May Fort Evegnée was hit by Luftwaffe bombers for the first time, and German artillery strikes continued. The bombing caused no significant damage but Private Gillis, one of the men sent out to survey the damage, was killed when he was struck by a shell that landed in the ditch. Another two-man patrol spotted German infantry approaching the fort. These were troops from 344 IR probing the intervals between Evegnée and Barchon. A four-man patrol encountered German scouts and a firefight broke out. Private Lejeune was hit and would later die of his wounds. Towards evening rifle shots were heard in the vicinity of the fort and some of the cupolas were struck by shells from Belgian 47mm AT guns left behind by retreating Belgian infantry.

Around 0100hrs the general alert sounded throughout the fort. Suspicious noises were heard in the barbed wire covering the glacis of Salient I. Flares were fired from the POC turret on top of the fort to light up the massif but nothing was spotted. The Germans, surprised to be lit up like daytime, opened fire. Lieutenant Decarpentrie, the battery commander,[11] ordered the 75s to open fire with case shot. The FM of the air tower and the MG turret also opened fire. The shooting continued until about 0300hrs and then calm resumed. German pioneers had dug in at the foot of the glacis and a couple of marksmen targeted the top of the fort, but they were unable to pass through the wire at any point. The superstructure of the fort and the air tower were hit by rifle and small-calibre artillery fire.

Throughout the day the investment of the fort was tightened and extended to the flanks of the fort and into the trenches formerly occupied by the Belgian infantry. The encirclement stretched to the rear of the air intake. The fort's 75mm howitzers and FMs in the air tower responded. Lieutenant Dinant, commander of the air tower, described some of the action:

> On Monday the 13th, at 0700, the crewmember at FM # 5 of the air tower spotted a group of Germans 300 meters away, at the crossroads of the Evegnée-Rétinne and Evegnée-Saive roads. I looked at the group with binoculars. There were seven Germans there, plus a civilian and a young girl. I did not order the men to open fire immediately. Having noticed me, the group broke up. The civilian and the girl were pushed forward towards Saive, a German following them very closely. The others moved into a trench along the road that had been prepared by the 12th Line Regiment prior to their retreat. I carefully indicated to FM # 5 and 6 their respective goals. I decided not to target the first group with the civilians, choosing instead the second group. At the right moment I ordered the guns to open fire. Three Germans fled to Rétinne, three others fell. Another group was alerted by the shots and tried to pass behind the Evegnée cemetery. They were stopped by FM

fire and forced to take cover between the graves. Fifteen minutes later, FM # 1 opened fire on a German soldier crawling towards the tower. He made it to cover below the tower. We opened fire but the bullets ricocheted off the concrete edge of the top of the tower. But the German screamed and stood up with his arms raised. I stopped shooting. He shouted at me: 'Kamerad – Fünf Battalion'. He took advantage of the pause in firing to fall out of sight and escape from the vicinity of the tower. A clever ruse.[12]

Around 1000hrs, the fort was hit by heavy Stuka bombs (250kg). The planes began their dive from an altitude of 1,000m, and pulled up at about 50m from the ground. The AA machine guns and the FM of the air tower came into action, but the Stukas sped away untouched. The bombing had a considerable effect on morale and caused a lot of damage. The fort shook and gave the men the impression of being lifted off the ground. The bombing was very accurate and here are some results:

- The 75mm turret[13] was put out of service. The bomb put a 15cm wide crack in the concrete turret housing. This would be repaired and the gun returned to action.
- The capital gallery leading to the head of the fort partially collapsed where it passed under the ditch. This collapse threatened to cut off the men in the head casemates (Sergeant Pierard and eight of his men).
- Large craters caused by bombs landing in the ditches caused the partial collapse of the counterscarp wall. In one location it was possible to walk down into the ditch from the counterscarp. The 75mm turret facing the wall was loaded with boîtes-à-balles and permanently aimed towards the collapsed wall, waiting for a grey helmet to appear.

Along with the aerial bombardment the Germans kept up a continuous shelling of the fort. Private Gillis, assigned to the Corps de Garde, was in the ditch on his way back from the kitchen when he was hit and killed. In the evening, his remains were carried to the morgue after which a religious ceremony was held by Chaplain Van Eycken and then the commander bade farewell to Gillis in the name of the garrison and the homeland. He was the first of Evegnée's defenders to die for Belgium.

The bombing, however, did not interrupt the fort's fire missions, and there were plenty of targets to choose from. The air tower was being hit by medium-calibre artillery fire – 100mm. The battery was located and the 105mm turret opened fire and silenced it. Another German battery firing from Cerexhe was hit and silenced by the 75s. The crew fled. The radio crew picked up a signal from Radio Stuttgart. The German announcer reported that Fort Evegnée had fallen. This false news helped to raise the morale of the garrison on a very difficult day.

On 13 May Fort Fléron was shelled heavily by medium-calibre guns, and bombed by Stukas. The AA guns installed on the massif were hit and destroyed. The AA gun crew set up in the Fléron cemetery was pulled back into the fort. Fort Boncelles requested support on the Pont de Tilff. Other action included support fire on Fort Pontisse and German gun batteries at Melen.

In the morning the observation team of bunker Mg 4 conducted a reconnaissance patrol to ensure there were no more Germans around the PO. When they arrived at Mg 1 they found it abandoned and maps and documents left behind. The documents were collected and Chaudfontaine's commander notified. The crew of Mg 1 had pulled out overnight and moved to the PO of Werister. Later that night Fléron and Chaudfontaine fired on Mg 1 and Mg 4 to clear it of Germans. One wounded German was brought back to the fort where he subsequently died.

Chaudfontaine spent a good part of the day firing on German troops from 251 ID attacking Fort Embourg. The Germans occupied Saint-Hadelin, Ayeneux, Bay-Bonnet, Casmatrie (600m west of the fort) and the quarries of Embourg and Magnée. Chaudfontaine intervened on behalf of Fléron, which was also under attack and at 2050hrs on Embourg to counter an attack on the air intake bloc and glacis.

Fort Embourg was now completely surrounded by troops of 251 ID. Around dawn, German guns installed in the Bois d'Oblusteine targeted the embrasures of Embourg's POC. Embourg countered with the close defence pieces, silencing the gun, but the damage to the post had been done and all of the optical instruments were destroyed. An unexploded shell was examined and found to be a 37mm anti-tank round. The bombardment continued and, along with 37mm guns, the Germans added 105mm and 150mm shells. The shelling was incessant and observers were unable to determine the location of the batteries. The AA gun positions reported they were being hit, forcing the gunners to take shelter inside the fort. Post BE 8 had not spotted any Germans at Tilff or Mery. EC 1bis was under attack and communications were cut off. Observers in the air tower spotted a line of Germans progressing along a ridge to the west of the fort called the *Bout du Monde*. The FMs of the tower opened fire. At 2200hrs suspicious noises were heard on the glacis, in particular at Salient III. The cupolas were alerted. Flares were fired and the fort's close-defence guns opened fire on German pioneers attempting to access the ditch with ropes and ladders. The embrasures of the ditch casemates were pounded by 37mm guns and machine guns. The barbed-wire network along Salient II–III was cut. The turrets swept the surface with *boîtes-à-balles* and the German attack stopped. One member of the gun crew recalled 'the calm that the *Maréchel des Logis* Courtois spread and communicated to us when he commanded [the direction and cadence of fire] which made a nice drum roll, but also a beautiful thing because the Germans did not expect such a reception from us'.[14]

For the first time Germans – scouts from 451 IR – were spotted by the observers of Fort Boncelles. The first enemy artillery bombardment of the fort started shortly after 0500hrs. German artillery batteries firing on the fort were located by forward observers from Fort Flémalle and its guns opened fire in support. Later in the day, the partially-destroyed bridge at Tilff was targeted because German infantry was still using a segment of the bridge to cross the Ourthe. Other targets included a motorized column at the Ferme Tombeur at Tilff and Chateau Plainevaux moving near the fort; troops on the Plainevaux-Seraing road; houses along the road from Boncelles village to the fort; and a battery in Esneux that was also hit by shots from Chaudfontaine. In the early evening, the PO of Famelette (Beauregard) was abandoned under German pressure. During the night of 13/14 May, Bunker FB 2 was also evacuated. BE 5 was attacked and abandoned. By nightfall the Germans were in the immediate vicinity of the fort and the close-defence pieces opened fire.

Enemy shells continued to land on top of Fort Flémalle. The AA gun position was hit and Adjutant Monjoie was injured in the foot. Four other men were hurt while providing first aid. Private Goossens, a medic, was killed by MG fire. Chaplain Lenniers was sent with four members of the medical staff to recover the injured men but they were prevented from reaching their companions by German shelling. The air tower, located some distance from the fort, was now serving as an observation post for the immediate surroundings. A group of Ju 52 transports landed at the airport at Bierset and Fort Flémalle was asked to fire on the airfield. Three planes were destroyed by the Belgian artillery fire.

The night of 12/13 May was relatively quiet for the men of Fort Battice. Around 0230hrs the commander of Bloc 1 reported that the Germans were firing on the observation embrasures of the bloc in an attempt to move in closer. The 60mm gun in Bloc 1 opened fire and was joined by MGs from Blocs 2 and 7. At 0700 large-calibre shells started falling on top of the fort. At the same time, German forces were spotted on the Chaussée Charlemagne moving from Henri-Chapelle to Battice and they came under

Machine-gun cloche of Bloc 4 of Fort Battice. The shell holes are probably from a 20mm or 37mm gun. (Bunkerfreaks Antwerpen)

attack from the fort. A little later cars and motorcycles were spotted at the Ferme Cesar along the same road. Observers suspected there was a command post set up at the farm and the fort's guns opened fire. In the afternoon the Germans launched an attack on Bloc 2. A German infantryman penetrated the anti-tank ditch and came within 20m of the bloc and opened fire on the embrasures. Bloc 4 responded to the attack with its own MGs. The German attack was supported by a PAK 37 and MG positions set up around Ferme Querette. All of these positions were fired on by Bloc 1's 60mm gun. The Germans could not move forward but beginning at dusk, they started digging-in close to Bloc 2. Sergeant Jorisson, the commander of Bloc 2, ordered the 75mm guns dropped to their minimum firing angle to strafe the ditch. Battice provided much needed support to the besieged forts of Aubin-Neufchâteau, Fléron and Evegnée throughout the day. Boncelles and Flémalle also requested support but they were out of the range of Battice's guns.

Strategic Situation in Belgium at the End of 13 May 1940

'Vesting-Holland' (Fortress Holland) was overrun at Dordrecht. The south flank of the German Eighteenth Army collided with the French Seventh Army, which, having lost Breda, was deployed along the line Bergen-op-Zoom–Turnhout.

On the Belgian front, forces deployed on the branch canal and on the river Gete fought a delaying battle. Violent fighting took place at Haelen and Tienen where the cavalry and the artillery distinguished themselves. In the afternoon the Cavalry Corps of the French First Army was violently attacked and withdrew to Perwez.

North of Namur the situation on the main line strengthened and became well organized, but south of Namur, on the First French Army front, the situation quickly became critical. Since 0700hrs, the Germans forced a crossing of the Meuse at Houx and infiltrated into the valley of Yvoir to Givet. The Meuse was also crossed at Monthermé.

On the Second Army front, the Germans seized a loop of the Meuse downstream of Sedan in the morning, then established a foothold on the left bank. In late afternoon, Von Kleist's Panzer Group captured Sedan.

Chapter 8

Tuesday, 14 May 1940

On 14 May, German units involved in the attacks on Liège and Namur were, according to the OKH *Lagekarten* West Front maps, at the following locations:

- 223 ID – To the north of Fort Barchon and attacking Forts Evegnée, Fléron and Barchon.
- 251 ID – South of Liège and attacking Flémalle-Boncelles-Chaudfontaine-Embourg.
- 253 ID – Had now moved off to the west.
- 269 ID – Had moved off to the west in the direction of Namur.
- 211 ID – South-east of Liège, probably 20km south of Tancrémont, headed for Namur.

The XXVII Corps report for 14 May stated that the 269th Infantry Division, with three regiments and vanguard units was already past Liège, heading towards Namur. 253 ID followed, the task of reducing the forts of Liège now left to the Corps' 223 ID (along with V Corps' 251 ID). Horse and vehicle crossings would take a few more days. The passage by the forts was difficult and accompanied by heavy losses because the forts continued to strike the flank and rear of the regiments. However, the performance of the two divisions and their willingness to continue to advance was remarkable despite the difficulties they encountered.

A number of air reconnaissance missions were carried out on 14 May. A 3 (H) 13 flight left at 1420hrs. No Belgian troops were detected north of the Meuse to the west of Liège. A small Belgian detachment was spotted south-west of the village of Lize, above Seraing and field fortifications south-west of Boncelles. German troops were marching west through Esneux. The flight took some fire from Fort Flémalle, possibly AA guns, but that was the only air defences noted. Another flight, piloted by Oberleutnant Schaefer and his observer Oberleutnant Scholz, took off from Spa at 1100hrs and flew over the city of Liège. No troops were seen along the inner fortress belt. All of the bridges over the Meuse were destroyed. No Belgian AA or ground troops spotted or encountered in the city itself.

Other flights noted the following:

- No moving targets detected in their flight area.
- No troops or vehicles spotted in the field fortifications and prepared battery positions.
- Herve-Fléron road and Soumagne-Fléron railway station, about 300m E and SE from the fort [Fléron] was blocked by heavy iron road blocks (Cointet gates).
- Romsée-Fort Chaudfontaine road at point 233 (approx. 2km NE) blocked by road block as above.
- Road south of Fort Embourg closed 300m from the fort.
- Flak was fired from Forts Evegnée, Fléron, and Chaudfontaine.
- Most road junctions made impassable by demolitions.
- Bridge over the Ourthe in Tillf blown in three places; but possible to cross on foot.
- All bridges over the Vesdre in the Fraipont-Chenée section intact.
- Forts Boncelles and Chaudfontaine firing their guns.
- No troop movements in Liège. Refugees moving over and west of the Meuse. Swastika flag flying over the Citadelle.
- All of the Meuse bridges destroyed in Liège; not all of the Ourthe bridges were destroyed.

251 ID,[1] attached to Fourth Army's V Corps of Army Group A, moved to the south of Liège and into place below Forts Chaudfontaine and Boncelles on 12 May. At 0700hrs on 14 May 6th Company of 2/471 IR attacked Fort Chaudfontaine. By 0830hrs all of the vacant field fortifications around the fort were occupied by German troops. During the attack the Germans were hit by heavy artillery fire from Fort Embourg and they were unable to capture the fort. At 0930hrs the company retreated due to the heavy Belgian fire, but only having suffered light casualties. It was decided to carry out an attack on Fort Embourg but it had to be abandoned due to darkness and heavy fire from Fort Chaudfontaine. Meanwhile, 451 IR reached Les Communes and worked its way close to Fort Boncelles. All roads and wooded paths around Boncelles were blocked, making the advance very difficult. The regiment was hit by fire from Forts Chaudfontaine and Embourg. The goal for the day was to continue to reconnoitre the three forts. 451 IR was to continue operations north and east of Boncelles while 459 IR moved to the west bank of the Ourthe. 223rd Pioneer Battalion, 223 ID's shock troops, arrived in the region. The bulk of the division crossed the Meuse. 1/344 IR, reinforced by 1/223 AR, was to remain 10km east of Liège and was tasked

with the capture of Fort Barchon. Terrible news reached the command staff of RFL via radio: The Netherlands had surrendered and the Germans had crossed the Meuse at Sedan. The Maginot Line was now in danger of being outflanked.

During the night of 13/14 May, Fort Pontisse resumed its fire missions at the surrounding crossroads and main traffic arteries. At dawn German troops were once again spotted in the vicinity of the fort. This time, however, they were digging in, not preparing an attack. One of the 75mm turrets chased them away and then shifted its fire to Oupeye. During the morning Fort Pontisse's observers watched the air strikes on Barchon that continued until about 1300hrs. Thirty minutes later Stukas appeared above Pontisse and started bombing the fort. This went on for about 90 minutes. Bombs fell on the S-II turret, causing serious damage and injuring some of the crew. A few hours later, around 1800hrs, the Germans launched an infantry attack. The fort's POs were hit by anti-tank guns. Around 1930hrs German artillery laid down a smokescreen on top of the fort, preparatory to storming it. All of the close-defence turrets and infantry weapons opened fire. When the smoke cleared the attack had not taken place. The Germans resumed heavy artillery fire on the fort.

Three kilometres to the east, the intensity of the shelling of Fort Barchon began to slacken around 0200hrs. A patrol was sent out at 0500hrs, led by Sergeant Danthine. They returned to report the presence of a 210mm mortar battery at Bacsay. The coordinates were passed on to Fort Evegnée. Around 1000hrs the fort's siren went off as German Stukas starting bombing the fort. It lasted a little over an hour. The explosions shook the fort to its depths and the men sheltering below moved into the air tower tunnel, the deepest part of the underground. When the bombing ended a patrol went out to inspect the damages. There were enormous craters all over the top of the fort and in the ditches. The concrete surrounding the left-side 150mm turret was cracked and the turret was noticeably sagging to the left. It was impossible to put it back into its normal position. The concrete around the right-side 150mm was also cracked but not as seriously as the left and the crack was quickly repaired. Two of the 75mm howitzers were damaged and out of service. The counterscarp wall across from Salient III was damaged along a 15m stretch. A large number of unexploded bombs were found next to the infantry sortie and in the gorge ditch. The 105mm turrets were in good shape and continued to fire, in particular on Bierset airfield where Colonel Modard reported the landing of Ju 52 troop transports. The 105s disabled some of the aircraft. Meanwhile German troops from 223 ID continued to pour into the perimeter of Barchon, Evegnée, and Pontisse. At 1705hrs

German infantry from 344 IR attacked the fort. The small-arms weapons in the fort opened fire and the assault finally stopped at 1945hrs. The Germans retreated, leaving many dead behind.

Commandant Pourbaix recorded the following fire plots in his campaign journal:

- 0045hrs – Battery situated at la Haute-Saive.
- 0152hrs – Troops passing through the Maréchal crossroads.
- 1325hrs – Haccourt village.
- 1326hrs – *Tirs fusant* [air-burst shells – see below] above Pontisse which was being bombed by aircraft.
- 1430hrs – Renewed friendly shelling of Pontisse.
- 1610hrs – Shelling of the airfield of Bierset where German troop transports were landing.
- 1827hrs – The remaining operational turrets, along with Evegnée and Pontisse, fired on multiple German targets.
- 2035hrs – Convoy at Withuis – shelling lasted two hours.

Just moments after midnight the Germans launched a major attack on Fort Aubin-Neufchâteau. Bloc 1 reported one of its MGs was under fire from a German MG in the anti-tank obstacles. One of the men inside the MG cloche was wounded in the head. The Mortar Bloc and the Bloc 1 turret responded and the German gun was neutralized. All three mortars

An unidentified MG cloche at one of the new forts of Liège. (Digital History Archive, German Military Study P-203)

responded to German fire coming from what could only be described as 'all directions'. An 88mm shell penetrated the observation cloche and embedded itself in the opposite wall but no one was injured. The crew evacuated the cloche. Another 88 damaged the embrasure but it was repaired with armour plates. A few minutes later the Mortar Bloc opened fire on German troops rushing towards Casemate 1. Movement was detected at various locations on the glacis and all of the fort's MGs opened fire. Bloc P came under fire from the direction of the former AA emplacements on the other side of the road at La Feuille. The Mortar Bloc fired twenty rounds. Bloc 1 fired on the Ferme Halleux, and twenty rounds on the Berneaux crossroads and the Goffard farm where lights were spotted.

At 0700hrs the Germans resumed shelling the fort. Muzzle flashes were seen near the Chateau de Clochettes. In the *Bureau de Tir* a map was examined and the location of the gun emplacement plotted. The coordinates were sent to both of the gun turrets. One hundred HE and twenty-five shrapnel rounds were fired on the target and the shelling of the fort ceased. Forty-five minutes later large shells hit the fort about every five minutes. One round landed on top of the Mortar Bloc but didn't cause any damage. At 1050hrs, fifty rounds from the 75mm guns were fired on a German convoy spotted near the Croix de Pierre crossroads in Battice. The location was quickly relayed to Fort Battice.

It seems that the very early morning attack on the fort was going to be the only one for the day. Some shots were fired at the fort in the afternoon but most of the activity was outgoing on German troops still marching to the west. At 1410hrs vehicles on the Mouland-Berneau road were fired on by the 75s. A German artillery battery was spotted setting up near the Ferme Smeet. It was immediately hit with fifty 75mm rounds. The MG cloche of Bloc 2 was hit by anti-tank guns. A few minutes later the Mortar Bloc observation cloche was also hit by the same guns. Bloc P reported enemy fire on the fort from the direction of Waides. Forty rounds from the Mortar Bloc put an end to it. At 1650hrs a German convoy was spotted at the Ferme Smeet and retreated after being hit by twenty-five rounds. Bloc 1 fired on the Ferme Weykmans which was being used by the Germans for ammunition storage. The 75 scored a direct hit and the farm buildings exploded.

The evening was quiet until 2300hrs. A searchlight suddenly illuminated Bloc 1. The Mortar Bloc fired at the light until it shut off. Forty minutes later a red flare was fired from one of the fort's outer posts. The guns opened fire in the direction of the flare. The Mortar Bloc fired sixty rounds over 360° around the fort.

By 14 May, Fort Evegnée was completely surrounded by 2/344 IR. German small arms, machine guns and artillery shot at anything that moved on the surface of the fort. The main targets were the viewing ports of the armoured observation post, the gun turrets and the air tower. The moment one of the 75mm turrets lifted into the battery position or turned to fire it was pounded by projectiles of all sorts that ricocheted off the top or smashed into the side. It would be a very long and terrible experience for the crews inside for the rest of the struggle. The only means of giving the Luftwaffe pilots something to worry about was to fire FMs from the top of the air tower but this didn't have much effect and the Stukas flew unscathed, leaving the fort at the mercy of the heavy bombs. Despite the loss of the AA guns the 105s and 75s could be used to harass the Stukas. The fuses of the explosive shells were set to detonate at a height of 50m over the adjacent forts. The air tower observers kept an eye for dive bomb attacks on Fléron or Barchon and when they took place the guns would fire in the air in suppression mode. 1st Lieutenant Dinant, who was placed in charge of the process, in the post-war report,[2] described it:

In the afternoon of 14 May, we first implemented the system in favour of Fléron. At the moment when the first Stuka dives, the Salient III turret, warned, opened fire. The fuse was set for a good height: 50 meters. The second Stuka followed in the wake of the first, but had to move up to a height of 100 meters. The guns were raised and now the shell exploded at 100m but the third Stuka had to climb to 150 meters. Obviously, the fusing fire impeded them in their action. I successively brought the bursts to 150 – 200 meters, Fléron was safe for the time being. Shortly after, we played the same game over Barchon. Our turn was coming. I led the defence, having at my disposal one of Barchon's turrets and another of Fléron. After ten or so rockets, the Stukas dispersed.[3]

Unfortunately this process could only continue for a couple more days as the supply of fused shells was quickly running out.

German infantry attacking the air tower was repulsed by the FMs. The observers in the tower and the POC, when they weren't under heavy fire, located some of the German batteries in action against the fort or its neighbours. They were then hit by Evegnée's guns and neutralized. Commandant Vanderhaegen asked for four volunteers to go out on patrol and assist with observation. Privates Wielmin, Colson, Lejeuen and Van de Myer headed out via the air tower exit and made their way past the Germans.

On the return trip Lejeune unfortunately was shot and killed only 100m from the house he had lived in all his life. The rest of the patrol returned safely to the fort.

Infantry assaults and shelling increased in frequency. To keep the Germans away from the fort, the commanders ordered the gunners to maintain fire on top of their neighbours, in particular on the glacis. Throughout the day Evegnée fired on Pontisse while it was under attack. Observers in the air tower helped to adjust the shots. Evegnée also countered attacks on Battice. This type of support became commonplace in the days and nights ahead. Communications between the forts by radio and telephone was excellent, and remained so throughout the defence. This helped to make mutual aid swift and effective. Evegnée intervened regularly in support of Pontisse, Barchon, Chaudfontaine, Boncelles, Flémalle, Battice and Tancrémont.

The 150mm turret, almost completely demolished by a shell exploding in the barrel, had to fire at a diminished rate of ten shots per hour. Manoeuvre by hand was very difficult and exhausting and it took an enormous amount of time to switch targets. The 105s, however, continued to manoeuvre well and responded almost immediately to target requests. The commander switched crews between the 150mm and 105mm to give the men a rest. Some targets and results are worth mentioning:

- The RFL commander, Colonel Modard, ordered Evegnée to fire on the Citadelle of Liège with its 150mm guns. The Citadelle was now occupied by a large concentration of German troops. The shots were sent towards the target and then adjusted by Lieutenant Dinant from the air tower. A few moments later he reported that the shots were effective. Buildings were hit and a cloud of smoke was visible over the old fortress.
- Colonel Modard also ordered all of the fort's guns to fire on the airfield of Bierset on a large number of German transport aircraft unloading troops. Evegnée's 150mm turret opened fire. A short while later, Flémalle reported great success: aircraft destroyed and ambulances heading to the airfield to tend to the wounded.
- Observers at Evegnée and Pontisse, working together, pinpointed the location of German batteries being assembled near Thier-à-Liège. Evegnée's 105s opened fire and neutralized the battery.
- An observer in the tower reported the presence of German observers in the belfry of the Tignée church.[4] This was an excellent location that provided high angle views over all of Fort Evegnée. With regrets, Vanderhaegen ordered the 105s to destroy the church steeple.

In the evening of 14 May, around 2100hrs, the radio picked up a message addressed by King Leopold to the defenders of the forts of Liège: 'I call the forts of Liège … Officers, NCOs and soldiers … Resist to the end for the homeland … I am proud of you … Leopold .'

Fort Fléron was hit by intermittent shelling from German artillery, mostly 75mm or 105mm. Some of the batteries were located and hit by counterbattery fire from Fléron and the adjacent forts. Fléron fired on several targets in support of Tancrémont. At 0800hrs the guns fired on a battery set up at the entrance to the Citadelle, but one of the guns was firing short and shells landed in the Saint-Leonard neighbourhood. A professor from the University of Liège contacted the RFL and the shelling stopped. At 0900hrs Fléron took part in the shelling of Bierset airfield with its 150mm and 105mm guns. After two days of firing, it was a surprise that the two 150mm turrets still functioned simultaneously. There were many mechanical difficulties with the 150s, previously mentioned, that frustrated the technicians. On the 14th, one of the 150mm barrels needed to be replaced. This process was very intricate and time-consuming and had to be done with extreme care.

Fort Chaudfontaine carried out various fire missions and Fort Embourg helped to drive off German attackers approaching the fort. Chaudfontaine also reciprocated for Forts Pontisse, Tancrémont and Embourg, and the Citadelle. Chaudfontaine was hit by 210mm shells. The aiming scope of Salient I's 75mm turret was hit and put out of service. At 0630hrs observers at EC 1bis spotted an assembly of German troops on the Plaine Grisard at the foot of the glacis of Fort Chaudfontaine's Salient I and II, preparing to attack the fort. Small squads were also forming up on the glacis on the Vesdre side of the fort. At 0830hrs Embourg joined in with Fléron to intervene against the German attack on the fort and the Belgian guns dispersed the Germans.

At dawn, the bombardment of Fort Embourg by 150mm field howitzers resumed. The turrets were hit and very badly damaged. In the early morning hours, post EC 1bis sent an alert to the fort regarding German troops preparing for the attack on Chaudfontaine. Embourg's gun turrets opened fire, guided by EC 1bis. The projectiles rained down on the German combat groups and they broke up and took cover.

During the morning the Salient 1 and II turrets took aim at a German reconnaissance unit using a building near Les Carrières du Fond des Cris above the valley leading from Ninane to Chaudfontaine. The building was pounded and turned into a ruin and the Germans fled. 37mm guns were set up in the quarries and fired directly at Embourg's turret visors. Other German guns fired on Chaudfontaine from the quarry.

Meanwhile, Fort Embourg was also taking German fire from heavier guns. One of the turrets firing on German troops in Beaufays was struck violently by counter-fire and had to retract. Nevertheless, damage to the fort was minimal. The kitchen could no longer be used; the central heating chimney was destroyed and there was a coal fire in one of the rooms of Salient I. In the afternoon the turret at Salient I fired on an armoured vehicle stopped in front of the destroyed EC 2 post. Observers in the tower of Chaudfontaine spotted the vehicle and opened fire but they were immediately hit by German 150mm and 88mm shells.

Fort Boncelles was now also within reach of German artillery and shelled regularly, beginning in the afternoon. German infantry from 451 IR were closely watching the fort, looking for blind spots to set up PAK 37s and 88s to fire directly on the armoured turrets and cloches. A German reconnaissance squad approached to within 500m and was hit by grenades from the Mi/LG turret. Stukas bombed the fort in the afternoon but then the aerial and artillery bombardment ceased.

Boncelles fired on a German observation post set up in a house close to the fort. They also fired on the Tilff Bridge and a 37mm gun located in a former Belgian infantry trench near the fort. Around noon a German detachment heading towards Freyhisse was hit. German troops were now moving freely through the city of Liège, which was now heavily occupied.

During the day, shelter BV 7 received an odd call supposedly from Fort Chaudfontaine. The caller's accent sounded suspiciously German. BV 7 notified Tancrémont and some shots were fired on Telephone Central #18. Later a German column was observed on the Polleur-Spixhe road. A vehicle in the column was transporting pieces of a gun that included a very large-calibre barrel. The fort immediately dispatched a salvo towards the column but results were unknown. At 1800hrs Tancrémont was called upon to provide protective fire on the woods near the PO de Haute-Fraipont. Inside the fort, rumours began to spread that the Germans were in the ditches of the fort at night and approaching the casemate embrasures and the walls of the ditch. At the end of the day two men were sent out to clear the opening of the grenade launcher in Casemate 2. They brought back a large piece of a 210mm shell.

From dawn, Fort Flémalle was under heavy fire from German batteries. The shots were very precise, damaging the access ramp and creating numerous craters in the ditches and along the massif. Around 0700hrs calm returned. The AA positions were now too dangerous and the guns were brought back to the fort that evening. The fort intervened on numerous targets throughout the day:

- 0300hrs: Destructive fire by the 150mm turret on the Ferme Thiry (on behalf of Pontisse).
- 0730hrs: Machine guns attacking the AA position, and on a 37mm near Xhorre.
- 0800hrs: Citadelle of Liège (150mm); on the exits of Tongres (105mm).
- 0900hrs: Airfields of Ans and Bierset (105mm and 150mm).
- 0930hrs: Pont de Tilff (150mm), and on a battery near Hony in support of Embourg.

Afternoon targets included a battery near Boncelles (105mm), again on the airfields of Bierset and Ans (150mm and 105mm); a German OP in the Chateau de Lexhy (105mm); suspected airfield at Chêne a la Croix (105mm); batteries firing on the fort and installed in the Bois de Moines and at Rugissant; motorized column at Dolembreux (105mm); crossroads at Beaufays (150mm), main intersections at Xhendremael, Velroux and Otrange (105mm) then on the exit roads of Tongres and Odeur (150mm). At night, the 150mm fired on a munitions depot at Fexhe les Slins and on a barracks at Villers le Bouillet.

In the early afternoon, after the fire on the airfields, Fort Flémalle was violently bombed by aircraft followed by an artillery bombardment of large calibre, then a second aerial bombardment that lasted 30 minutes. The bombing blocked the embrasures in the wartime *Corps de Garde*, forcing the position to be abandoned. A large pile of debris thrown up from the bombs blocked the embrasures of the gorge casemates. It was now impossible to provide flanking fire in the gorge ditch. Coverage of the other ditches was also degraded. Around 2115hrs about thirty Germans were discovered in the ditch of Salient I–II. The Salient II casemate lit them up with its searchlight and opened fire with machine guns. This small battle went on for 15 minutes and then calm returned, but it was anything but calm for the garrison, knowing that German pioneers had penetrated into the ditch. Later that night the sentries heard something in the ditch of front III–IV and the 75s opened up with *boîtes-à-balles*. Calm returned at night and Colonel Modard took the opportunity to attempt a getaway from the fort.

Observers at Fort Battice spotted German troops near the toboggan. Fearing they may be trying to unblock the entrance, a patrol was sent out but did not see any evidence of engineering work to clear the debris. Upon their return to Bloc Waucomont the patrol was shot at from the road leading to the village of Battice. The Belgians took cover in the trenches of the AA battery, but the Germans did not pursue or attack. At 2200hrs, suspicious noises were heard coming from a blind spot on Bloc 1's escarp wall. Three men went out through Bloc 5, armed with an FM and accompanied by an engineer to determine if explosives had been set. Two men went out from Bloc 1, tossed grenades into the ditch and the others from Bloc 5 spotted a German on the wall and another jumping into the ditch. They were killed by the FM fire.

Commandant Guéry was seriously concerned about the deteriorating situation of the POs which had been kept under enemy fire the entire night, and had suffered a number of infantry attacks. The fort was running out of ammunition and because of this the bloc chiefs had determined they would be unable to respond to a request for fire from MN 29. Guéry considered this to be unacceptable and directed that from now on firing requests to protect the POs would not be ignored or refused and would be executed with priority. Ammunition was set aside to support the POs.

Strategic Situation in Belgium at the End of 14 May 1940

On 14 May the army dispositions of the Antwerp–Dyle–Meuse line was established. The order of the day was to hold this position at all costs.

In Holland the situation was desperate. Fortress Holland was outflanked and captured from behind, the position of the Grebbe was overrun, and the end was near.

The French Seventh Army was pushed back on Antwerp and the islands of the Escaut estuary. In Belgium, the German Armies made contact on the line Antwerp–Namur.

The Germans attacked the French Ninth Army with tanks and aircraft, and their breakthrough was expanding on a large scale. The Dinant pocket was growing and a violent battle was taking place at the junction of Ninth and Second Armies.

Chapter 9

Wednesday, 15 May 1940

O
n 15 May, German units involved in the attacks on Liège and Namur were, according to the OKH *Lagekarten* West Front maps, at the following locations:

- 223 ID – North-east of Liège.
- II/253 ID – Attack on Fort Pontisse (II/425 IR).
- 251 ID – Attacks on the southern forts.

Liège

On 15 May the 42nd Battalion of 620th Pioneer Regiment (Sixth Army) was called in to support II/425 IR in the attack on Fort Pontisse, which was planned for 19 or 20 May. 344 IR was tasked with the capture of Fort Barchon. The attack was to be supported by flamethrower and demolition

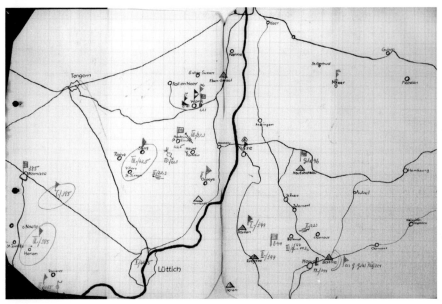

German unit positions at Liege. Probably around 15 May. (Digital History Archive, Microcopy No. T-315)

squads from the 223rd and 42nd Pioneer Battalions. These squads fell under command of 344 IR. 251 ID scouts – *Spahtruppen* – crossed the Meuse at Ougrée to set up a camp at Sclessin. 473 IR troops from 253 ID were now moving into the city of Liège.

At 1030hrs 251 AR scouts reported that Angleur, on a salient between the Ourthe and the Meuse, was free of enemy troops. The railway bridge 800m south-east of Angleur was destroyed along with all other bridges over the Meuse and Ourthe. 471 IR sent scouts to Forts Chaudfontaine and Embourg, where the Belgian status remained unchanged. The German attack on the southern forts was scheduled to commence on 16 May. It would include units of 451 IR against Fort Boncelles, 251 AR and 471 IR against Forts Chaudfontaine and Embourg, 459 IR against Flémalle, and other units of 451 IR to subdue the adjacent forts. At 1645hrs a reconnaissance flight from Recon Group 13, 3rd Squadron, flown by Lieutenant Schneider and the observer Private Kirschey, dropped leaflets over Fort Boncelles at low altitude. They landed at the front entrance to the fort. No one from the fort came out to pick them up. What they said is unknown but most likely a request for the fort to surrender.

The Germans were moving very heavy artillery pieces to Liège. They set up a 42cm battery at Dalhem assigned to *Schwere Artillerie-Abteilung* 820[1] to use against Fort Barchon. Sixth Army's *Eisenbahn Batterie* (Railway Batteries) 717 and 718, with 17cm *Kanone* (E), attacked the eastern forts, including Fort Battice, from the vicinity of Vaals.

The men of Fort Pontisse were exhausted after another sleepless night. Morale was at a low point. At 0600hrs large-calibre artillery shells began to land on the fort which lasted for about an hour and then it was quiet. Patrols were sent out by Captain Pire to determine what the Germans were doing. They reported that the barbed wire surrounding the fort was almost completely destroyed. Large quantities of weapons and equipment left behind by the Germans testified to the failure of the infantry attacks. The calm gave the cook time to bake some fresh bread. It would be the last time. The men enjoyed a hot meal and a shower before fire orders resumed in the afternoon.

Around 0200hrs the POC at Fort Barchon spotted a concentration of Germans on the perimeter attempting to get into the fort. The Mi/LG turret opened fire and the Germans cleared off. Between 0700hrs and 1000hrs, a work detachment was sent out to block up a breach in the counterscarp wall caused by a heavy artillery shell the previous day. The crew placed anti-tank mines and barbed wire in the gap. Two patrols were sent out, one led by Lieutenant Mans with Privates Grevesse and Leveque, and a second led by Sergeant Ghislain with two other soldiers (not identified). At 1100hrs, Lieutenant Mans's patrol was shot at from the church tower of Barchon village and the Rousseau farm, which was located along the road from Blegny to Troisfontaines. Grevesse was hit and not moving. Both patrols quickly ran back to the fort, leaving Grevesse behind. At 1130hrs Mans and Ghislain attempted to retrieve Grevesse but when they reached him he was dead. In response to the shooting, the church of Barchon and the Rousseau farm were set on fire to dislodge the Germans. From 0800hrs to 1000hrs the remaining 150mm turret fired on the old airfield at Ans when it was discovered that the Luftwaffe was using the site to refuel and rearm the Stukas.

At 0030hrs the following message was sent from Aubin-Neufchâteau to HQ: 'Received multiple coded telegrams. [Decipher] Key not working.' At the same time Bloc P reported seeing a red flare north-west of the fort, and vehicle headlights near Warsage. A few minutes later both gun turrets were ordered to fire *boîtes-à-balles* in a 360° arc. The casemates flanking the ditch were ordered to fire 47mm shrapnel shells over the top of the massif by ricocheting the shots against the outer walls. All three mortars fired twenty-five rounds per barrel on all three sides of the glacis. Another coded message was received from HQ but it was impossible to decipher as the key was still not working.

At 0510hrs another indecipherable telegram was received. At the same time Bloc O detected another convoy, this time with infantry escort. The 75mm of Bloc 1 fired twenty rounds. Thirty minutes later they spotted a large convoy on the Mouland-Fouron road composed of horse-drawn vehicles[2] and trucks. One of the gun turrets was ordered to engage with forty rounds and the column was scattered. The Germans left their dead and wounded horses behind. At 0812hrs a new convoy was moving on the Mouland-Fouron road and Bloc 2 fired fifty rounds at the maximum rate of fire. Several trucks were hit and blocked the road. From mid-morning to late afternoon the fort responded with 75mm shells on German infantry and convoys at Chateau Regnoul, Mouland and the Berneau Bridge, where German sappers were attempting to repair the bridge. A German artillery battery was being set up near the Berneau railway crossing. The battery was hit with fifty rounds from the 75. Germans were spotted at the Goffart farm and the gun turrets were ordered to fire fifty rounds to destroy the farm. At 1800hrs German infantry with horses were seen near a farm in Warsage. They appeared to be orderlies tending to officers' horses. Ten rounds were fired on the farm and it caught fire. At the same time, Fort Battice was warned that a military column was heading in their direction from Thiernagant.

On several occasions throughout the evening and after nightfall, German troops attempted to set up guns and jump-off points for assaults on Fort Aubin-Neufchâteau, such as the ruins of the Weykman Farm, the Fouron crossroads, in the ruins of the peacetime barracks and on the road leading to the cemetery. The mortars and 75mm guns responded but there were no direct attacks on the fort.

The morning was relatively calm around Fort Evegnée. No new attacks took place with the exception of shelling by small to medium-calibre guns against the fort and the tower. The 75mm turrets fired back but had to play a game to keep from being hit while in battery. The turret would lift quickly and then drop down immediately without firing. The Germans would open fire on the now-retracted turrets. Then, while the German guns were reloading, the turret lifted, fired and dropped back down. The Germans had better results against the cloches, firing *obus de rupture* (AP shells) to break through the metal walls, causing steel, copper and concrete splinters to fly around inside. Several of the men were wounded, with minor injuries to the face and hands. Most were able to resume their duties.

In the afternoon there was a heavy air raid on the fort and the air tower by Stukas. Fléron and Barchon tried to protect Evegnée with high-angle fused shots, while Evegnée responded in kind. This was the first time the Stuka pilots attacked the three adjacent forts simultaneously to prevent them from providing mutual support. The heavy bombs had a considerable effect on morale. With each hit, the fort seemed to lift up and drop back down. The air tower felt as if it was swaying and could collapse at any time. The bombs also caused serious damage to the fort:

- Landslides of debris and concrete in the ditches, in particular the counterscarp of Salient I. A huge crater formed in the gorge front ditch.
- One of the FMs in the head casemate was torn off of its mounting and thrown, along with the gunner, against the armoured door at the back of the room. An unexploded bomb was stuck upright in the ground.
- There was so much debris in the ditches in front of the casemates that Commandant Vanderhaegen ordered the guns to be moved up to the second level.[3] Even from the upper level, getting good shots was difficult due to the condition of the ditch.
- Damage to the walls of Salients II and III was profound and there was a large crack in the ceiling of the tunnel leading to S-III.

- The ceiling of the former troop assembly room in the central massif was cracked and pieces of concrete fell on top of the plotting table in the adjacent fire-control room.

To avoid further casualties, Vanderhaegen ordered the evacuation of the turret gun chambers during Stuka attacks. The crews moved down to the quadrilateral.

Following another bombing, German infantry attacked the breach in Salient I and attempted to jump down into the ditch. They were immediately fired on with *boîtes-à-balles* from Salient I's 75 and the attack was stopped. Germans attempted to infiltrate the ditch in other places but were hit by MGs, FMs and the Mi/LG turret.

In the evening, Privates Wielmin and Colson volunteered to go out on a night patrol. Under cover of darkness they exited the fort through the breach at Salient I, dressed in civilian clothes and carrying a basket of pigeons to send messages back to the fort. They did not return to the fort. Only one pigeon came back with the coordinates of a German battery. The men were never heard from again.

Fatigue and low morale were taking their toll. The disappearance of Wielmin and Colson added to the dark mood of the fort. It was not safe from the Stukas anywhere inside the fort and the men now fully realized that any hope of rescue was long gone. The PFL was now many miles behind enemy lines. Some men began to spread rumours or suspicions that, because the forts were causing heavy losses among the Germans, they might take revenge on the garrison after they were captured. Vanderhaegen, aware of what was going on, gathered the men in the main tunnel of the fort and spoke:

> Your comrades Wielmin and Colson acted heroically. You must give me all of your confidence; I will not needlessly sacrifice any of your lives. The fear of being shot by the enemy because of a stubborn defence is absurd. The German army, too, has traditions of honour; it knows how to recognize and respect courage and its respect for you will grow as your resistance continues. If captivity becomes inevitable, we will leave together, with our heads up, after having accomplished our duty. After I am no longer your commander I will be there, for as long as possible, as your defender. We may know some painful days ahead but the hour of deliverance will come.

The men replied with shouts of 'Long live the King – Long live Belgium – Long live our commander.' The entire crew shook hands with Vanderhaegen. Peace and courage returned for most men for the time being.[4]

On 15 May Fort Fléron was shelled intermittently by medium-calibre guns. The Germans were concentrating on Fléron's neighbours to the north. Fléron fired suppression rounds in support of Flémalle which was under heavy Stuka attack. Other than that, the fort fired on German observers in the steeple of the church at Retinne and on two German batteries that were spotted by patrols.

During the night of 14/15 May, Brigadiers Delaurier and Heusking and Privates Cellars and Peeters left Fort Chaudfontaine to resume their duties at Mg 1 in Magnée. They arrived around 0330hrs. Around noon, the surface of Fort Chaudfontaine was shelled at its own request by the 150mm turrets of Flémalle and Fléron. The shell fuses were set to explode a few metres above the ground to chase off German infantry.

Fort Embourg was hit by heavy artillery, suspected to be 150mm guns. In mid-afternoon the Stukas struck and their bombs fell until nightfall, causing heavy damage to Salient IVs turret. The three remaining turrets took up the slack. Observation Post EB 8 at Tilff was attacked and the fort landed shells in the immediate vicinity of the PO. During the night the heavy artillery shelling continued. The Germans attempted to move onto the glacis but were chased off by *boîtes-à-balles*.

At 1130hrs the Luftwaffe resumed the bombing of Fort Boncelles, knocking out three of the four turrets in a matter of minutes. Two men were killed inside the S-III turret and Sergeant Louis in S-IV. The fort was left

Gorge ditch of Fort Embourg with postern entry in the centre. (Digital History Archive, 'Bunkers of the Blitzkrieg')

with only the Salient II turret and its close-defence weapons. When the aerial bombardment ended, German 88s, set up about 1km from the fort, opened fire to finish the job. Despite this, S-II continued to fire throughout the night. The tower was hit by 37mm and 88mm guns. Fine dust was sucked into the vents, severely hampering the function of the fort's ventilation system, a gross oversight in the design of the system. Small German squads attacked the fort throughout the night, looking for a breakthrough but the FMs held them off until morning.

Sometime during the day, a letter was dispatched to Captain Charlier (exact means unknown – most likely German parliamentarian under white flag or this may be the leaflet that was dropped) that read as follows:

THE GENERAL COMMANDANT OF THE SIEGE ARMY OF LIÈGE

To

Commandant of Fort de Boncelles
Monsieur le Capitaine Charlier

Fort de Boncelles

Monsieur le Capitaine,
I suppose that you are aware that on 10/5/40 the Ouvrage of Eben-Emael was conquered in very little time by a new method of combat employed by our troops.

I have the honour to inform you that the same method will be used by me, if necessary, against Fort Boncelles. As a consequence it is inevitable that your soldiers will be lost. The local population as well as the surrounding villages in the countryside will be swept up in this catastrophe.

I have no interest in killing either Belgian soldiers or the civilian population, because Germany did not want war with Belgium.

So as not to uselessly spill blood I ask that you, by 1700 hours this evening (Belgian time), today, 15/5/40, hoist the white flag.

If this term is not met, the fort and those who occupy it, will be destroyed.

The responsibility for this wasted blood will fall only on you.

COMMANDING GENERAL COMBAT TROOPS OF GERMANY

Fort Boncelles did not surrender.

Fort Tancrémont had a fairly quiet day. The only setback being the loss of the PO in Vesdre near Verviers. Late in the day the ventilation Bloc O was fired on at close range. Return fire from the bloc killed two of the German gunners and a third was captured. The prisoner reported that his team had been tasked with firing (poison) gas grenades at the air shaft. He was most likely bluffing but as a precaution the fort was put under pressure to keep outside air from being sucked inside the fort.

Fort Flémalle had a quiet night and early morning and carried out interdiction fire on numerous roads and intersections, including a truck on the Route de Mons carrying ammunition and German columns approaching Liège. Tancrémont was under attack by bombers and requested AA fire from Flémalle. Around 1000hrs the Stukas returned for the third time and the fort was blasted for about three hours with medium-calibre and incendiary bombs. The first bombs fell on the infirmary and on Salient IV. Bombs also fell on the AA position, pounded the barbed-wire perimeter and reached the glacis between Salients III and IV. The craters created by the bombs would later provide concealment for German troops. An hour after the Stukas flew off, German artillery took over, and then the bombers returned again to finish the job. The gun turrets, which had been evacuated of its crew earlier, were taken out one by one.

Around 1300hrs German pioneers moved on to the glacis of lateral I-II and II-III and the central massif. The S-III turret intervened with case shot and the Mi/LG opened fire with MGs and grenades. The bombing lasted until 2030hrs. During the bombardment the turret crews were evacuated and the minimum number of men needed to fire the guns waited at the foot of the turret for the bombing to stop. The rest of the crew waited in the lower level of the fort.

Damage to Flémalle included blockage of the gorge ditch and escarp casemate embrasures with earth and blocks of concrete. The guns could still fire towards Salient I but at a reduced angle. Two of the head casemate embrasures were partially blocked. The escarp tunnel was blocked by pieces of concrete that had fallen from the ceiling. The S-IV turret was badly damaged, its shell lifts wrecked and the turret inaccessible. The corridor leading to the *Salle de Détente* (rest room) in the quadrilateral had partially collapsed. S-II turret's cap was jammed against the forward armour; the 105mm turret was also jammed and inoperable. The S-I turret was out of service. The 150mm turret was jammed and unable to turn. The Mi/LG received a very serious hit from a shell and the turret housing was cracked, allowing access into the turret from the outside. The ditches were heavily cratered. The commandant sent engineers to block the gap in the Mi/LG.

The bombardment of the fort by German artillery continued all night long. Fléron intervened with shells set to explode just above the ground on the massif and glacis to break up any potential enemy infantry attack.

Activity from and against Fort Battice was minimal. The fort targeted roads and intersections with interdiction fire and against a small number of German columns. All in all, infantry activity was minimal as 253 ID moved off and 223 ID units moved in to take their place and make plans to finish off the forts.

Namur

At 0830hrs on 15 May the smell of smoke hung over Namur. Worse, the Belgian VII Corps had been ordered to move its divisions west to Flanders. The defence of the PFN now fell to the forts. General Deffontaine, commander of VII Corps, decided to take the RFN staff along with him, leaving the strategic defence of the PFN to the fort commanders. RFN's last message was: 'You must consider that from now on the forts are isolated. Resist to the end of your means. Goodbye and good luck!' The commanders felt as if a lead weight had been dropped on their heads. They were now in charge of their own fate. There would now be no chance of relief or resupply of food or ammunition. The interval troops were gone. This terrible news now had to be passed on to the men. The morale of the troops was, up to the point they were notified of the withdrawal of field troops, still excellent. The abandonment by the infantry, as it was depicted by the men, brought on a general despondency. Like being stuck on an island after all the boats have left. The officers tried to add a positive note but the men weren't ignorant and had a pretty good idea of their fate – to end up as prisoners of war. After the infantry left the interval positions, patrols were sent out to recover abandoned food supplies and to destroy weapons and ammunition left behind.

Because of the new circumstances, and the steady approach of German troops from the east, the commanders began to essentially rewrite the manuals in order to work out a mutual support plan. When the enemy appeared, or his approach was detected, the forts would provide mutually supporting fire to scour the vicinity of enemy troops. However, since the infantry was gone, and most of the POs were empty, the only way of knowing what was happening in the distance was to send out reconnaissance patrols. Composed of volunteers, these missions were fraught with risk as the men moved along deserted roads and through abandoned villages, avoiding detection at all costs. Danger was everywhere, especially since the enemy was now anywhere and everywhere, and he was also looking for information. Meanwhile, the Germans formulated their attack plans for the PFN. Forts Marchovelette and Suarlée would be attacked by 269 ID, followed by an attack of 211 ID south of the Meuse and Sambre.

At 0700hrs the gunners of Fort Saint-Héribert were placed on alert and directed to fire the turret guns as follows: 75mm GP on the crossroads at Six-Bras; two howitzers on the Bourdon d'Hiver crossroads; and two howitzers on the Route Royale at marker 7. At 1000hrs the PO de Pruniers reported the sighting of Germans at the Chateau Mariensberg. The howitzers opened fire on the target.

Around noon, French and Belgian troops withdrew between Fooz and Profondeville, falling back on the line of Fooz-Ferme–Potisseau–Portique–Ri de Flandre. Troops to the south of Profondeville moved along the Route des Morts and Route Royale to occupy the line Ri de Flandre–Six-Bras. Saint-Héribert's artillery intervened sporadically on the Route des Morts and the Route Royale in support of the retreating troops. The fort's POC spotted French tanks, cavalry and artillery pieces passing by the Ferme du Laquisse in the direction of the crossroads of Provis and Six-Bras. It was also noted that 1/13th Line Regiment, coming from Andoy, had stopped and was occupying shelters at Cabacca.

Beginning at 0030hrs, the 75mm turrets fired on the right bank of the Meuse, at the level of the Rivière lock, at the rate of fifty shots per piece per hour. At 0200hrs the rate was increased to seventy-five shots per piece per hour. At 0410hrs the 75mm howitzers opened fire on the southern outlet of the Lustin railway tunnel, at a tight bend in the Meuse across from Profondeville. At 0520hrs the order to cease fire was given as the guns could not keep up the pace for too long.

In the meantime, Saint-Héribert experienced its first death – a gruesome accident. A patrol was sent out overnight to the Bois-de-Villers to investigate the civilian telephone exchange, which was apparently not responding to calls. Along the way a wounded French soldier from 8th Infantry Regiment was found and treated. Upon returning to the fort around 0220hrs, one of the men from the patrol, Private Radu, fell into the water-filled ditch at the base of the access ramp. All attempts to save him were futile and he drowned in the pit.

The Luftwaffe bombed the fort's AA guns, a testament to their lack of usefulness. Around 1500hrs, the PO du Manoir no longer responded to calls. PO des Pruniers reported the withdrawal of the last French troops, followed closely by the Germans. In support of the French, the fort resumed its fire. The order was given to the crew of PO des Pruniers to fall back towards the fort. By the evening, except for a few small groups, the French were gone. It was now up to the officers of the fort to try to raise the men's spirits, a very difficult mission on this day of abandonment.

Elsewhere, Fort Maizeret fired in support of Marchovelette. Fort Malonne fired long-range shots to interdict the crossing of the Meuse by the Germans. Its external observation posts were evacuated and the men returned to the fort. Fort Marchovelette's external POs were also evacuated. Captain Georges De Lombaerdt, the fort's commander, sent out two patrols. One, led by Sergeant Lemineur with eight soldiers, bumped into the Germans at the tram stop of Gelbressée. A skirmish followed and there were losses. Lemineur was hit in the abdomen and fatally wounded. He begged his men to leave him so they could report back to the fort. The men returned to inform the commander of their findings and to tearfully apologize for leaving Lemineur behind. His body was recovered after the fall of the fort. Under cover of darkness the Germans attempted an infantry attack on the fort but they were spotted and repelled. Support fire was also conducted by Fort de Suarlée to cover the French retreat. The fort's external POs no longer responded to calls. The fort was bombed by medium-sized projectiles.

Strategic Situation in Belgium at the End of 15 May 1940

In the north the Dutch Army surrendered. The German Eighteenth Army completed the occupation of the country. The French Seventh Army was sent to reinforce the crumbling Ninth Army.

In Belgium the Germans continued to make contact and their artillery was violent and relentless. The forts of Liège were holding out.

The withdrawal of the French Ninth Army forced the French First Army to pivot on its left flank and withdraw its right along the Sambre River. General Blanchard, First Army Commander, requested the withdrawal of the Belgian VII Corps from Namur to support the Allies. Ninth Army began its withdrawal at 1100hrs. By 1600hrs its commander, General Corap, was relieved of command and replaced by General Giraud, but by that time the army was in tatters.

Von Kleist's Armoured Group drove west through the breach at Sedan. In the morning, General Erwin Rommel's 7th Panzer Division had established a bridgehead across the Meuse. His next objective was Philippeville. On his right, 5th Panzer Division reached the bridgehead around noon. Both divisions came in contact with the French 1st Armoured Division at Flavion, which had been sent there the previous day from Charleroi. By the evening of the 15th the tanks on both sides were engaged but the French were running short of fuel. In the morning a bridgehead was created for 6th Panzer Division at Monthermé. From now on the French front would be continuously pushed back. At Sedan, the Germans exploited their bridgehead, although at Stonne the intervention of 3rd Armoured Division Reserve threatened their southern flank.

Chapter 10

Thursday, 16 May 1940

Liège

2 51 ID's plans for 16 May called for a continuation of the attack on Fort Boncelles by 451 IR, 1/2/231 AR and 88mm Flak batteries. 471 IR was ordered to keep watch on Forts Chaudfontaine and Embourg and 459 IR on Fort Flémalle. During the night, artillery batteries kept up fire in the area of the forts and on the 16th would support the attack of a reinforced 451 IR by holding down the adjacent forts. Boncelles, the weakest fort at Liège, was destined to be the first casualty.

At 1530hrs German aircraft left Spa with orders to drop leaflets on the southern forts of Liège and to perform photo reconnaissance. Leaflets were dropped on Forts Tancrémont, Chaudfontaine and Embourg. Photos were taken of Forts Flémalle, Boncelles, Embourg, Chaudfontaine, Fléron and Tancrémont. Air defences were very light. Machine-gun fire from Fort Fléron hit one of the aircraft but it returned to Spa. Random gunfire came from Chaudfontaine.

At dawn, an observation team from Fort Pontisse moved to the Thiry farm (about 150m west of Salient I) to direct the fire of the 105mm turret and observe enemy movements around the farm and the fort, in particular the slope of Fond de la Vaux, which was hidden from the fort. Telephone lines were laid from the fort to the farm. The Germans left the fort alone for the time being. Enemy formations were fired on but there did not appear to be an attack in the works. At 0900hrs PO AC 1 notified Pontisse that a column of about 200 men was heading from Haccourt to Vivegnis. The 105mm guns opened fire on the column. Small groups of Germans were also spotted by observers in the POC and the Thiry Farm moving in the direction of Oupeye and on the perimeter of the Bois de Pontisse. The fort's guns drove them off.

At 1430hrs German infantry were moving on the Rue de Hermée, directly in view of the Thiry farm observers. The Salient I turret opened fire. At 1930hrs more German infantry crossed the Haccourt Bridge and began marching south along the canal. The area was targeted by the fort.

The crew of Pontisse was exhausted by the continuous alerts, artillery shelling and bombing from above. Rest did not come easy and nerves were on edge.

During the night, German infantry again crept through the surrounding fields towards Fort Barchon. Some had reached the glacis and opened fire with small arms. They were spotted and fired on with shrapnel rounds from the 75mm turret and the Mi/LG strafed the perimeter. The Germans pulled back to Housse. During the day various other targets were hit. At 0927hrs the airport of Ans was shelled and at 1100hrs a German artillery battery in Trembleur was also shelled. Between 1600hrs and 2100hrs Barchon was shelled by heavy-calibre guns, some estimated to be 305mm. The second 150mm turret had been knocked off balance during the bombing of 14 May and with each shot from the heavy guns the pins holding the platform in place were sheared and around 2200hrs the turret was finally put out of operation altogether.

Aubin-Neufchâteau reported that since 10 May it had fired almost 6,700 artillery shells. The Germans continued to launch probing infantry attacks against the fort. From midnight to dawn the mortars and gun turrets fired at random times around the glacis to deter German movements in the close proximity of the fort. At 0600hrs Bloc 2's observer noticed that the shutters on the Trois Cheminées farm were all closed. Just yesterday they were all open. Suddenly the bloc was fired on by a PAK 37 near the farm. The gun turret fired ten rounds on and around the farm and the PAK was silenced. By mid-morning observation post NV 5 was surrounded by Germans and had run out of ammunition. The post commander called to announce they were surrendering. Commandant d'Ardenne congratulated the men for a job well done, having provided the fort with a goldmine of information on the location of German troops over a very difficult six-day period.

At 1144hrs Bloc P called the command post to say that three Germans carrying a white flag were approaching the bloc's entrance. They had what appeared to be three hostages with them. The commandant agreed to see them but only if they released the hostages which the Germans agreed to do right away. One of the hostages was Brigadier Raemackers who had been taken prison at bunker NV 5. The fort's doctor was sent out to make contact with the Germans and came back with a colonel and a captain. According to the message sent by 223 ID at 1915hrs,[1] this was Colonel von Mayer of 253 ID. Here is an account of the meeting from the point of view of Von Mayer, which is very close to that of Commandant d'Ardenne:

Around 1300, as the commissioner of the commanding general I arrived at the entrance to the fort and was led alone to the entrance bunker. There I informed the commander of the fort, *Kapitan* d'Ardenne, who was standing behind a wall:

'On behalf of the commanding general, I ask you to hand over your work [fort]. The crew can move unharmed into captivity in Aachen. You may keep your weapon in recognition of your heroic defence.'

Kapitan d'Ardenne informed me that he had already participated in the previous war and that I would therefore understand if [he] had to refuse my request and keep the work to the last man. He especially acknowledged that the German Wehrmacht had fought heroically in the crackdown on the Neufchâteau fort. The fallen German soldiers were buried in honour.

I replied that, as an old soldier, I could understand *Kapitan* d'Ardenne's opinion, but I had to point out that it was completely pointless in view of the modern methods of combat used by the German Wehrmacht when taking Fort Eben-Emael, sacrificing a crew of 700 men.

I concluded the negotiations with the request to be able to extend a hand to Kapitan d'Ardenne as a comrade and out of respect for the defence of the work. I was then blindfolded at the entrance of a bunker equipped with two observation domes. While saying goodbye I asked the adjutant accompanying me if he would notify his commanding officer that if he should make the decision to hand over the fort during the coming fight to show a white flag because we had a particularly good observation of the fort.

As the Germans departed, the fort's officers were expecting to be pounded by German artillery due to their refusal to surrender. Both gun turrets were ordered to stay closed. The troops were ordered to remain in the lower level of their blocs. Only sentries were allowed to remain above.

Commandant d'Ardenne contacted HQ to report the encounter with the two German officers. HQ replied: 'Admired and approved.' A moment later seven aircraft released their bombs over the fort. They detonated but no visible damage was reported.

Aubin-Neufchâteau continued to respond to German sightings with 75mm and mortar fire. At 1530hrs they opened fire on the Moudrerie and Fouron crossroads. At 1614hrs a large number of horses were spotted near the Moudrerie farm. Several aircraft were spotted flying over the fort. Infantrymen and two horsemen (officers) were seen travelling on the Warsage crossroads. One hundred rounds were fired at a mass of infantry in Bombaye village. The Germans attempted to evacuate the village and were hit by the 75s as they fled. Other targets included the Mouland and Witthuis crossroads and the Scheur Farm. At 1945hrs another group of ten aircraft flew over the fort. A message was sent to HQ to close out the day: 'Everything under control. 7,854 rounds of all calibre fired so far.'

The situation at Fort Evegnée was the same as the previous day. The fort was closely surrounded and guarded on all sides. The Germans kept up a continuous fire on all of the visible works of the fort. Work crews attempted to repair the damages and to move debris away from the embrasures but it was too dangerous. Men clearing debris from around the turrets that was hindering the firing of the guns had to quit and take cover. Being outside on the superstructure, even at night, was suicidal. The functioning 75mm turrets continued to fire on enemy targets. Despite the heavy fire coming at them from the Belgians, the Germans didn't give up, and resumed the work of digging towards the fort hour after hour. The 75s fired almost continuously on targets directed by the air tower observers. Towards evening German actions at the tower became more violent. Sous-Lieutenant Dinant recounted:

Around 1900, a hail of shells fell on the top of the air tower. The circular parapet collapsed. I spotted two German automatic guns positioned in the pits dug for the alternate location of our Mi/CA. A violent fire also erupted from a crater sixty meters from the tower that was formed when Belgian engineers blew up the road at the turn of the Evegnée – Heuseux road.

I threw grenades through a gap at the top of the tower but my situation became untenable. Some of the enemy shells embedded themselves, intact and unexploded, in the crumbling wall of the circular parapet. I ran down to the firing chamber. The embrasures were also under enemy fire. One of my men collapsed, shot in the chest. He treated his own wound and then descended alone twenty meters down the straight ladders of the shaft of the tower to find a doctor to help him. Shells penetrated through the embrasures, and crashed against the central column. I gave the order to close the metal shutters but to leave a gap large enough to fit the barrel of the FM. A duel commenced between my FMs and the Germans, who continued to close in.

Not being able to neutralize the German machine guns by my own means, I asked the commander of the fort to intervene with the 75mm turrets. Shortly after, the entire area around the tower was pounded for about thirty minutes. The crater on the Evegnée-Heuseux road and the

Mi/CA pits were effectively neutralized. Enemy shots began to taper off, little by little. The systematic firing of the large turrets continued, but at reduced density.[2]

Fort Evegnée also participated in the defence against infantry attacks on Forts Flémalle, Boncelles and Chaudfontaine. This included targets identified by Fort Aubin-Neufchâteau. A large body of troops near Mouland and German troops operating in the region of Louveigne were hit by the 150mm turret. During the night several incidents occurred. The Germans became very daring, going so far as to set up guns in craters on the counterscarp and fire MG bursts into the ditches, making movement there very dangerous. Night fell and calm returned to Fort Evegnée but the men remained on high alert.

In the evening Forts Boncelles and Flémalle no longer responded to calls. There was also no news on the fate of Colonel Modard who had his headquarters at Flémalle. Fort Chaudfontaine responded.

The fall of Forts Boncelles and Flémalle
At dawn the Stukas resumed their bombing of Fort Boncelles. Waves of fourteen planes each dropped a bomb every couple of minutes. There was so much activity that one of the aircraft was hit by bomb fragments and crashed.

At 0900hrs, Commandant Charlier and Lieutenant Lhoest went outside to inspect the damage. All of the turrets were destroyed and the wartime *Corps de Garde* abandoned. At 1030hrs Charlier called his officers together to discuss the feasibility of continuing the defence. They agreed that further losses should be avoided and beside that, the fort was running out of supplies. Charlier stated that he didn't want to give up and was looking for other options. It was agreed that a small staff of five officers and twenty-five volunteers would remain behind at the fort, while the rest would attempt to join the field army by escaping through the tower exit. Defensive tasks were split up among the men. A request for support was sent to Fort Flémalle but it had run out of ammunition.

The crew of about 100 men selected to re-join the army made their way through the tunnels to the tower, only 200m from the massif. The first group left but sadly they did not get very far. German machine guns opened fire and many of the men were captured in the Bois de la Marchandise. The bombing made it impossible for the remaining men to get away.

Meanwhile, Charlier ordered the destruction of confidential documents and surplus material. While this was going on German pioneers noticed

The air tower of Fort Boncelles pounded by German artillery. (Bunkerfreaks Antwerpen)

the ditch casemates were no longer defended. They climbed down into the ditch and placed a large explosive charge against the entrance to the central part of the fort. At 1230hrs the TNT exploded, destroying the airlock at the entrance and sending shockwaves throughout the fort and flames down the main tunnel. Commandant Charlier and Lieutenant Hurlet were in the telephone exchange near the central gallery and were killed by the blast. Nearly everyone left in the fort was injured or burned. German medics rushed into the fort to treat the wounded.

Fort Boncelles' struggle was over, but no white flag ever flew over the fort. The fort was a wreck. The abandoned *Corps de Garde* was full of shell holes. Most of the embrasures guarding the ditch were blocked. The capital gallery under the ditch collapsed. Breaches all along the counterscarp formed what looked like a staircase leading into the ditch. Bomb and shell craters covered the surface of the fort. The previous day, three of the turrets were knocked out of action in a 20-minute span, with the exception of the turret at S-II, which was also now out of commission, and only a couple of the ditch guns could fire. Finally, the air tower was heavily damaged. By 16 May there was nothing left to fight with. Eight men had been killed and twelve wounded. Boncelles was considered by the post-war investigative commission to have been captured by the Germans. The second fort of Liège had now fallen.

Captured Belgians leave the escarp entrance of Fort Boncelles. The casemate guarding the postern is on the left. (Digital History Archive, 'Bunkers of the Blitzkrieg')

Flémalle suffered the same fate from the air as Boncelles and from heavy artillery fire. German pioneers closed in on the fort. At 1200hrs Colonel Modard attempted to leave the fort through the air tower with twenty of his men but they were unable to get away.[3] At 1400hrs the aerial bombardment resumed and the tower was hit by 150mm shells plus 88s and 37s, blowing a hole in the side and killing two men. This put the ventilator out of action, allowing dust and gas from the shells to permeate the fort. The defence council met and voted to surrender the fort. At 1430hrs the white flag was raised.

The situation at Fort Fléron was becoming dire. Because of the continuous shelling and power failure, life inside the fort became particularly difficult. Bombardment by medium-calibre guns continued. Heavy aerial bombing started at 1320hrs. The whine of the engines and whistling sounds made by the Stukas was a terrifying thing to hear. Heavy bombs landed on the fort. The cap of the 75mm turret of S-I was completely lifted off. The infantry exit was blocked.

At 0255hrs, while Fort Chaudfontaine was undergoing sustained heavy shelling, an attack was carried out on the air tower by German infantry. The neighbouring forts responded and the attackers were pushed back.

Three aerial bombardments took place at 1110hrs, 1200hrs and 1320hrs. Fléron and Embourg were included in the third attack. At 1500hrs a new bombardment caused additional damage to the 75mm turrets. Chunks of concrete became lodged in the space between the forward armour and the turret cylinder, preventing the turrets from turning or retracting, making them sitting ducks for the German high-powered anti-tank guns. The 105mm turret was out of service and the embrasure was heavily damaged. The embrasures in Salient I's ditch casemate were destroyed by PAK 37s. Patrols reported that the centre of Chaudfontaine village was occupied and three enemy guns were spotted at Vaux on the Quai des Ardennes and at Olne. Chateau Ancion was occupied by the Germans.

Captain Clobert received a letter from the Germans:

COMMANDING GENERAL ATTACK TROOPS IN FRONT OF LIÈGE 16/5/40

To the Commander of Fort Chaudfontaine

Monsieur le Commandant,

Fort Boncelles was conquered after the employment of a new combat method.

I will employ the same method after the fort that you continue to hold.

In order not to waste blood needlessly that is not to be regarded as in the best interest of Belgium, I will be sending to you today a Parliamentarian. He will come with a white flag.

I direct your attention to the articles of the laws of war which guarantee the inviolability of a Parliamentarian. A violation of these articles will have the gravest of consequences for the commander and his men.

THE COMMANDING GENERAL OF ATTACKING TROOPS IN FRONT OF LIÈGE

Similar letters were sent to the commanders of Forts Tancrémont and Embourg, encouraging them to surrender. Each one mentioned a 'new combat method', alluding to the shaped charges used at Eben-Emael.

Fort Embourg was pounded by aerial bombing and artillery. A shell got stuck in the breech of the S-III 75 and it was unable to fire. This pause allowed German engineers to climb on top of the turret to finish it off but they were driven off by shells from Chaudfontaine. As night fell the guns fired *boîtes-à-balles* in close proximity to the fort to prevent German movements.

Near Fort Tancrémont, the Germans were moving through the hills around Vert Buisson, Johoster and Haut-Regard. Tancrémont shelled the ridge in response. Otherwise the fort was left alone.

Fort Battice's day started quietly and for the first time since the start of the war, there were no infantry attacks on the fort. Forts Evegnée, Embourg, Barchon and Fléron sent requests for assistance throughout the day. In the afternoon Aubin-Neufchâteau and Tancrémont also requested support. Contact with MN 29 was broken off around 2100hrs. MN 12 reported they had witnessed an explosion at MN 29. Battice tried in vain to restore the connection with the PO.

After dark, Sergeant Fischer took a patrol out. On the way back the patrol came across two German trucks that had been abandoned on the Aubel–Charneux road. They recovered weapons, maps and vehicle documents before destroying the trucks. They also investigated the empty Border Cyclist barracks at Henri-Chapelle which had been used by the Germans until recently. Plans had been left behind outlining an attack on the fort. The empty barracks and the plans led Fischer to believe that this particular attack was now in the works.

The crew of MN 29 withstood multiple attacks during the final days. At 1900hrs they noticed that a new attack was being set up and this time the Germans approached through the blind spots of the observation cloche. In this way German engineers were able to place an explosive charge against the bunker's entrance door. At 2100hrs the post commander requested an artillery strike, but it was too late; the door blew up and was thrown into the bunker with a loud bang and killed Sergeant Servais and Private Burton, and the other two soldiers were seriously injured. This was the explosion seen at MN 12. MN 29 was seized by the Germans at the same time as the requested artillery fire arrived. The Germans left the bunker behind. The two surviving soldiers spent the night of 16/17 May in the bunker.

At 1915hrs, 223 ID sent out a message[4] regarding the attacks on the eastern forts.

1) Last night, scouts were turned away everywhere: Neufchâteau, Barchon, Evegnée, Battice.
2) Yesterday, Colonel von Mayer (253 ID) asked Neufchâteau to surrender. The fort commander refused and stated he will defend the fort to the end.
3) Reconnaissance of Fort Barchon by Pi. Bn. 51 is being carried out now.

4) Hill 267 was suspected of having a Belgian observation and fire control bunker. An attempt by II/IR 344 to take it away the previous night was rejected. A shock squad also failed and the squad leader was killed. 2/Pi. Bn. 51 was ordered to take the bunker that night.
5) Battice was suspected of having an underground connection with the Herbe coal mine. According to statements by residents of Herve the owner of the coal mine was the commandant of Battice. II/IR 344 dropped grenades into the mine shaft and destroyed the lift, on the assumption that the supposed exit was there.[5]
7) Flak-Abt. 246 (FA 246) participated in the attack on Barchon and the other works.

223 Inf. Div. (HQ Wonk) – 5/16/40 – 2245hrs
Orders to attack Fort Barchon

1) The attack is set for 18.5.
2) Units participating in the attack:
   a) 344 IR as determined by the regiment commander. To include 13th and 14th Companies and parts of the Pi. Bn. 51 subordinated to the 344 IR.
   b) 223 AR: Gamma Batt. 820 (42cm); also requested 8.8cm and 2cm Flak.
3) Implementation:
   a) From 0730 preparatory and disruptive shooting of the entire artillery group according to the fire plan.
   b) Artillery commander will notify 344 IR when shelling of Barchon begins. Shelling of Fort Barchon, in agreement with 344 IR, will then be interrupted in order to enable the request for surrender.
   c) If there is no surrender, artillery commander, through 344 IR, will be notified that fire should continue.

The beginning of the attack is determined by commander of 344 IR, in coordination and agreement with artillery commander. The attack on the fort must take place immediately after the last shot of the Gamma battery, which must be reported to the attacking force in good time.[6]

Fire plan for the spread of the attacks on Fort Barchon on 18.5.40

Time	Unit	Harassment Fire	Destruction Fire	Ammunition Use by Department		
				Light Field Howitzer	Heavy Field Howitzer	42cm Mörser
0800	Battery 820		Fort Barchon			Total 10 shots
0730–0800	One battery of IV/AR 223	Fort Barchon			20	
0730–0800	One battery of IV/AR 223	Fort Pontisse			20	
0730–0800	One battery of IV/AR 223	Fort Evegnée			20	
0730–0800	One battery of I/AR 223	Fort Battice		40		
0730–0800	One battery of I/AR 223	Fort Evegnée		40		
0730–0800	One battery of I/AR 223	Fort Barchon		40		
0830?–0855	III/AR 223	Fort Pontisse		Each battery 40		
?–0800	II/AR 223	Fort Pontisse		Each battery 40		

41st Flak Regiment Operations Order

Operations order for FA 246, commanded by Hauptmann Lorentz, regarding bombardment of the forts north-east of Liège.

1) On 17.5 and 18.5 FA 246 will support 344 IR and 425 AR in the attacks on forts Barchon, Evegnée, Battice and Fort Pontisse. The bombardment of the fort will be done using pieces with calibre 8.8cm and 2cm.

2) FA 246 is subordinate to 41st Flak Regiment and dependent on cooperation with 344 IR and 425 IR.

3) Preparatory shooting will begin on 17.5, and full fire on 18.5. On 17.5, in connection with 425 IR, the main target is the armoured turrets and cloches of Fort Pontisse.

4) FA 246 will move on the night of 16 to 17 May to Homburg and Montzen (Strasse Aachen-Aubel)

[Orders 5, 6 and 8 omitted]

7) Use the Homburg-Aubel-Fawes-Charneux-Strassenkreuz not far from Battice-Hacboister. Road is under fire in some places.

9) If parts of FA 246 are not used for ground fire, they are to be used for air defence at the Meuse crossing at Visé on the east bank. 3/711 of 41st *Flakgruppe* is already there.[7]

Namur

On 16 May, German units involved in the attack on Namur were, according to the OKH *Lagekarten* West Front maps, at the following locations:

- 211 ID – Had crossed the Ourthe.
- 269 ID – Had moved off to the west.
- 253 ID – Moving north of Namur.
- 267 ID – Moving north of Namur.

The bombardment of Fort Marchovelette began at 0700hrs and ended 12 hours later. Two of the 75mm turrets were put out of action. The cap of the armoured observation post was cracked. The last of the external observation teams were recalled to the fort and it was completely locked up. The gunners traded shots with several German batteries. The air tower was hit by a battery deployed at Franc-Waret.

Fort Maizeret was cut off by advancing German forces. The close defences were activated to keep them away from the fort, and also intervened in support of Marchovelette. No patrols were sent out. It was otherwise quiet.

The modified escarp entry at Fort Marchovelette. (Bunkerfreaks Antwerpen)

During the night, the Germans made their first attempt to capture Fort Andoy. It was quickly repulsed by the fort's howitzers. Andoy also fired on numerous targets identified by the external observation posts and the armoured observation post and in support of Marchovelette and Maizeret.

Fort Dave shelled several positions on the Lustin lock and along the Meuse as daylight arrived. Five hundred shells were fired on a group of German engineers building a bridge over the river. Three of the fort's external posts – Troonois, bunker SD 1A and DA 24A – remained occupied by Belgian troops. A patrol was sent out and while collecting intelligence near Abbe Claver, they stumbled upon a German patrol coming from Naninne. They managed to stay out of sight of the Germans. Another patrol was sent into the Bois de Dave and spotted a German observation post about 1,800m from the fort. Several shells were fired on the woods. Dave also participated in counterbattery fire with Fort Saint-Héribert. At 1020hrs Captain Noel was informed that RFN staff was leaving Namur. The men were beginning to realize that they would most likely end up as prisoners of war.

At midnight, Fort Saint-Héribert intervened in support of Fort Dave, which called for a shot at the Tailfer Lock #8, then an hour later, at Dave North railway station. At two in the morning, the last French troops withdrew. At 0220hrs a patrol was sent to find out what was going on at Shelter 12, which was no longer responding to calls. They found the shelter

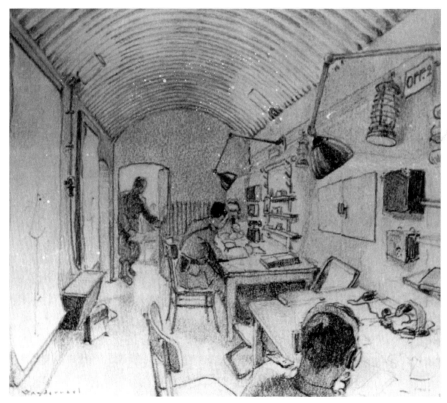

A sketch drawn by Chaplain Xandremael, member of the garrison of Fort Saint-Héribert, of the Bureau de Tir. *(Copyright @Fortsaintheribert.be)*

and everything inside destroyed. They also found that PO des Ruines was abandoned; perhaps the men had retreated with the French. Now there were four external posts remaining: PO du Carrefour, PO de Bois Spinette, *Abri* 17 and the Casemate Wépion. The decision was made to reoccupy the PO des Pruniers and some of the veteran observers volunteered.

At 0930hrs, artillery shelling of the fort began. With the help of Fort Dave the artillery battery was located near Chapelle de Clovis. The two forts fired on the German batteries, off and on, until 1730hrs. At 1030hrs Dave called to report that the Germans were building a bridge near Rivière. A patrol consisting of Privates Lorand and Mottet was sent to gather information about the bridge. They were not heard from again until 21 May when the Germans informed Commandant L'Entree that the two men had been taken prisoner on the heights overlooking Rivière.

The PO des Pruniers reported seeing Germans at la Sibérie, located on the heights of Profondeville. Two observers sent out earlier encountered a

German patrol at Fontaine Meurette, and exchanged fire. Only one of the men returned and reported he had seen muzzle flashes in an orchard near the former PO de St-Hubert. Dave and Saint-Héribert opened fire on the orchard and the bombardment stopped. At 2130hrs PO des Pruniers found itself surrounded by German infantry. The crew destroyed everything inside the post and escaped towards the fort. At the same time the PO de Bois Spinette called to say that the crew of *Abri* 17 was now with them. The stove at *Abri* 17 had exploded and everything inside the shelter was burned and destroyed.

The Germans were approaching Fort Malonne and the men took steps to strengthen the approach defences. The fort's guns successfully destroyed a German battery firing on the fort.

Fort de Suarlée was bombed from the air, putting the 75mm out of action. The concrete of the former German observatory was cracked and no longer useable. German troops fired on the air tower with a PAK 37, followed by two infantry attacks which were repelled by FMs in the tower and the fort's howitzers. Suarlée also provided support to Marchovelette. Several enemy columns were spotted on the road to Nivelles. Retreating French troops passed by the vicinity of the fort.

Strategic Situation in Belgium at the End of 16 May 1940

At Liège, Forts Boncelles and Flémalle had fallen.

The First French Army had been badly battered by the Sixth German Army and had to yield ground.

At 1000hrs General Gort of the BEF received the order to withdraw gradually on the Escaut. He anticipated one day's resistance on the Zenne, and one day on the Dendre. Operations were timed to start on the night of the 16th to 17th.

Ninth French Army continued to fall back. General Giraud was captured at his command post.

Chapter 11

Friday, 17 May 1940

Liège

Army Group B Report – 17 May 1940 – 1900 hours

1) 223 ID is now under command of the Army Group.
2) Mission of 223 ID remains as before: removal of the remaining Liège fortifications. For this, 126 AR is made available to 223 ID.[1]

Sixth Army High Command – 17 May 1940
To: 223 ID

1) 223 ID is immediately subordinated to Army Group B (HQ Aachen).
2) The following units of Sixth Army remain subordinate to 223 ID:

   • Special MG Battalion
   • Battery 320
   • 42 Pi. Bn. (minus one cy)
   • 51 Pi. Bn. (minus one cy)

3) Supply of the division continues to be through Sixth Army.[2]

From V Corps – 17 May 1940
To: 223 ID

1) Attack on Fort Chaudfontaine has not been successful in so far as the fort continues to provide artillery support to Forts Evegnée and Fléron. Infantry attacks continue.
2) V Corps asks for immediate shutdown of Fort Evegnée's artillery capability and if possible, Fort Fléron as well. V Corps has requested Stuka attacks on Fort Evegnée and Fort Fléron beginning at 1800h.[3]

A reconnaissance flight was sent out to check reports of a Belgian battery in the area of Fort Embourg, shooting from an open fire position. 10th Battery of 251 AR was set to engage this battery. The observer reported no battery position was found and there were no Belgian troops outside the fort. There was no fire coming from either Fort Embourg or Chaudfontaine. A Stuka dropped four 25kg bombs in a tight circle on the north-west turret of Fort Embourg. The results were not observed. This same turret was fired on by 88s and 20mm AA guns from a position on the south edge of the woods 600m north-east of Ninane. The armoured turret fired but was then enveloped in a cloud of smoke from an impact of the 88. Most of the shots by the 20mm bounced off the armour.

Other reconnaissance flights reported:

- Field fortifications were not occupied. German infantry was notified.
- German infantry digging in along the east and west side of Fort Chaudfontaine. Some resistance encountered.
- German infantrymen on the fort.
- Fort Chaudfontaine was shelled by Fort Embourg.
- Forts Fléron and Embourg shot at by Belgian artillery and Stukas with average bomb loads. Later, Fort Fléron does not fire. Fort Embourg fired only intermittently.
- One turret of Fort Evegnée is firing towards Chaudfontaine.
- Fort Fléron is shooting south-east with two turrets.
- Fort Evegnée is shooting at Chaudfontaine.
- German artillery firing on Fort Fléron.
- Stuka attack on Fort Fléron.
- German pioneer group at Fort Chaudfontaine.
- Enemy anti-aircraft defences from Fort Fléron and Fort Evegnée.
- 1/607 is firing at Forts Fléron and Evegnée.

The eighth day of war for Fort Pontisse began with a very heavy bombardment by Stukas. 88s also poured in shell after shell. The bombing started at a slow pace but picked up intensity throughout the morning. Fort Barchon was also under aerial attack. Forts Pontisse and Evegnée fired fused shots into the air above Barchon to drive off the Stukas. One was hit and crashed near Barchon. All of Pontisse's guns fired clearing shots in the ditches of Barchon, as well as the northern edge of the fort and the road to Housse. Around noon the telephone connection with Barchon was cut.

In the afternoon, German reconnaissance aircraft flew at low altitude over Pontisse and soon after, the bombing resumed with more violence than before. Large-calibre shells smashed against the roof of the fort, taking the men's breath away. German light field guns fired at will from the Bois des Trixhes and on the La Vaux ridge, peppering the fort's defences. High-velocity 88mm shells struck the armoured pieces and embrasures. The POC was taking direct hits. The S-III turret was destroyed when a shell passed right through the armour and reduced the interior to scrap metal. Two of the crewmembers, Heusy and Bajard, were seriously injured. Heusy died as the doctor arrived at the scene and Bajard died in the infirmary. On the wireless, Fort Barchon reported a German heavy battery in the vicinity of Wandre, but due to lack of observation and patrols, efforts to locate it were unsuccessful.

At 1930hrs the POC was hit again by an 88mm shell that penetrated inside the post. The observers dropped down the shaft and ran for cover. As night fell, the Germans attempted to locate one of the remaining POs at the Thiry Farm but were unable to find it.

At 0500hrs a general bombardment of Fort Barchon began with guns of all calibres. It lasted for five-and-a-half hours. At 1125hrs an aerial bombardment began that lasted 30 minutes. A squadron of Stukas returned at 1310hrs and dropped over 100 bombs. This assault lasted for about 50 minutes. One bomb fell on the door to the escarp entry, jamming it in the closed position. The Stukas returned again at 1420hrs and this time the bombing lasted for 20 very long minutes. Commandant Pourbaix went out afterwards through the infantry exit and noted the following:

- The walls of the airlock (escarp entry) were half-crumbled.
- The appearance of the ditches was barely recognizable as such; they were filled with mounds 2m, sometimes 3m high, hardened as if they had been trampled for a long time.
- The ditches in front of the casemates were filled with hardened earth up to the top of the embrasures and the guns were unable to fire. Crews were put to work to create firing lanes with the aid of picks and shovels. This work was often interrupted by visits from German aircraft. Fortunately there were no losses.
- The access ramp was in the same condition: mounds of earth covered the *chevaux de fries*, seriously compromising the ability to impede German infantry on the ramp.
- The wall of the *Corps de Garde* had collapsed to a great extent. The front wall at this location was very close to collapse.
- The escarp walls of the curtain were completely broken up.
- Everything was in ruins; everything was cracked inside and outside the fort.
- There was a huge crack in the well of the Salient I turret lift that extended to the ammunition gallery 20m underground.
- The greatest destruction was done to the counterscarp. The whole gorge front wall was full of cracks, some several inches wide.

At 1522hrs Pourbaix received a call from the air tower: the Germans had dug in near the Ferme Nanet at Couvelence, from where they were firing into the embrasures of the tower. Private Willems was wounded. The 75mm turret responded. At 1930hrs observers noticed German troops in the convent of Blegny and the two 105mm turrets opened fire.

The aerial bombardment resumed at 1730hrs. This time bombers dropped 'paquets' that opened on contact with the ground and released a thick blue/black smoke. Was this gas or smoke to cover an attack? Fortunately the wind picked up and blew the smoke away towards Housse.

One of the crew of the 105mm turret describes an incident inside the gun chamber:

It was at this moment that, finding myself with Joseph Simonis in the airlock of the 105, the door suddenly jumped out of its hinges. We were indeed trapped in the airlock. We both screamed for someone to come and help us. With our bare hands, we tried to open the door; we even tried to go down through the freight elevator which transported the shells. The bombs ceaselessly fell on the fort. The roar of the sirens which the Stukas made while they dropped their bombs on the fort made us crazy. Finally, after a time that seemed like hours to us, a comrade heard us and, with a lever, managed to open the door. I assure you that, when you feel stuck like that, your thoughts turn to your Mom (I even think we shouted after her). After all these emotions, we rested for a while. This day of May 17 (which I will never forget) ended at around 2200 with the sounds of automatic weapons fire. At the fort, a few friends shot at any looming enemy. Of course, he responded with his weapons.[4]

Throughout the day Barchon continued to fire on nearby targets including German troops at Withuis and Riemst, at a battery firing on Pontisse from Sabare and Charatte-Hauteurs, and at German troops in close proximity to the fort. Otherwise the Germans were biding their time until the next day.

At 0100hrs German aircraft flew over Fort Aubin-Neufchâteau. Blocs 1 and 2, Casemate 1 and 3, and the Mortar Bloc fired randomly around the fort to secure the perimeter. The mortars and 75mm guns continued to actively strike targets in the area: muzzle flashes near Mauhin; German trucks near Trois Cheminées; a German motorcycle convoy on the Visé–Julémont road; and an artillery battery near Julémont. German sappers were spotted attempting to repair the Warsage Bridge and were hit by twenty-five rounds from the 75. The guns had fired more than 10,000 shells since the German invasion. Captain d'Ardenne learned of the precarious situation of

Forts Pontisse and Barchon, and that it appeared they would not be able to hold out much longer. German small-calibre shells continued to fall on Aubin-Neufchâteau.

Most of Fort Evegnée's crew was sheltered deep under the fort, but they were well aware of the heavy attacks on their neighbours and there was no doubt they would soon suffer the same fate. In the afternoon, German artillery and infantry were beginning to pay more attention to the fort. Heavier bombs were dropped and the crews of the guns and observation posts were forced to move deeper inside the fort. Small cracks appeared everywhere in the concrete. The fort shook. Before the men could take up their positions in the turrets the Germans, now surrounding the fort from all sides, attempted a probing attack but it was repelled. All of the turrets were targeted. They needed to be retracted or turned to protect the barrels, rendering them useless. During the shelling the telephone lines were damaged, cutting Evegnée off completely from the outside.

Sous-Lieutenants Dinant and Dubois were both seriously injured by the same enemy fire while manning the Mi/LG turret. Dinant recalled the event as follows:

> From my observation post [in the air tower], around 0900, I could see the approximate location of a heavy machine gun on the glacis of Salient II – III, near the anti-tank rails. I decided to go [over] to the Mi/LG turret to fire back with the right machine gun. Second Lieutenant Dubois, the firing officer of the 105, accompanied me. He told me that Flémalle and Boncelles no longer responded, and that the five men in the turret of Salient I were injured by machine-gun fire. I sat on the right machine gun. In the telescope, I focused in on the glacis and saw the German machine gun, concealed within the anti-tank rails. One of the gunners held the band of 250 cartridges and I was ready to open fire. Too late! The enemy gun, coming into action, fired a volley directly into the turret's aiming port. I fell backwards, my left eye punctured and a bullet in the right shoulder. I warned the *Bureau de Tir*. The commander ordered the 75mm turret to open fire with *boîtes-à-balles*. I headed to the clinic and laid down on the operating table. I was declared out of action and transported to the infirmary. Sous-Lieutenant Dubois was also hit with shrapnel and suffered an eye injury.[5]

On the same day, the two 105mm turrets ceased firing, their ammunition exhausted. Commandant Vanderhaegen ordered the preparation for destruction of the guns inside these two turrets. Lieutenant Decarpentrie misinterpreted the order and blew up one of the two turrets. Although having taken refuge at the base of the turret shaft to light the explosive fuse, he was violently shaken by the explosion. His helmet was torn off and he was thrown to the ground, his face and hands blackened but he escaped without any serious injury. Vanderhaegen intervened so that the second turret was not destroyed immediately. He thought there would be time to take care of that later. Corporal Denis, who for several years had zealously maintained the 105 turrets, with tears in his eyes helped the lieutenant to destroy the guns. In the evening enemy infantry made a new attack on the fort. The 75s fired in series with *boîtes-à-balles* and the Germans pulled back.

The end of Fort Fléron
Heavy bombing of Fort Fléron began at 0700hrs. At 0900hrs the bombing intensified and was joined by artillery. This time the bombs were much heavier. At 1000hrs the decontamination room and the airlock (escarp entrance) were heavily damaged. The shaft of the POC was blocked and the men inside were trapped. The embrasures of the two casemates flanking the gorge ditch were blocked by large chunks of concrete and churned-up earth. The *Bureau de Tir* was damaged for the first time and the commandant's room destroyed. One of the doctors was badly wounded and later died at the hospital. Around 1130hrs the garrison moved down to the lowest level of the tunnels for shelter.

The embrasure of the casemate defending the postern entry was also blocked by debris. Volunteers went out with picks and shovels to try to clear it but a huge chunk of concrete blocked the field of fire and it was useless to continue. A large explosion at S-I forced the crew to rush back inside. One hour later the *Bureau de Tir* was hit again. The right side of the room was crumbling and the telephones were pulled out of the wall. The plotting table was covered with concrete that had fallen from the ceiling where the corrugated steel was open in places. The left side of the room was still intact. The men in the munitions room were extremely nervous that they would be next. Maréchal des Logis Lequeu and Private Monseur of the telephone crew were killed. Private Digneffe was gravely wounded and buried under debris but he was pulled out still alive. The telephone system was completely knocked out. One of the elevators fell into the underground gallery and the wall of the gallery was cracked along a 20m section. Lighting and ventilation was cut off and the control panel to the ventilator destroyed.

At this point the account of the final hours differs between that of Lieutenant Henry and Captain Glinne and several other men and is quite confusing. The fort was being systematically destroyed. In normal circumstances a Council of Defence would have been assembled to vote on what to do – keep fighting or surrender. Henry seems to have, in essence, assumed command in the absence of Captain Glinne, who had disappeared. His account follows.

Henry, who had just left the *Bureau de Tir* after its destruction, bumped into Lieutenant Delheid in the hallway of S-III. He told Henry that the men below did not want to come back up to their posts. Henry climbed down into the munitions tunnel and asked for six volunteers but there was no reaction. Six men were ordered to follow him back up to attempt to clean up some of the mess. As soon as they started to work there was a large explosion from the direction of the centre of the fort. Cries were heard and the electrical control panel blocked the passage. Delheid went off to locate Captain Glinne. Henry went down to the quadrilateral and located the 75mm turret crews who had been sent to check on the status of their turrets. Arriving at the 105mm turret, Henry found two gunners who told him the guns were functional. The turret moved well except for some minor damage. The 75mm turrets were still intact.

Despite this news, it was discovered that several of the men were gravely wounded. Only three officers were left in the upper level along with the six volunteers. There was no electrician or doctor. Due to the condition of the fort, it was prepared for destruction and some key pieces of the guns were tossed into the well. A fire was set in the motor room and the remaining men left via the air tower tunnel. The commandant was still nowhere to be found. After the Henry group left the fort they found Private Brouillard in one of the houses at Fléron and he told Henry that as they were exiting the fort from the air tower, the captain let the men go who wanted to leave and he left with the rest in the direction of Moulin-sous-Fléron. Meanwhile the Stukas continued to bomb the fort. It was around 1700hrs.

Opinions differ on what happened during the last few hours. The stories concerning the evacuation of the fort do not agree. Henry seemed to imply that the turrets were still working. He was not correct as we will see below. He stated there was no Council of Defence, but was that true or did it take place down below without him in attendance? Regardless of the exact account, there was definitely a lapse of communication between the officers during the chaotic last hours. After the war and after testimony from others, the '*Service Historique*', while not making conclusions about the evacuation, prepared an assessment of the damages to the fort.

In summary:

a) Artillery material:

- Two 150mm cupolas out of service (off-centre); two cupolas with two 105mm guns intact, but ammunition exhausted;
- 75mm turret S-I out of service by bursting in the barrel on 11/5;
- 75mm turret S-II left intact;
- 75mm turret S-II right intact;
- 75mm turret S-III repaired at 1400hrs; hit a second time and almost repaired at the moment of the departure of the garrison;
- Freight elevator crashed into the bottom of its well at the level of the bombardment gallery.

b) Fortifications:

- Airlock entry: large cracks at the chicane and in the airlock;
- Disinfection room: raised floor, deformed ceiling, large cracks in the wall, ruined doors, front door lying in the airlock;
- *Bureau de Tir* completely ruined, floor raised, ceiling smashed and sagging, concrete ceiling fallen, entry into gallery in danger of collapse;
- POC shaft obstructed by concrete debris;
- *Salle de Détente* in Salient I, part of the concrete vault collapsed into the room;
- Capital gallery wall right footing leaning towards the gallery (location of the distribution board of the electrical panel), ground raised, broken slabs;
- Escarp gallery to Salient III wall right footing off and inclined in the gallery 7m long, raised floor, broken slabs;
- Quadrilateral with munitions gallery: cracks in the main tunnel and in the first two lateral tunnels;
- Escarp gallery to Salient I fissured;
- Escarp gallery to Salient III fissured;
- Underground bombardment gallery: horizontal cracks exceeding 20m in length;
- Air tower intact;
- Infantry sortie in ruins, cracked ceiling;
- Massive upheaval of earth, especially at the gorge front; craters from 8 to 12m deep, a lot of earth and large blocks of concrete blown on top of the massif.

(c) Flanking casemates:

- 15m of escarp wall in front of the airlock and flanking the postern cracked;
- Two gorge casemates and the casemate flanking the postern: cracked faces, large pieces of debris obstructing the embrasures and the entrance to the airlock;
- Double head casemate concrete above the emergency exit damaged;
- Gorge ditch: counterscarp strongly affected in three places:
  - 1) cracked 3m long and 2m high;
  - 2) 15m long and 3m high;
  - 3) Salient I, vault collapsed. Large amount of debris in the ditches;
- Ditch I – II: Five large cracks at the base of the counterscarp, large craters in the embankment, huge pile of dirt making shooting impossible;
- Ditch II – III: craters in the embankment, a pile of earth one of which is 3 to 4m high;
- Wartime *Corps de Garde*: piles of earth in front of the embrasures.

While one or two of the turrets may still have been able to fire, it didn't really matter because there was nothing left of the rest of the fort. Fort Fléron did not surrender. In the end its ruins were simply abandoned to the Germans.

The fall of Fort Chaudfontaine

Bombing of Fort Chaudfontaine began at 0655hrs, followed by a heavy artillery pounding that did considerable damage to the fort. The Germans were now hoping to quickly end the resistance of the rest of the PFL forts. The POC was heavily damaged by German artillery, blinding the fort. At 0900hrs the air tower was targeted by Stukas and guns for two and a half hours, opening up a large hole in the side and causing an ammunition explosion that destroyed the FMs. The tower could no longer provide any close-proximity defence. PAK 37s, which had been moved up very close to the fort, concentrated on the embrasures of Salient III's casemate, reducing it to a useless ruin. At 1010hrs a bomb put the S-III turret out of action. Large calibre shells poured in, followed by an infantry attack directed towards the superstructure. The Mi/LG turret fired in an attempt to drive them off but the Germans tossed grenades at the embrasure of the grenade launcher and into a breach in the wall of the POC.

The 105mm turret of Fort Chaudfontaine. The Basilique Notre Dame de Chèvremont is in the background. (Emil Coenen Collection)

Calls to Fléron for artillery support went unanswered. Embourg could only fire a few rounds that had no effect. All of Chaudfontaine's turrets were now out of action. The Germans seized the *Corps de Garde* casemate and now had free reign to enter the fort. This was followed by an attack by AT guns on the casemate guarding the postern. The Council of Defence took this opportunity to meet and voted to surrender the fort. An envoy was sent out to request a parley with the Germans and that was the end.

The fall of Fort Embourg

Under cover of heavy shelling, German infantry crept closer and closer to the fort. The turrets were very badly damaged so Embourg was no longer able to provide support to its neighbours. The shutting-down of both Embourg and Chaudfontaine was a heavy blow to the other forts. In addition, the turret crews had already moved underground to escape the destruction taking place above. However, prior to their being put out of action, attempts were still being made to provide support. When a fire command was received the crews rushed to their stations, loaded the guns, raised the turret and fired. Salvoes of six shells were fired then the crews moved quickly to shelter. During one of these fire missions the S-III turret was hit in such a way that the armour shattered, exposing the gun chamber to the outside. Private Kiprag was killed and that was the end of S-III. The POC shaft was smashed to pieces. At the entrance to the fort a huge block of concrete fell into the armoury of the *Corps de Garde*. The turrets of S-I and S-II were also

Postern entry to Fort Embourg. The Corps de Garde *is on the right. Large blocks of concrete have fallen towards the entry ramp.* (Digital History Archive, 'Bunkers of the Blitzkrieg')

eliminated, their caps blown off, and with that, the Germans were free to move into the fort.

Having no means of close-range defence, and since Chaudfontaine had surrendered, there was no sense in continuing the struggle. Around 2000hrs a white flag was hoisted over Embourg. All material left in working order was sabotaged, documents burned, and the crew left the fort.

Analysis of the facts- Fort Embourg:

- The four 75mm turrets were out of action and the instruments of the armoured observation post were destroyed. As a result, the Germans were free to occupy the glacis and move on top of the flanking ditch casemates. No support came from any of Embourg's neighbours, despite the sending of signals for help.
- The demolition, in two places, of the counterscarp of the gorge front and especially that of Salient IV made access to the ditch by the Germans possible, and they were able to move through a dead zone

in the angle of S-IV. The top of the massif was breached in three places, one directly above the *Bureau de Tir*.
- The casemate defending the postern was wrecked and there was no way to stop the Germans from accessing the gorge front ditch. One of the casemates defending the gorge front ditch was blocked by a landslide on the right side.
- For several hours the Germans had the postern and the air tower under fire, thus preventing any patrols from leaving.

Conclusions
At the time of surrender:

a) Artillery equipment:

- S-I 75mm turret out of service since 15 May (centre shaft broken by a Stuka bomb);
- Turrets of S-II and III caps blown off;
- Turret of S-IV advance armour hit by bombs, put out of service.

b) Structure:

- Access to the well of the POC damaged;
- Escarp wall near the 1914 infirmary sagging towards the ditch;
- Emergency exit of the infirmary hit by a bomb on the counterscarp side and collapsed;
- Counterscarp wall collapsed at Salient IV, allowing easy access into the ditch;
- Escarp wall on the right crushed.

c) Flanking ditches and ramps:

- Ditch casemates destroyed; unexploded bombs in front of the casemate at S-I and S-II;
- Wartime *Corps de Garde* view to the outside blocked and no possibility of firing on the ramp;
- FM flanking the postern hit by a shot through the embrasure, pushing the gun away.

d) No help from neighbouring forts forthcoming.
With the loss of Fléron, Chaudfontaine, Embourg, Boncelles and Flémalle, the southern flank of Liège was open. Only Barchon, Evegnée and Pontisse remained, along with three of four modern forts. The former would be tested in the next two days, and the latter after that.

No information was available on the events at Fort Tancrémont on 17 May. The Germans were, for the most part, leaving the fort alone. It was far enough south to not impede the movement of the army to the west. The same could be said for Fort Battice, which lost telephone contact with Fort Aubin-Neufchâteau, but other than that, it was relatively quiet.

Since 13 May, 211 ID was moving south-east then west of the PFL, destination Namur. On 13 to 14 May they marched on the line Born–Meyrode–Honefeld–Mürringen, and on 14 to 15 May Chevron–Menil–Vielsalm–Recht–La Gleize. 14 May was a scorching hot day and the men rolled up their shirtsleeves. The streets of the villages resounded with the clatter of wagons and drivers urging on the horses. The men were bathed in sweat and a cloud of swirling dust rose into the air above the roads. On 15 May the division reached My, and the next day Tohogne, north of Durbuy, about 40km from the fortress of Namur.

Namur

On 17 May, German units involved in the attack on Namur were, according to the OKH *Lagekarten* West Front maps, at the following locations:

- 267 ID – Arrayed against the southern front.
- II/253 – Crossing north of Namur above Suarlée.
- 211 ID – Now approaching from the south just past Cindey.

Fort Marchovelette was under direct attack from all sides. Captain De Lombaerdt asked for volunteers to go out on patrol in the vicinity of Gelbressée. Nine men stepped up and, equipped with a light machine gun and rifles, left the fort via the tower exit. The men used the anti-tank ditch to reach the railway station at Gelbressée. They encountered a German patrol and exchanged fire. Corporal Lemineur was fatally wounded and would later die at the fort. Upon their return and after hearing the news the Germans were close by, the turret guns were loaded with *boîtes-à-balles* in preparation for an attack. The Germans, meanwhile, were moving to the edge of the fort, the Belgian shells whizzing over their heads.

Support was requested from Maizeret, Andoy and Suarlée. Observers in the tower directed Maizeret's shots and its 105mm guns were effective in hitting the glacis. Meanwhile, Marchovelette's 75mm turret which had been repaired after the bombing of the previous day was hit again and put out of action permanently. At 1400hrs a German shell hit the left barrel, breaking the embrasure. Sparks showered down inside the turret onto the floor of the gun chamber. Bolts broke off and flew violently around the inside of the turret. Thinking the turret might explode, the crew evacuated to the central massif. Upon inspection it was learned that the barrel was permanently out of order. The next day the embrasure was sealed up with concrete. The day ended calmly.

It was a much quieter day at Fort Maizeret. The howitzer fired some rounds at a German patrol in the Samson Valley, plus support was provided to Marchovelette, as described above. During the day the fort received a visitor (identity unknown) from the PFL who provided information on German methods being used to attack the forts of Liège. This information was passed on to all of the forts of Namur.

Fort Andoy's air tower was targeted on 17 May but otherwise there was very little action.

At Fort Dave, several patrols were sent out to explore Naninne, Dave, Lustin and Mont de Godinne. All returned by nightfall, bringing valuable information. German columns were seen moving in just about every direction. The Troonois shelter fired on motorized troops that ventured into its sights. The 75mm howitzers took part in this action. This combined action resulted in significant losses of enemy personnel and equipment.

Around 1030hrs, an armoured car coming from the direction of Dave Nord stopped in front of the anti-tank rails. An officer stepped out of the car, waved a paper, and began to climb up the slope of the railway tracks. It seems the Germans were attempting to bring an early end to the resistance of Namur and Fort de Dave. The chief of the bunker guarding the anti-tank rails came out and met with the German. He agreed to pass on the text of the communiqué from the German to Commandant Noel. As expected, it was an ultimatum to surrender the fort within the hour or face a certain number of threats. The Belgians responded frankly and negatively to the ultimatum and the German left.

A short time later a convoy of cars and trucks were spotted on the Namur-Dinant road, on the left bank of the river, pulling into a Shell petrol station. Taking advantage of this 'stop for gas', the guns of Dave opened fire, causing panic among the Germans. A vehicle arrived at the petrol station with a red cross painted on it and the guns ceased fire. At that very moment, a call came in to the forts from the INR – *Institut National de Radiodifussion* – to listen to a broadcast. It was as follows:

> Calling the forts of Namur. Calling the forts of Namur. Commanders of the forts; officers, NCOs, and soldiers of the *Position Fortifiée de Namur*, resist until the end for the homeland. I am proud of you. Leopold.'

This message resulted in a significant boost to the morale of the garrison. This was the final communication from the outside.

The supply situation was bad. Until 14 May the forts were resupplied by the depots but since then, they were cut off. Also on 14 May, trucks carrying a resupply of ammunition attempted a delivery from the depot of Fort Cognolée but after a harrowing journey the driver discovered only a small amount of supplies were left that were not of much use to the fort. Fatigue began to sap the men's energy. The many patrols and the continuous work of clearing the trees were the main cause. To top it off, the cramped spaces inside the fort, the permanent nervous tension and the incessant noise of machinery and guns made sleep next to impossible.

At noon, three more observation posts had been evacuated. At 2020hrs a patrol returning to the fort reported that a bridge was being built at Godinne and artillery positions were being prepared near the d'En-Haut farm. These two objectives were harassed by Dave and Saint-Héribert all night long. Around 2200, PO Troonois spotted Germans between La Brèche 43 and the villa Bella-Vista. The artillery of the fort intervened. The Germans responded by firing red flares, an indication they were under fire. During the night, the last external observation post of the fort was abandoned.

Fort Malonne was bombed from 0400hrs to 1600hrs. The fort provided counterbattery fire but due to insufficient observation there was no way of pinpointing targets, therefore a massive amount of ammunition was wasted carpeting the suspected areas. Stocks were now running very low.

Fort Suarlée was also being hit by a German battery but a lucky shot from Malonne put this one out of action. The Germans launched a nighttime attack on the fort but it was repulsed with close-range weapons.

Strategic Situation in Belgium at the End of 17 May 1940

The occupation of Holland by the Germans was nearing completion, freeing up Eighteenth Army for use against Belgium. In Belgium, German vanguard units skirmished along the Willebroeck Canal. The Belgian 15th Infantry Division was attacked but held its position.

At Liège, the forts of Fléron, Chaudfontaine and Embourg fell.

The BEF withdrew in stages. The French First Army was thrown back on a line Tubize–Charleroi. Ninth Army was in full retreat. Touchon's Sixth Army marched towards the area of Rethel.

The Belgian Army carried on with its withdrawal. Brussels was occupied the night of 17/18 May.

Chapter 12

Saturday, 18 May 1940

Liège

Message sent by 223 ID in the evening of 5/17/40:
Artillery order for the attack on Fort Barchon on May 18, 1940:

1) IR 344 and Pi. Bn. 51 will attack and take possession of Fort Barchon.
2) Battery 820 to be placed under AR 223 on May 18, 1940 and from 0730 onwards fire disruption and destruction shots on the forts of Barchon, Pontisse, Evegnée and Battice.
3) Starting at 0530, artillery batteries to open according to the enclosed firing plan.
4) After the fire of Battery 820 on Fort Barchon is complete, all batteries assigned to Barchon to cease fire. Fort Barchon will then be requested to hand over the fort. If there is no handover, fire will be continued according to orders of the regiment and the infantry will wait for attack orders from the division. When the attack begins, the batteries will cease fire. The batteries assigned to suppress the fire of the other forts will then increase their rate of fire.[1]

Message from V Corps HQ at Schloss Trihosdin 6km west of Esneux – 18.5 0450
Morning message:
First: Fort Chaudfontaine was handed over to the JR [*Jäger Regiment*] 471 around 1900, Fort Embourg at 2030.

- Chaudfontaine captured: eight officers and 180 men
- Embourg captured: three officers and 165 men.
- Chaudfontaine guns captured: four armoured turrets each with 75mm guns; two armoured turrets for 105mm gun; one turret with a 150mm gun; one turret with a machine gun and grenades.
- Fort Embourg guns captured: four armoured turrets each with 75mm guns.

- In Fort Chaudfontaine, the commander of southern front with Forts Flémalle, Boncelles, Embourg, Chaudfontaine and Tancrémont, Major Parmentier, was captured. Interrogation revealed, in addition to the commander of the fort, the commander of the fortress artillery regiment of Lüttich (Colonel Modard) was captured at Fort Flémalle.[2]

From: *Heeresgruppe* B – 17.5.40 – 1900
To: 223 ID

223 ID with immediate effect is now under the direct orders of *Heeresgruppe* B's *Kommandatur* 126
    Task of the 223 Div. remains as before: Removal of the still fighting Lüttich fortifications.[3]

From: *Oberkommando* Sixth Army – 17.5.40
To: 223rd Infantry Division

223 ID becomes effective immediately directly subordinate to *Heeresgruppe* B. The task remains the same.
    The following are subordinate to 223 ID orders:

- Battery 820
- Pi. Bn. 42 (minus one company)
- Pi. Bn. 51 (minus one company)[4]

From: Commander 223rd Infantry Division – 18.5.40 – 0730
To: 425th Infantry Regiment

Koluft 6[5] reports that the requested Stuka attack will be flown today on the 18th against Pontisse in the form of a prolonged rolling attack from 12-13 o'clock. Infantry attack 1 pm.

Körner[6]

Belgian perspective on the capture of Fort Pontisse

Beginning at dawn, Fort Pontisse was shelled by large-calibre artillery (*Schwere Artillerie Abteilung* 820). At the same time the armoured structures and the air tower were struck by 37mm and 88mm shells. The periscope in the POC was hit and put out of action. Around 1030hrs the 105mm turret was put out of commission, the barrel having been cracked. The fort continued to reply with the remaining turret in S-IV. Barchon intervened but this ended around noon.

From 1030hrs the fort was bombed by Stukas dropping heavy bombs (250kg). The Thiry Farm observation post was bombed and communication with the fort was cut off. The bombing ended around 1130hrs. German infantry leaving Oupeye was hit by salvoes from the 75mm howitzers and by fused fire from the 105mm. The S-IV turret intervened against German troops gathered on the edge of the Bois de Pontisse. The S-I turret was hit and put out of action. Repairs on the turret were attempted. Suddenly there was a large explosion and the 105mm turret was blown out of its shaft.

German infantry approached the air tower shelter and hit the openings with flamethrowers.[7] Thirty minutes after the beginning of the attack a German on top of the shelter let down explosives tied to a rope in front of the embrasure. The German was shot. The S-IV turret attempted several short-range shots to clear the attack in front of the air tower but the gunners couldn't see it over the crest of the hill and the shots went wide.

After about an hour of Stuka attacks, a heavy bomb fell into a hole in the top of the massif and down the stairs leading below. A second bomb fell in the same location and destroyed the infantry sortie, cutting off all access to the top of the fort from the inside. The Germans placed small calibre guns on top of the glacis to fire down on the ditch casemates. Debris was now blocking the casemate embrasures so they were not able to respond. The S-IV turret swept the surroundings with case shot.

The Germans finally captured the air tower shelter. Observers in the shelter spotted a German sapper team closing in on the shelter with flamethrowers. The crew guarding the entry was warned and just as they evacuated the shelter entry and closed the armoured door the flamethrower team attacked. The flames caused ammunition, tracer rounds and grenades in the shelter gun room to explode, sending thick smoke into the ventilation tunnel. The ventilator was shut down as a precaution but the S-IV turret crew claimed they couldn't breathe and requested that ventilation be restored. Fumes spread throughout the fort, causing irritation to the eyes and throat. A request to Barchon for support went unanswered.

All efforts to repair the S-I turret were unsuccessful and orders were given to blow it up. S-IV continued to fire but was rapidly running out of ammunition. The situation in the ditch casemates had become unbearable. Due to the smoke coming through the ventilation, the crews were unable to respond to the German encroachment into the ditches. When the MGs in the casemates attempted to fire they were hit by German guns installed on the glacis which fired point-blank on the embrasures. To make matters worse, the casemates were also hit by flamethrowers.

From inside the fort the soldiers heard noises that sounded like the Germans were placing explosives to break into the massif. The men were now completely cornered with no means of defence. S-IV finally ran out of ammunition. At 1345hrs a white flag was displayed at the entrance to the fort. Pontisse's long and gallant struggle was over and it had fought to the very limits of its capabilities.

The Germans allowed the crew of Pontisse to bury two of their dead comrades and they were given full military honours. The wounded were evacuated along with the German major who led the assault troops, whose leg had been crushed by a shell. A Belgian doctor provided first aid. Major Simon, commander of RFL Group II and Captain Pire, commander of Fort Pontisse, were permitted to keep their sabres.

223rd Infantry Report of the Attack on Fort Pontisse – 18 May 1940[8]
(Translated language style left for emphasis)
After an attempt on May 17th to take Fort Pontisse by surprise, in combination with an 8.8cm anti-aircraft battery, the regiment received the message on May 18th at 0730 that a Stuka attack would take place on the fort from 1200 to 1300 and the regiment was ordered to take the fort afterwards [see message above]. 2nd and 3rd companies of Pi Bn. 42 supported the II/425 IR deployed against the fort.

Since 0730 there had been a combined type of fire, light and heavy, on the fort with some interruption, in order to eliminate resistance against a planned attack on Fort Barchon. This artillery fire and the fire of the 8.8cm battery were very good, and contributed significantly to the moral shock of the crew.

Three mixed groups were formed for the attack.

1. Northern group – Five companies with a shock troop led by Lieutenant Schuster, in cooperation with a shock troop of the 2/Pi. Bn. 42 under Oberleutnant Orschel, against the north-eastern tip of the fort. The rest of the company against the bunker in front of the north-west tip (air intake shelter), here also 14 [Pz. Jag.] Kompanie.
2. Western group – Against the western front and the courtyard (gorge front) 7th Company.
3. Southern group – 6th Company in cooperation with a shock troop of the 3rd Company of Pi. Bn. 42 under the leadership of Lieutenant Kinders. Here also a platoon from 14. [Pz. Jag.] Kompanie. Rest of the company behind it.

A squad from 8th Machine Gun Company was attached to each shock squad.

Since the time for readiness was very short, the request was made to postpone the Stuka attack by half an hour, but this did not succeed because the connection to the *Fliegergruppenkommando* failed.

1220, while the attack groups were still in readiness, the Stuka attack took place and lasted until 1245. As it turned out later, it was very effective, especially in terms of morale.

The fort could no longer be considered fully defensible at this point in time. As I convinced myself, the 10cm gun tower [105mm turret] was lifted out of its concrete bedding by the fire of the morning of the previous day and lay overturned on the concrete ceiling. The armoured turret in the north-west corner of the fort [S-II] was apparently unusable due to the bombardment of the 8.8cm Flak battery on May 17th and was largely covered with earth. To what extent the other turrets had suffered could not be determined at first.

The attack began at 1330. Troops climbed down to the inner ditch of the fort and as they headed for the top, Fort Battice opened fire with 12.5cm [either 75mm or 105mm].

The northern group was observed from different places from the viewing slits of the overturned gun tower and from the adjacent observation port of the tower of the rifle and M.G. [Mi/LG], which opened fire. 1st MG Company replied immediately and in a short time silenced this fire. Despite the repeated heavy shelling from Battice, the shock squads under Lieutenant Schuster and Oblt. Orschel approached the armoured cupolas. The pioneers attached shaped charges to two turrets, blew up the turrets and threw hand grenades inside, which were now open at the top. The overturned gun turret was also overturned again by a new explosion and thereby silenced. I succeeded in directing our guns on to the Battice Panzer Group, which stopped firing on Pontisse after the start of our bombardment.

The Western group had initially bypassed the courtyard west of the fort with light patrols and was already standing between the courtyard and the inner fort entrance when they were hit by rifle and MG fire from the gorge front casemates. Once again our MG Company fired, silencing the enemy guns and the gorge front casemate was taken by our company. The men spread out along the ditch, but did not get any further intervention.

According to the reports I received, the fight by the southern group went as follows:

Lieutenant Kinder of the 3rd Company, Pi. Bn. 42 went with ladders into the east part of the south ditch with his pioneer shock troops. Here he came across a ditch casemate, not initially recognized as such. He was able to place and detonate three explosive charges in the various embrasures and, after the detonation, attacked them with flames. Immediately afterwards a steel door opened at the bend of the southern trench and an officer with a white flag appeared. Lieutenant Kinder began handover negotiations with him, which were most assuredly influenced and accelerated in our sense, by the blowing up of the armoured turrets by the northern group.

At 1440, the northern group, without knowing about these negotiations, displayed the *Hackenkreuz* [German battle flag] flag on the heavily damaged armoured dome of the observation post. Since none of the turrets could defend themselves, the company was master of the top of the fort. A short time later, the commander of the Pi. Bn. 42 reported the handover negotiation was successfully concluded. Seven officers, three doctors, one clergyman, and 203 NCOs and men were captured.

From: Commander 223rd Infantry Division (Körner)
To: Commander 42nd Pioneer Battalion

I express my full appreciation to the battalion for the brilliant achievements in taking away Fort Pontisse.

For the removal of the Neufchâteau works, the battalion is placed under Colonel Rünge, HQ at Dalhem. Immediate contact (this evening) is necessary. Review the exploration results of Pi. Bn. 51, which has been deployed there until now and which will remain there. Attack on Aubin-Neufchâteau planned for 20.5.40.

/s/ Körner[9]

* * *

Since dawn, Fort Barchon had been shelled by guns of all calibres, up to and including 305mm. But it was the AP shells fired from the trenches left behind by the Belgian infantry that brought about decisive results in the destruction of the fort's guns. At 0630hrs a heavy shell struck the right 105mm turret, destroying it and wounding four of the crew. At 0900hrs German 88mm and 37mm guns opened fire on the embrasures of the air tower. At 0940hrs the Stukas returned in nine subsequent waves and dropped bombs throughout the morning.

The Belgian perspective on the capture of Fort Barchon
Barchon maintained its firing missions, to the maximum possible extent. At 0615hrs the 75mm of S-II fired on the Ferme Nanet. At 0730hrs the same gun destroyed a German battery on the football pitch of Housse. The 75mm of Salient I fired on the Mohring and Nanet farms after which German fire coming from there ceased. Brigadier Deprez was killed by an anti-tank

shell, the fourth death at Barchon. At 1014hrs the S-III 75 took out a mortar section in Marechal. The right S-II 75mm fired on Riemst, and the last shells fired by the 105mm before it ran out of ammo targeted and destroyed an enemy battery at the Trembleur coal mine. Shelling was soon replaced by a fierce aerial bombardment.

At 1215hrs, three German emissaries from 4/344 IR approached and demanded to speak to the major or commandant of the fort. They noticed that, beginning 30m from the entrance, there were only small obstacles (*chevaux-de-fries*, barbed wire) and an iron gate. Soldiers in the fort were alerted and went to find the commander. Lieutenant Wehner, Feldwebel Rentasch and Unteroffizier Klemm, were received by Commandant Pourbaix and Lieutenant Jungling. Pourbaix bade the men approach closer to the gate and directed them to a path through the obstacles to the main gate. The rolling bridge had been moved to reveal a 3m-wide trench filled with water. Pourbaix apologized that the men could not come any closer. With Klemm interpreting, the ensuing conversation[10] went as follows:

> 'We are the official emissaries sent by the Division General to demand a surrender of your fort. We are charged to tell you that German troops now surrounding the fort are full of admiration for your courage and tenacity over the course of seven days' siege. The fort defended to the last and left no handful of soil to their enemies voluntarily. My General affirms that the garrison of the fort will receive all of the honours of war and that the officers may keep their swords. We have assembled a vast quantity of artillery around the fort and we have the means to destroy [the fort] to the point where your resistance is impossible and useless. Your only alternative [other than to surrender] is to be bombed by shells and bombs of all calibres in a continuous manner. Our heavy artillery is set to fire and will result in the fort's destruction; your situation will become quickly untenable.'
>
> Pourbaix: 'I will not surrender the fort.'
>
> Wehner: 'Remember that your situation is desperate. I ask that you go back inside the fort and confer with your officers.'
>
> Pourbaix: 'I will not surrender the fort. We will defend until the very limit of our ability.'

The emissaries left and the Belgian officers returned to the fort. The Council of Defence was assembled, composed of Pourbaix, Jungling, Doctor Dessart and Lieutenant Mans, the youngest officer. The commandant related to the men what happened with the Germans. The conclusion was that the morale of the men of Barchon was good and the fort should not surrender.

At 1315hrs a violent bombardment resumed with shells of all calibres. At 1345hrs the 75mm of S-III was put out of action. At 1430hrs the shelling let up. The POC reported that Germans were on the glacis and in the surrounding fields and approaching the fort. The last shots – *boîtes-à-balles* – were fired from the 75mm of S-I. The Mi/LG turret also launched a barrage but the turret could only turn very slowly, taking 45 minutes to make a complete revolution. The short-range guns continued to fire and the German advance was held in check temporarily but the Germans had found a way into the fort through a gap in the wire where the counterscarp wall was damaged. At 1720hrs Pourbaix requested assistance from Pontisse and Aubin-Neufchâteau but there was no response from either fort. Moments later an AP round landed on the Mi/LG and 75mm of S-I, forcing the evacuation of both turrets. The only close proximity defences left were FMs guarding the ditches. The ditch casemates were attacked by flamethrower squads. German shells also targeted the embrasures from the glacis of S-III. By 1800hrs the Germans were on top of the central massif and German infantry raised the German flag over the fort. The Council of Defence reassembled and decided to surrender the fort, even though, technically, the fort had already been captured.

The garrison of the fort departed from the air tower exit, after nine days of siege. The men formed up in three ranks along the military road that ran adjacent to the glacis. German MGs were trained on them. The Belgians could now see the Germans occupied the entire area surrounding the fort, as well as the inside. About 1,500 Germans participated in the final attack. Colonel Von Mayer, commander of 344 IR accepted the surrender but returned Pourbaix's sword. More than 50,000 bullets and 11,000 shells were fired by the garrison of Fort Barchon. Four men died and twenty-two were wounded. The men marched into five years of captivity.

Capture of Fort Barchon from the point of view of the Germans
On 15 May 344 IR surrounded the fort while I/AR 223 kept the fort under fire. The outer defences stretched 1,000–1,500m from the fort. On the night of 16 May this outer band was penetrated. At this point the telephone network was still in working condition and allowed for a joint defence of the group of forts (Barchon, Evegnée, Fleron and Battice). The attack resumed on 18 May as planned. 51 Pi. Bn., which for a time had occupied Eben-Emael, became available for the destruction of Barchon. On the night of the attack, things were not calm. The fort fired in all directions. On the morning of 18 May the following troops were assembled and ready for the final attack on Barchon:

1/IR 344:

- Three medium and small flamethrower squads of Pi. Bn. 223.
- 3rd Company of Pi. Bn. 51 (Captain Parchow).
- I and IV Regiment of 223 AR.
- Battery 820.
- 3 sections of 13 Pz. Jg. Company of IR 344.
- 2 sections (squads/platoons) of 14 Pz. Jg. Company of IR 344.
- II/Flak Regiment 246 with two batteries of 8.8cm.
- V/Flak Regiment 29 with 1 section of 2cm Flak.

The attack began at 0830hrs with an artillery barrage. After the first shots there was a pause until 1030hrs. During this time the fort received only fire from MGs, PAK and Flak, but the fort's response was still strong and forced several of the guns to be moved to different locations. The artillery mixed in some heavy shells to good effect. At 1545hrs the Flak and infantry fire stopped on the western side of the fort after which began the assault of this side by the shock troops of 3/Pi. Bn. 51 coming from the north, north-east and east.

The southern flank was attacked by the flamethrower squads of Pi Bn. 223 and by squads from 3/Pi. Bn. 51, and the barbed wire entanglements and anti-tank obstacles of the north-east were demolished. The Belgians fired with all of their small arms, especially with case shot from the 75mm turret and the two Mi/LG of the central turret. The observatory and three 75mm turrets were demolished by German fire. The ditch was made accessible and was crossed with the work of the pioneers from Pi. Bn. 51 with smoke and demolitions. The PAK, which targeted the anti-tank obstacles, fired now from closer range on each turret that had not yet been put out of action by demolition charges.

The FMs of the air tower fired for the longest time. During the attack, the medium-calibre German artillery blinded the embrasures. The light and medium mortars put out a continuous harassing fire. At 1815hrs the flag of the Reich was raised on top of the fort. Following an attack by sappers and infantry the fort fell 10 minutes later when the white flag was shown.

The forts showed all of the weaknesses of the old forts of this type where, in a confined space of long- and short-range guns in a massif, allowed the concentration of fire. Just as at Eben-Emael, the garrison was composed solely of artillerymen and technical personnel to care for the equipment. Infantry and engineers were absent. After the retreat of the main army in the intervals, the fort was forced to defend without coverage of the intervals and without any depth of defence. Because Pontisse also fell, the two adjacent

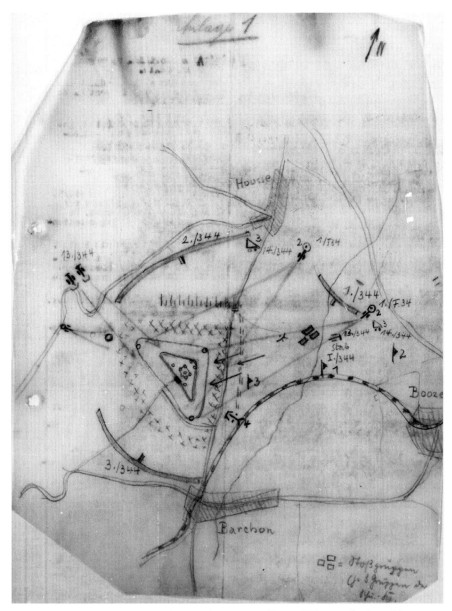

The attack by 344 IR on Fort Barchon on 18 May 1940. (Digital History Archive, Microcopy No. T-315)

forts were unable to provide mutual defence. The central massif was also defended by firing embrasures and barbed wire entanglements. The only entrance was through a narrow doorway. The fact that the troops planned for the defence of the PFL were pulled back let the Germans advance quickly which simplified the capture of the forts.[11]

344th Infantry Regiment Combat report on attack on Fort Barchon (dated 20.5.40)
Attack to include:

- I and II/344
- 3/Pi. Bn. 51 and
- I/223.

Gamma batteries (42cm *Mörser*) opened fire from 0830. Attack troops of I/344 pulled back to safe distances. Battery fired one shot and then stopped. Enemy artillery defensive fire missed but shelling was strongly felt. I and II/34 Flak had to leave their positions temporarily. Gamma fire recommenced at 1038. At 1230 battalion units returned to their previous positions. Firing ceased at 1255 to request surrender of the fort. Lieutenant Wehner with two officers from I/344 approached the entrance to the fort. The commander of the fort rejected the offer of surrender.

At 1436 shelling resumed and at 1545 infantry attack began. At 1547 the first pioneer and infantry squads moved forward. Shock troops proceeded with wire cutting and blasting and expansion of attack paths through the wire. Enemy MG and 75mm *boîtes-à-balles* was fired from the north armoured cupola and west turrets plus strong MG fire from the Mi/LG turret.

At 1633 pioneers used flamethrowers on the south side armoured cupolas. The ditch was overcome with use of smoke and blasting teams from 51st Pioneer under fire protection from MGs of 4 Company I/344. 14 Company and I/344 also attacked and stormed the tank obstacles and successfully entered the fort on the south side. PAK and MGs were used to suppress enemy fire, which became weaker and weaker. At 1635 troops from 51 Pi. Bn. advanced towards the turrets under cover of fire from I/344 and used explosives and grenades to disable the turrets. MG fire from the turret on the north-west side of the fort was stubborn. 14 Company I/344 responded and used a 60kg charge to put the north turret out of action. With enemy guns suppressed, I/344 now attacked from all three sides. The remaining turrets and embrasures were blown up by Pi. Bn. 51. Obstacles in the ditch were taken individually under fire. The air tower west of the fort was hit by 8.8cm Flak.

II/344 from the north-west and III/344 from the south-west arrived towards the end of the assault and moved into the fort. III/344 and IV/344, in reserve, provided additional explosive materials for Pi. Bn. 51, but were no longer needed in the attack. At 1900 there was no further action from the fort. Men began to step out of the air tower exit where they were assembled on the road on the south-west side of the fort.

Number of prisoners taken: 13 officers including medical staff and clergy, 53 NCOs, and 221 soldiers.[12]

From 0020 to 0315hrs, protective rounds were fired around the perimeter of Fort Aubin-Neufchâteau by the Mortar Bloc to secure the perimeter. Bloc P spotted a German artillery battery near Julémont and fifty rounds were fired from the 75mm. The Germans evacuated the position. At 0545hrs the Mortar Bloc fired at German troops moving on the road leading from Julémont to Mortier.

Between 16 and 18 May, Fort Aubin-Neufchâteau had been hit by about 1,000 tons of German shells and bombs. The outer wall facing east, near Casemate II, looked to be in very bad shape. The glacis and massif were covered by craters. Rubble and dirt was accumulating in the ditch. Bloc 3, the main entrance, was being pounded by direct hits coming from the direction of Val-Dieu. The incoming shells were concentrated on the exact same spot on the bloc. This had been targeted for over 24 hours, leaving a crater 1m deep on the face of the bloc.

The bombardment of the fort on 18 May had been quite heavy until dawn. The Belgians took advantage of the short period of quiet to place about 265 anti-personnel mines they had remaining in storage in front of breaches in the counterscarp walls. The postern entrance was also mined. All combat positions were ready for whatever would come. In the late hours of the morning and into the early afternoon the fort fired on several German targets: the Heuzière and St. Andre crossroads where a German column with motorcycles, tanks and trucks travelling in the direction of Julémont; road traffic moving between Julémont and Bombaye. German troops near the Coolen farm were hit by ten rounds from the 75mm.

The command post received a message from Barchon indicating the Germans requested the surrender of the fort. Another message arrived shortly after, this one partially indecipherable, indicating Barchon was on the brink and the Germans were preparing for an assault on the fort. Fifty rounds were fired in support. Pontisse also requested support and then it went silent.

Interdiction fire continued in the late afternoon against a German battery and a convoy at Trois Cheminées. Casemate 3 engaged the convoy with its 47mm gun but the gun jammed after firing twelve rounds. Bloc 1 took over with the 75mm. More Germans were spotted near La Sablière and Bloc 1 opened fire again. Several vehicles were destroyed. The German tried to escape on foot but were hit by the fort's MGs.

The fort's situation was as follows: two out of the four 75mm guns were still in operation (one gun per turret); all three 81mm mortars were in working condition. Four of five 47mm guns were operational. 8,017 rounds had been fired so far. As for the crew, six were dead, fifteen wounded and twenty-four

81mm mortar inside the Mortar Bloc of Fort Tancrémont, the same as at Fort Aubin-Neufchâteau. This is the French version of the 81mm mortar found in the Maginot Line. (Bunkerfreaks Antwerpen)

missing (mainly the crews from the external bunkers from which the fort no longer received any news).

Throughout the day the crew could hear the violent pounding of Pontisse and Barchon in the distance. Major Simon, commander of RFL's Group II and his staff, trapped inside Fort Pontisse, sent a telegram to Captain d'Ardenne asking him to maintain courage and keep up the attack. Within an hour both forts surrendered. Four forts now remained in operation at Liège; three of the modern forts – Aubin-Neufchâteau, Battice and Tancrémont – and Fort Evegnée.

The situation at Fort Evegnée remained unchanged. All the attention was on Pontisse and Barchon but the men of Evegnée knew their turn was coming. The Germans continued to target the air tower and the S-III turret with AP shells. The 150mm turret finally gave out, having exceeded its wear and tear limit. Even so, Captain Vanderhaegen ordered the replacement of the barrel, an operation that took at least 24 hours as long as there was no outside interference. This left only three partially-damaged 75mm turrets, each quickly running out of ammunition. Every time the turrets rose up to fire they were hit once again, causing additional damage.

Sadly, Fort Evegnée had to bear witness to the violence taking place at Pontisse and Barchon and to watch helplessly. Pontisse called to request support from Evegnée but its 75mm guns were out of range. Observers in the air tower reported that Pontisse was enveloped in a thick cloud of smoke. At that point the fort no longer responded. Evegnée provided as much support to Barchon as possible with its 75mm guns, but it was futile and soon Barchon too succumbed to the German onslaught.

Since the previous night there was no response from Embourg, its fate unknown. The sense of isolation of the men in Evegnée was awful. It seemed that all of the other rearmed forts had surrendered. Evegnée was still in contact with Aubin-Neufchâteau, Battice and Tancrémont, but the telephones were cut off and the only communication with the latter two was by radio. Belgian General HQ radio was also silent and all attempts to reach them failed.

In the evening, Lieutenant Decarpentrie, observing from the top of the air tower, noticed that the shells falling on the fort burst with less noise and more smoke than usual. He immediately reported this to the *Bureau de Tir*. Could it be a gas attack? The commander alerted the entire garrison as the fort disappeared little by little under an opaque white cloud. No toxic gases were detected; it was smoke shells. It seems Evegnée would soon suffer the same fate as Pontisse and Barchon.

The 75mm turrets and the flanking casemates were blinded by the smoke. The guns fired continually, especially the FMs flanking the ditches. The 75s' supply of *boîtes-à-balles* was low and they were unable to fire the maximum number of rounds lest they run out of ammunition altogether. Also, these close-range shells were much less effective against the lunar landscape the ditch had become. However, when the cloud of smoke cleared, no German troops were visible on the glacis or in the ditch, or in the fort's vicinity. Was this a new tactic? Did the fort's defences drive the Germans away? Were the Germans trying to exhaust the fort's ammunition supplies? The men kept up their vigilance throughout the night. Morale was now at its lowest point.

Things were very quiet during the day at Forts Tancrémont and Battice. MM 305 was captured, leaving MN 12 as the only external post remaining in support of Fort Battice.

Namur

At approximately 1430hrs on 18 May, 211 ID arrived at Assesse, just a few kilometres south of the Namur fortress line. The division was ordered to take over from 267 ID and to protect the flank of the army against the occupied forts and to prepare for their removal. To do so, the division was also given the use of 125 AR, commanded by Colonel Siry, whose HQ was at Rouillon. The regiment was equipped with 100mm and 150mm guns. 607th Heavy Artillery Regiment, previously subordinate to 267 ID, was made available to 211 ID. General Renner, commander of 211 ID, met with Siry, who informed him that the five forts on the southern front of Namur were still completely intact and occupied. With their fire they blocked all traffic on the roads going past Namur from the south-east, south and south-west. German troops, including SS units, were regularly fired at, especially from Fort Saint-Héribert. The forts had been approached by German envoys but they refused to surrender. In one case, the envoy was told that if he showed up again he would be shot.

There was no precise information on the forts in the north and north-east. They had possibly already fallen but this was currently unknown. The general was taken to an observation post in a water tower at Six Bras where he could get a good overview of the battlefield and from where he could develop his initial attack options. 267 ID departed Namur at 2200hrs. 211th Division's units included 2/317 IR, 14/317 IR, 211 AR, and 14/306 IR on the line Lesves–St. Gerard.

German troops had now completely surrounded Fort Marchovelette, which called for support from Maizeret, Andoy and Suarlée to drive them off. Fire control was now being managed by the air tower observers and from the glacis of the fort. Around 1400hrs the left 75mm gun of turret S-III was hit and put out of action. German shells struck the top of the turret with extreme violence. The crew was afraid that the turret cap would fly off, leaving them in the open, so they evacuated to the lower level of the fort. The second barrel of the same turret was destroyed when a shell created an opening in the top of the turret and exploded inside.

In the morning, three civilians with a white flag approached the fort to request its surrender. These were residents of Gelbresée sent by the Germans to deliver an ultimatum written in French. The commander sent Lieutenant Wilmet, along with the three civilians and an interpreter, to meet the Germans at the anti-tank ditch. Wilmet delivered the commander's scathing response that he had no intention of surrendering.

Around 1230hrs the bombardment resumed with extreme violence. Around 1500hrs, soon after Wilmet returned to the fort, there was a new attack near the air tower. The top of the air tower was heavily targeted. The turret in S-I opened fire but was hit by anti-tank guns. Private Moens was killed by an explosion inside the turret. He had been busy loading the piece when a shell hit the barrel, causing the projectile he was handling to explode. The Germans had meanwhile advanced and moved on top of the air tower shelter and were lowering explosives in front of the embrasure from above. The men in the air tower evacuated into the tunnel between the tower and the fort. Moments later a box of shells exploded, causing severe damage and smoke inside the tower. Concrete dust fouled the ventilator fans and the tower was evacuated.

The 75mm howitzer of S-II was also put out of service. The turrets that were now disabled were sealed off with concrete.

Maizeret and Andoy fired at the German batteries that were overwhelming Marchovelette. One battery was destroyed, and others neutralized, but the shelling continued. The remaining turrets of S-II and S-III were put out of action.

German infantry, remnants of 267 ID, reached the summit of the glacis preparing to launch an assault on the fort. Only the two Mi/LG turrets remained in defence but their action was too slow and did not have the same effect as case shot fired by the howitzers. German sappers used ladders

Damage to the lower tunnels of Fort Marchovelette caused by German bombs and/or shells. (Bunkerfreaks Antwerpen)

to climb down into the ditch. They approached and occupied the massif and destroyed the Mi/LG. Explosive charges were dropped down through the exhaust chimneys into the fort. The ditch casemates were neutralized by flamethrowers. The Council of Defence met and voted to surrender. A white flag was pushed out through the *Corps de Garde* and at 2030hrs the fort surrendered.

Fort Maizeret intervened with a bombardment on the upper structure of Marchovelette. In addition to the immediate surroundings of the fort itself, the 105mm turret also bombarded German troops on an airfield north of Hannut. Patrols were sent to Bonneville and one of the fort's non-commissioned officers was sent on a mission to reach Namur. A civilian appeared outside the fort, his mission unknown. The commander ordered him to be chased off. He was not interested in allowing civilians to negotiate a surrender, nor did he want this one hanging around in case he was there to disrupt the fire of the fort. The commander was clearly aware that the Germans were going to attack the fort and took this time to place anti-tank mines on the glacis.

Fort Andoy provided support to the surrounding forts, and Marchovelette in particular. Andoy was out of range of Fort Marchovelette but could strike targets in the Forêt de Boninne.

Fort Dave provided support to Saint-Héribert, which was shelled violently. Sometime during the day an armoured car approached bunker SD 1d carrying German envoys. They pulled up in front of the Cointet gates and asked to speak to the commander. Captain Noel sent one of his men with a brief statement that there would be no question of negotiating a surrender of the fort. The Germans replied with a threat to bomb the fort but this had no effect on the commander's decision. Later on, shelling of the fort began.

The morning was relatively calm around Fort Saint-Héribert. The fort fired on German troops spotted by a patrol. Around noon a powerful bombardment began with 150mm and 210mm guns, causing damage to some of the rooms in the counterscarp and the postern entry. With the help of Fort Dave, the German batteries were located on the plateau of the Chapelle de Clovis and the En-Haut farm. Counterbattery fire significantly reduced the German rate of fire but it continued intermittently throughout the day and night.

In the afternoon the POC and the observation cloche between Salients II and III spotted a group of about thirty men on the St-Gérard road, between the Café Le Relais and the Maison Falise. The fort's howitzers opened fire and the group was dispersed. Three other enemy groups were similarly dealt with.

In the evening the 75mm guns fired on the bridge near Godinne and the valley of Burnot. The howitzers fired on the Chapelle de Clovis, the En-Haut farm and route des Morts. The Germans were harassed as much as possible throughout the night. Up until now the damage suffered by the fort from the bombardments was not serious. Only the counterscarp chambers had suffered heavy damage. The concrete of the *Corps de Garde* to the corner of the postern entry was equally affected.

Around 1700hrs Fort Maizeret called to announce the fall of Fort Marchovelette.

Fort Malonne's day consisted of firing interdiction rounds on German infantry troops. No other events are recorded.

Fort Suarlée's howitzer destroyed a German aircraft landing on the plain of Belgrade. That was the highlight of the day. German shells and bombs rained down, causing much damage to the fort. The 75mm gun jammed and the 75mm howitzer was put out of service. The S-III howitzer turret was covered over with piles of debris thrown up by large shells. The infantry exit and the disinfection room were also blocked by debris.

Strategic Situation in Belgium at the End of 18 May 1940

In Holland the war was over. On the Belgian front, the German Eighteenth Army entered Antwerp and attacked the Escaut loop. The Sixth German Army skirmished with the *Chasseurs Ardennais* and the British rearguard. The forts of Pontisse and Barchon fell. At Namur the fort of Marchovelette was captured. General Gort ordered the completion of the withdrawal to the Escaut the night of the 18th/19th. The First French Army was retreating. On the Ninth Army front, Von Kleist's Panzer divisions reached the Escaut at St. Quentin and nothing could stop their momentum. The Seventh Army assembled to block a breakthrough on the Oise. Sixth Army now entered the line.

Chapter 13

Sunday, 19 May and Monday, 20 May 1940

Liège, 19 May

Fort Aubin-Neufchâteau was now the only fort remaining from RFL Group 2, which, due to the capture of Major Simon at Pontisse, had technically ceased to exist.

Action began shortly after midnight. The greatest fear was the infiltration of German troops onto the fort and precautionary measures were taken. All blocs were ordered to drop a grenade through their respective grenade chute into the ditch, and to fire over a 360° arc to secure the perimeter and over the massif. Ten rounds were fired on each side of the fort to secure the glacis. The Germans attempted to fortify a position within the ruins of the Weykmans farm. Bloc 1 fired twenty-five 75mm rounds and twenty-five 81mm bombs on the farm.

At 1130hrs a German battery firing on Fort Evegnée was hit by fifty rounds from Bloc 1. The German battery stopped firing when the twelfth round landed directly on top of their position. By the thirty-second round, the battery was completely destroyed. Bloc 3 fired fifty rounds on German infantry trying to set up a position near bunker NV 25. Twenty-five rounds were fired on German activity at a farm along the Chemin des Waides. Another twenty-five were fired on the woods they fled to. German infantry on the Julémont–Mortier road was engaged with both gun turrets, one firing HE shells, the other firing shrapnel. In mid-afternoon Fort Battice reported its 75mm guns were showing serious signs of wear, significantly reducing their rate of fire. The commandant of Fort Evegnée called to say goodbye; they could no longer carry on the fight.

As night fell Bloc O spotted a tank and a truck in front of the Café Bellevue near Julémont. The 75mm turret fired twenty-five rounds in that direction. As soon as the first rounds landed, the vehicles escaped but German infantry suddenly appeared and ran in all directions. Twenty-five more rounds were fired and the vehicles were scattered even further. German traffic was also hit on the Houssière crossroads. The last action of the day took place at 2135hrs. All machine guns and mortars were ordered to fire over the glacis to secure the perimeter.

The fall of Fort Evegnée

The pounding of Fort Evegnée continued throughout the night of 18/19 May and into Sunday morning. Since the German batteries no longer had any other targets, the density of the shots increased. Evegnée's large turrets remained silent. The 75mm turrets still had a few explosive shells and could fire in close proximity to the fort to keep the Germans away, but there were no enemy troops approaching the fort at this point. They were waiting for the guns to finish the job.

Around 1230hrs the bombardment stopped. A group of Germans approached the fort with a large white flag. They moved down the access ramp and asked to speak to the commander. Captain Vanderhaegen, accompanied by Lieutenant Decarpentrie, left the postern to speak with a German officer accompanied by an interpreter. Vanderhaegen understood German and had no need for the interpreter. The German officer stated:

> Fort Evegnée is the only one of the rearmed forts that still resists. The Germans surrounded the fort to prepare the final assault, using all of the same means under which the other forts succumbed. They have felt the degree of destruction handed out. If the fort does not surrender it will be bombarded by artillery and Stukas, then the fort will be attacked by flamethrowers, among other things. In order to avoid a massacre that is useless, the commander was asked to surrender his work which will be received with the honours of war.[1]

Commandant Vanderhaegen dismissed the parliamentarian by inviting him to come back in an hour to receive his answer. Returning to the fort, he assembled the Council of Defence that consisted of: Lieutenant Decarpentrie, 2nd Lieutenant Dubois and Doctor Demelenne. He asked the commander of RFN Group 3, Major Herbillon, to attend the meeting. The major refused at first, but then, at the insistence of Vanderhaegen, accepted. Vanderhaegen briefed the council on the parliamentarian's message. He then summarized the situation of the fort: food, equipment, ammunition, remaining possibilities of defence against the artillery, against the planes, and against assault.

Major Herbillon stated that his mission ended as a result of the fall of the other rearmed forts and the decommissioning of the large turrets. The fact of his presence in the fort must, therefore, in no way influence the decision to be made by the fort commander. The group commander stated that the coordinated defensive phase of the forts was over. Since Evegnée no longer had any artillery capable of denying the enemy access to Liège, its role had become that of an isolated infantry support point in the rear of the enemy. Its only task was to hold up enemy forces. Further resistance could prolong this for perhaps one hour, perhaps two. In view of this fact, the fort commander would have to weigh the fact that the fort includes the personnel of the disabled turrets and that these personnel could not be evacuated or sheltered against the effects of the bombs. Finally, the commander must weigh the fact that, once the assault is triggered, he will probably no longer have any way of stopping the course of events.

Dr Demelenne stated that his infirmary was filled with seriously wounded men who have been there for several days. To save their lives, they need improved care as soon as possible that could not be provided by the fort. The garrison was physically and morally exhausted. It would be an act of humanity to end the fight.

After listening to the advice of the council members, Vanderhaegen dismissed them and thought for a long time. He knew that the moment was serious and that his honour as a soldier was at stake. He felt the responsibility for the nearly 200 human lives entrusted to him and who depended on his decision. The fort was defenceless against aircraft and artillery. Against infantry, the 75mm turrets would exhaust their last shells within a few minutes. The flanking of the ditches was no longer ensured; the embrasures of the FMs could be attacked by flamethrower with no reaction possible. He therefore decided to surrender the fort. He made the following conditions:

- The wounded shall be evacuated forthwith to a hospital.
- The garrison to be treated with respect.
- The surrender will take place only at 1600hrs.

At 1400hrs, the Germans returned and the conditions were accepted. The German commander, to pay tribute to the valour of the defence, allowed the officers to keep their swords. Captain Vanderhaegen assembled his men and thanked them for their courageous service. Major Herbillon congratulated the fort commander for his good defence and declared that he approved of his decision. Prior to 1600hrs, all the turrets and all the weapons were destroyed, the water, electricity and heating installations were put out of service, and the documents, maps and fire plots were destroyed. The officers led the garrison out, carrying their sabres, followed by the wounded on stretchers, then the troops in rank. The defenders of Fort Evegnée marched to Germany and into captivity.

Further south the Germans attacked bunkers BV 6 and BV 7 in Spixhe. Fort Tancrémont intervened but the bunkers were heavily damaged. The fort fired at targets in La Reid and Haut-Regard. German envoys approached the fort and asked to see the commander. He was accompanied by Commandants Clobert and Jaco of Embourg and Chaudfontaine. Captain Devos had no interest in negotiating and the delegation was sent away. Around 1900hrs the bombardment of the fort resumed.

It was a very quiet day at Fort Battice.

Namur, 19 May

It fell to 211 ID's 12,000 men to encircle Namur and to guard the flanks of the Fourth Army as it moved west towards Flanders. The emphasis was on the five forts south of the Sambre and Meuse valleys. The 211th was commanded by Major General Kurt Renner, veteran of the war of 1914–18. He ordered the regiments already across the Meuse to concentrate on the forts of Saint-Héribert and Malonne. Troops further east were to keep watch on Dave, Andoy and Maizeret. 306 IR was deployed on the line of Gesves–Sorinne–Courriere–Lustin. Renner's artillery support included AA guns to guard against an attack by Allied aircraft against the German regiments, plus the 88mm and 20mm guns to be used against the forts. Renner took note of the continuing important role of the forts to interdict the movement of German forces towards Namur and slow the reinforcement of the army in Flanders. Renner thus decided to attack the five forts south of Namur and break through the blockage of the road and rail traffic.

In the PFN Fort Maizeret fired on enemy vehicles and on the railway. Two wounded German soldiers were captured.

It was a quiet day for Fort Andoy. A skirmish took place between PO BM 24b and German motorcyclists. Andoy provided artillery support to the shelter. The Ausse Bridge was shelled and the Germans turned towards Sart-Bernard.

It was also a quiet day for Fort Dave with the exception of a friendly-fire incident near the fort. Around 1030hrs, four individuals were spotted on the railway embankment at the end of the village of Dave near the Chapelle Notre Dame de Bon Secours. Mistaken for a German patrol attempting to get through the anti-tank rails, one of Dave's shelters opened fire. It was discovered they were four women, residents of Jambes who had taken refuge in Namur for several days and were attempting to make their way home. Only one of the women survived. As a result, Captain Noel had barbed wire placed across the pathway leading to the railway underpass. Captain Noel, in agreement with Captain Degehet of Fort Andoy, also took the necessary steps to prevent a surprise attack from the rear of shelters BM 24a and BM 24b by adding additional barbed-wire entanglements around them.

The night passed without incident for Fort Saint-Héribert. Around 0900hrs the POC spotted German troops between le Relais and the Maison Falise. The 75mm guns pounded the route de St-Gerard as far as Six Bras. At 0930hrs the bombardment of the fort resumed with greater intensity and its effects were beginning to show on the concrete of the fort where bits were slowing being chipped away. The turrets were still in good condition. Various targets were struck throughout the morning: on the route du Portique; German observers on top of the water tower of the Bois-de-Villers; observers on the Focroulle farm; and the Daoust Farm where an observer was spotted at one of the farm's windows. Later in the morning the bombardment of the fort concentrated on the turrets and the POC. As the morning wore on the bombardment diminished in intensity and stopped altogether by mid-afternoon. The rest of the day was relatively quiet. The fort continued to target suspected enemy movements with its MG and artillery. In the evening news arrived that Fort Suarlée had surrendered. During the night some repairs were made to the inter-fort communications. A sentry was placed in one of the embrasures of the air tower confirm. Two MG positions were dug into Salients I and III.

Shelter BM 4 near Fort Malonne was attacked during the evening. The Germans were driven off by the fort's howitzers. At the end of the day the crews of the POs were ordered to evacuate to the fort after the destruction of their weapons.

Fort Suarlée came under heavy artillery fire from units of 267 ID. The ventilation and lighting were knocked out. Several of the gun turrets were irreparably damaged by the shelling. The 75mm howitzer turret at S-III was repaired and able to fire within a 500m radius. Around 1000hrs an officer and two German soldiers appeared on the massif. After some confusion it was realized that they were envoys requesting the surrender of the fort. This was refused. Later, at 1345hrs the same officer, this time accompanied by a large detachment, approached with a white flag. He again requested a surrender. He stated, and this was confirmed, that German sappers had penetrated on top of the fort unobserved and placed explosive charges on the top of the turrets. Whether this news was the determining factor is not known but Captain Tislair, commander of Fort Suarlée, surrendered the fort at 1515hrs.

Strategic Situation in Belgium at the End of 19 May 1940

On the 19th the Belgian Government notified Paris of the great danger of encirclement threatening the Armies of the North.

The withdrawal of the British behind the Escaut neared completion under cover of rearguards. These units broke contact on the Dendre early in the morning, thus exposing the right wing of the 1st Division of the *Chasseurs Ardennais* which continued to fight until about 1230hrs.

The Escaut loop at Antwerp was taken by surprise with the help of Stukas but the Germans were held off by a vigorous cavalry counter-attack. Elsewhere, German attempts to cross the Escaut were repulsed. At night the Cavalry Corps fell back on the Ghent-Neuzen canal. At Liège Fort Evegnée and at Namur Fort Suarlée had fallen.

On the French front, the German thrust continued without stopping. Cambrai was captured.

Liège, 20 May

Of the Liège forts, only three of the four modern forts remained in action. Fort Aubin-Neufchâteau had now fired more than 10,000 rounds since the beginning of the German invasion. Around 0600hrs the Germans launched an infantry attack on Bloc 3. This was repulsed. This was followed by an intense artillery bombardment. The Germans were going to push for a surrender as quickly as possible. More than twenty infantry attacks were launched against the fort throughout the day. Casemate 2 was blown up by the Germans, creating an opening in the central part of the fort. Blocs 2 and 3 were also attacked. In addition to explosive charges the Germans were using 88s to target the concrete. The following units were arrayed against Aubin-Neufchâteau and opened fire on 20 May:

- AR 223 – twelve 150mm howitzers (420 shots).
- Battery 779 – two 305mm mortars (24 shots).
- Battery 810 – one 355mm mortar (15 shots).
- *Eisenbahnbatterie* 695 – two 280mm guns (25 shots).
- *Eisenbahnbatterie* 696 – two 280mm guns (25 shots).
- *Eisenbahnbatterie* 717 – two 170mm guns (40 shots).
- *Eisenbahnbatterie* 718 – two 170mm guns (40 shots).
- Flak R. 246 – in association with infantry.

Here is a detailed, hour-by-hour account of the final combat of Fort Aubin-Neufchâteau on 20 May 1940:

0002hrs – Twenty-five *boîtes-à-balles* rounds fired in all directions on the massif in case German troops attempted to penetrate through the damaged eastern wall near Casemate 2. Fifty rounds of 75mm were fired on the Ellenooz road to harass potential German traffic.

0100hrs – All MGs were ordered to fire a couple of rounds across their field of fire; the Mortar Bloc was ordered to fire ten rounds on each side of the glacis to secure the fort's perimeter. All sentries were contacted to ensure they were at their stations and, more importantly, awake.

0225hrs – Ten 75mm rounds were fired over the massif. Red flares were fired over the Trois Cheminées crossroads; white flares near Canelle to illuminate the surroundings. It was suspected that German troops might be moving around the fort under cover of darkness.

0410hrs – The Mortar Bloc was ordered to fire twenty-five rounds on each of the three sides of the fort.

0510hrs – Bloc 3 was attacked. German infantry infiltrated the moat and tossed grenades and satchel charges over the rolling bridge protecting the main entrance. One of the charges tore the FM protecting the bridge from its mount. The gun was still working and the sentry manning the position opened fire again. All of the MGs of Bloc 3 fired at will. The Germans deployed smokescreens all around the bloc. The MG in the casemate overlooking the access ramp was completely destroyed by an explosion. What remained of the MG and its mount was removed and an FM used instead. Armour plating and sand bags were put in place for additional protection.

The commandant sent volunteers to Bloc 3 to make sure it hadn't fallen to the enemy. Only the one rolling bridge and a double set of armoured doors remained between the Germans and the inside of the bloc itself – the main gateway to the fort.

0557hrs – German troops carrying a large white flag approached Bloc P. They wanted to speak with the commandant. They were accompanied by a priest from the Val Dieu monastery and delivered a letter addressed to the commandant who refused to read it. He refused to surrender or even discuss surrendering the fort. Less than 30 minutes after the envoys left, the fort was heavily shelled.

0648hrs – Casemate 3 and Bloc 3 were heavily targeted for more than an hour by German artillery firing from Maison Simonon. Both turrets were authorized to engage with fifty rounds each.

0655hrs – The Mortar Bloc fired fifty rounds on two artillery pieces near bunker NV 7 and near the Mortroux–Warsage road.

0710hrs – One of the two observation cloches on Bloc P was hit by a lucky shell that entered cleanly through one of the viewing ports, killing one sentry and wounding his colleague. The cloche was evacuated. Both gun turret blocs (Bloc 1 and 2) came under heavy shelling.

0720hrs – All blocs were now under intense shelling that grew heavier by the minute. All non-essential personnel were ordered to the lower levels. Both gun turrets were retracted. Only the sentries were allowed to stay at their combat stations in the cloches and casemates. A sentry in the remaining cloche in Bloc P spotted enemy movement near Maison Delacroix and fifty mortar rounds landed on the objective.

0745hrs – The Germans started to specifically target the fort's ventilation system. First the remaining cloche of Bloc P received two direct hits and was temporarily out of order. The main air intake tube on Bloc P was damaged. This tube supplied 35,000m^3 of air per hour to the fort's main blocs, galleries and barracks and its loss would be critical. The Mortar Bloc fired fifty rounds on the perimeter of Bloc P. Bloc O, the other ventilation bloc, was also pounded by enemy artillery.

0800hrs – The observation cupola of Bloc O took a direct hit. Both sentries were badly hurt. There was also a direct hit on the air intake at Bloc O. The fort's chaplain was helping with the wounded men inside the bloc when a piece of German shrapnel hit his helmet but he was not hurt. The gun turrets were authorized to open fire in the vicinity of Notre-Dame on a suspected German battery. Another German battery located near Appelboom was engaged with fifty rounds from Bloc 2.

0820hrs – Another German position was detected near the Moudrerie crossroads. It was engaged by both the Mortar Bloc and B2's gun turret. The commandant was expecting a German assault. Fire support was requested from Battice to assist in shelling the German gun position near Appelboom. One of the three mortar tubes in the Mortar Bloc was temporarily put out of action. Bloc O was now very badly damaged, including the air shaft, and the men were evacuated. Inside the fort's combat blocs, soldiers started putting up sandbags and steel beam barricades to close up the inner fort. A German penetration of one of the blocs was now expected.

0920hrs – One of the German gun positions firing on the fort was hit. Sentries could see German trucks evacuating their wounded and dead from the position. A tractor approaching one of the guns in an attempt to tow it away was fired on.

0950hrs – One of Casemate 3's two gun cloches received a direct hit fired from the Trois Cheminées crossroads. The aiming scope on the gun was damaged.

1020hrs – One of Bloc 1's MG cloches received a direct hit. The shell came from the Coolen farm. The order was sent to the Mortar Bloc to fire fifty rounds on the farm.

1025hrs – Muzzle flashes were seen near Goffman farm. The Mortar Bloc engaged with fifty rounds.

1045hrs – Casemate 3 opened fire with its 47mm gun on a German armoured vehicle. Bloc 1 was engaged by a gun position near the Ferme DuBois. Fort Battice responded.

1100hrs – A German gun position in Hecheberg opened fire on the fort. The battery was neutralized with fifty mortar rounds. Bloc 1's turret opened fire on Ferme DuBois but its remaining gun jammed. The turret was retracted and engineers were called in to make repairs. It took the engineers 25 minutes to repair the gun and it resumed firing.

1200hrs – A German observer was spotted near a house by the Trois Cheminées crossroads. Ten 75mm rounds were fired on his position. The German shelling intensified again. The crew could feel the reinforced concrete walls vibrate. Casemate 3 was targeted by direct fire. Bloc P was under heavy shelling. The Mortar Bloc was violently targeted by shelling.

1215hrs – Bloc 3 was shelled again. Non-essential personnel were sent to the lower level, leaving only the sentries on the surface. German shelling was now so heavy that the vibrations were felt inside the command post, 35m underground. A German observer was spotted in a farm near Les Waides and hit by mortar rounds.

1335hrs – Bloc 1 was being hit by heavy siege artillery.

1410hrs – Casemate 3 was now being hit by MG fire coming from the cemetery. German shelling suddenly stopped. Everyone was ordered to rush to their battle stations, as an imminent German assault was expected. The Mortar Bloc was ordered to fire 100 rounds all around the fort's perimeter. Bloc 1's gun turret was ordered to fire on the cemetery and around Bloc P to secure it.

1415hrs – German shelling resumed but at a slower pace. MG fire targeted one of Bloc 3's MG cloches. One of the rounds hit the viewing scope. The soldier at that position was cut in the face by flying glass shards.

1438hrs – A German infantry assault was launched against Casemate 2. The bloc defended itself with its machine guns, 47mm guns and grenades. The gun turret on Bloc 2 provided cover with *boîtes-à-balles* rounds. German guns engaged the MG cloche on Bloc 2 with direct fire. Both MG cloches were evacuated but the gun turret remained in action. Casemate 3 spotted a large number of German infantry in the shell craters all around the fort. The Mortar Bloc was ordered to fire along the three sides of the fort. Explosions were felt inside the fort. The Germans were trying to breach Casemate 2 which continued to defend itself. Bloc 3 reported smoke grenades being used by the Germans.

1455hrs – German shock troops carrying scaling ladders were now attempting to rush through a breach in the outer wall near Casemate 2. The men in the casemate fought back and Bloc 1 fired *boîtes-à-balles* in support. There was now an all-out German infantry assault on the fort. All guns still in working order were in action. The Germans suffered heavy losses. (The fort repulsed twenty-four infantry assaults in total.)

1456hrs – Casemate 2 was breached. Explosive charges were detonated against the bloc's searchlight and 47mm gun embrasures. One Belgian soldier was killed on the spot, crushed by the gun. Another was wounded and died in the fort's infirmary the next day. The Germans used grenades and flamethrowers. Casemate 2 was now compromised and the survivors rushed down the stairs to the lower level. The Germans were about to enter the bloc where they could reach the main part of the fort. The Belgians placed a 280kg explosive charge at the bottom of the stairs leading to Casemate 2, and sealed the bloc's access with steel beams and sandbags. They closed the armoured doors and detonated the charge as German pioneers started to make their way down the stairs.

With the loss of Casemate 2, two out of the three laterals of the ditch were no longer protected (Casemate 2 was a double coffer, simultaneously protecting two laterals of the ditch). The Germans took advantage of the situation to rush on the top of the fort and attack the gun turrets and cupolas with flamethrowers and explosive charges. A distress call was sent to Battice and its 120mm and 75mm guns opened fire on Aubin-Neufchâteau. The Germans were caught in the open and retreated. The German assault was repulsed, but at great cost.

1523hrs – The chief of the gun turret in Bloc 1 reported that the gun assembly showed serious signs of wear and tear. Despite that, the turret was ordered to fire *boîtes-à-balles* rounds on the glacis. Bloc P now came under small-arms fire. Bloc 3 lost one of its three MG cloches. It was utterly destroyed and being unable to provide any protection for the men inside, was evacuated. Battice called to say they could see preparations for another assault on Aubin-Neufchâteau. Battice fired 120mm shrapnel and 60mm HE shells. Casemate 1 was now under attack but resisted. German smoke grenades were deployed. The Mortar Bloc opened fire along the fort's perimeter. The Bloc 1 gun turret fired *boîtes-à-balles* over the massif. All battle stations were ordered to fire at will. Casemate 1 fired its 47mm gun over the massif by ricochet fire.

1545hrs – German infantry assembling near the Sart farm was engaged by Bloc 1's gun turret. Bloc P was also under infantry assault. The Mortar Bloc fired seventy-five rounds to repulse the German attack.

1610hrs – German troops moved up on to the roof of Bloc 2, and were engaged by twenty-five rounds of case shot from Bloc 1. A fully-fledged assault was now under way. Battice was once again called for help. The German assault teams placed shaped charges on top of Bloc 2's turret. While the explosions did not penetrate all the way through the metal, they created enough damage inside the turret that it could no longer be raised. The crew suffered burns on their hands and faces but made it back down to the lower level alive. The fort now had only one gun turret with one gun remaining.

1630hrs – Bloc 3 was under attack. One soldier was wounded by shrapnel. The Germans were still trying to get by the rolling bridge and the casemate defending the bloc using explosive charges and grenades.

1648hrs – Bloc 1 reported that its gun was completely worn out and both its MG cloches obstructed by debris and rubble. Small cracks were now visible on the concrete walls of the Mortar Bloc. To make matters worse, the fort was now being bombed by Stukas. The vibrations caused by the heavy bombs were enough to cause leaks in the central heating pipes running along the galleries and corridors 35m below ground.

1705hrs – Bloc 3 was attacked once again but was still holding out. Both Bloc 3 and Bloc P received the order to resist *à outrance* – till the end.

1725hrs – The Germans moved inside Casemate 2 again. The staircase leading down to the lower level and the corridor leading to it were destroyed and the Germans were unable to use them. Another distress call was sent to Battice. Aubin-Neufchâteau's one remaining 75mm gun in Bloc 1 was so worn out that it barely worked at all, but it was still used against the Germans at Casemate 2.

2200hrs – Over the past couple of hours, German activity continued around the fort but the attackers were fired upon wherever they were detected and the attack ended. Engineers were ordered to repair whatever could be repaired. Crews inside the fort were asked to clean their quarters and combat blocs. The Mortar Bloc was now fully operational with all three mortars in working order.

2300hrs – The Mortar Bloc fired 100 rounds along the fort's perimeter. The commandant congratulated the garrison for its defence of the fort. Soldiers were handed extra rations.

Somehow Fort Aubin-Neufchâteau had survived this brutal day. The operations of 20 May was a perfect example of the ability of one of the forts of the PFL to defend itself against a close-proximity attack. But the defenders could do nothing about the damaged and destroyed weapons and armour, and the end was just a matter of time.

During the night, Fort Tancrémont suffered a three-hour heavy artillery bombardment. In the afternoon, German infantrymen gathered at the unmanned bunker BV 6 and prepared to attack bunker BV 7. The Germans succeeded in placing a hollow charge in the anti-tank gun's barrel. Corporal Hanquinet lost consciousness when the charge exploded. BV 7 asked the fort to fire on its own position. The Germans fled when artillery shells exploded around the bunker. Two enemy pioneers hid in a trench and, when the shelling died down, tried to place a second charge. The fort intervened again and the Germans pulled back.

For two days, Fort Battice's external shelter, PO 305, commanded by H. Xhonneux, had not responded to calls. A patrol was sent out to find out what was happening. The Germans fired on the patrol at the Beau Buis farm and on the Chaineux road. The men retraced their steps but were ambushed at the Beau Buis and a firefight broke out. The Belgians finally ran out of ammunition and were captured. The fort also lost PO MN 12 and could now rely only on observers inside the fort. The Germans continued to harass the fort but could not stop the Belgians from responding.

Namur, 20 May

There were no German attacks on the forts on 20 May. 211 ID was planning the details of the attacks, scheduled to start the next day, and 267 ID had moved on. German artillery fired throughout the day. The forts responded to sightings of German activity in the region.

Fort Maizeret carried out artillery missions in the region of the fort, including the destruction of a bridge and railway line and the external barracks of the fort. Shots were also fired towards Fort Andoy. Several patrols were sent out, indicating that the fort was not yet locked down by the Germans.

The ditch casemate of Fort Malonne. Note the second row of embrasures. If the bottom embrasures were covered by debris the guns were moved up to the second floor. (Digital History Archive, 'Bunkers of the Blitzkrieg')

The situation at Fort Andoy was identical to the previous day. Several German targets were hit, in particular along the Marche road. Andoy's stock of ammunition was running out. At dawn on 20 May the fort was in very bad condition. Around 1215hrs heavy shells started to fall on the fort. Unexploded shells lay throughout the ditch. The men were pinned down.

Beginning at 1000hrs Fort Saint-Héribert was shelled by heavy-calibre guns that caused serious damage to the counterscarp chambers and the *Corps de Garde*. The fort kept up shelling on route de St-Gerard, on the crossroads of Six-Bras, the water tower and the roads and crossroads of the route des Morts. At 1930hrs, calm returned.

Fort Malonne suffered very heavy shelling. A civilian visited the fort to bring information about the occupation of the village of Malonne and the Bois de la Vecquée. Guards and patrols were reinforced.

Strategic Situation in Belgium at the End of 20 May 1940

The Allied position was now astride the Neuzen–Escaut canal. The King, in the face of the fall of Cambrai, the German push towards Abbeville and the obvious weariness of the French troops in the North, informed London of the situation. At 2000hrs German armour, having moved another incredible distance, reached Abbeville, completing the encirclement of the forces in the North. Allied actions in the region of Maubeuge–Valenciennes were of no importance. A counter-attack by a French armoured division south of Laon achieved only local success.

General Gort intended to mount a counter-attack towards the south with two divisions. The French would also cooperate in this action with two divisions. Gort asked the Belgians to prolong their front in order to free one of his divisions. King Leopold agreed.

Chapter 14

Tuesday, 21 May 1940

Liège: The Fall of Fort Aubin-Neufchâteau

The bombardment of Fort Aubin-Neufchâteau began at midnight on 21 May. The main target was Bloc 3, which, if it fell, would mean the end of the fort. But that was not the only thing that Commandant d'Ardenne would have to be concerned with throughout this very long day.

As the shells poured in, the Mortar Bloc fired a hundred 81mm bombs on all sides of the fort. Twenty minutes later Casemate 3 reported hearing noises around the bloc. Twenty-five mortar rounds were fired on top. Casemate 1 and Bloc 1 were also being shelled. Engineers attempted to repair Bloc 2's gun turret, which was stuck half way. At 0105hrs the turrets of Blocs 1 and 2 were shelled. In this situation it was not possible to raise the guns to fire.

At 0500hrs the fort's ventilation shafts were targeted along with Bloc 1 and Casemate 1. German infantry carrying a small-calibre gun of some type were spotted near the false turret. The Mortar Bloc fired twenty-five rounds. The Germans then tried to run for cover into the ruins of the peacetime barracks but were pinned down by mortar rounds. Fort Battice was asked to fire on the glacis to protect the perimeter. All of Battice's guns were beginning to show significant wear and tear. A few minutes later the Germans tossed a smoke grenade in front of the Casemate 1 embrasure. The casemate responded with its MG and 47mm gun. Casemate 3, meanwhile, fired its 47mm gun on a PAK 37 near the Trois Cheminées crossroads.

Throughout the morning, German infantry continued to move in to attack the fort but it was not a concerted effort. Artillery shelling also continued. Bloc O was not occupied but its air intake shaft was still vital to the fort. German infantry was spotted near it. The Mortar Bloc lobbed twenty-five rounds and Bloc 3 fired its MG towards Bloc O. The Mortar Bloc was also shelled and observers were unable to spot the location of the German gun. At 0925hrs the MG cloche engaged German infantry near Casemate 2, location of a large breach in the outer wall. A smaller breach was visible near Casemate 1. An hour later Bloc 1 fired fifty rounds on German troops at the Trois Cheminées crossroads. A few minutes after that the first squadron of Stukas flew over and an aerial bombardment began. At the same time Bloc P was attacked by infantry. Mortars and MGs from Casemate 3 fired to repulse the attack.

At 1130hrs the engineers abandoned the gun turret in Bloc 2 as it could not be repaired. Explosives were planted at the base of the bloc and detonated, sealing it up. As the German assault mounted in intensity another distress call was sent out to Fort Battice. Battice responded but its rate of fire was much slower than before. The German assault was stopped for the time being. At Casemate 1 and Bloc 3, grenades were dropped down the chute into the ditch to prevent the Germans from approaching the blocs. At 1210hrs Bloc 3 was attacked. German bodies were seen lying in front of the entrance, victims of the blockhouse gun defending the rolling bridge and the main entrance to the fort.

At 1215hrs Bloc P was being shelled. Its two observation cloches were now useless. The bloc's only defences were the two FMs in the casemates and grenades. Suddenly a TNT charge exploded on the cover of the telescopic ventilation tube. The ventilator was still working but the tube was no longer covered and the Germans dropped more explosives inside, which detonated inside the bloc. The ventilation was shut off to avoid pulling smoke and dust into the fort. At the same time the fort was bombed and shelled again. Bloc O was heavily damaged and presented a significant risk because it was no longer being defended and could be accessed by the Germans. Charges were placed by the Belgians to seal off the bloc. Orders were also sent to prepare for the possible destruction of Bloc 1 and the Mortar Bloc if necessary. The morning ended but the afternoon would be worse.

German shelling and infantry assaults were now relentless. What guns could fire did so on top of the fort in an attempt to disperse the German attackers. At 1310hrs there was a large explosion over the mortar bloc, either a very heavy shell or more likely a Stuka bomb. Two of the three mortar embrasures, located in the ditch below the ground level, were now completely buried by debris and unable to fire. The remaining mortar's barrel was completely out of alignment causing it to misfire. The mortar bloc, which had fired 5,260 rounds, was done. Another distress call was sent to Battice. The 47mm in Casemate 1 ran out of ammo and attacks could only be met by the FMs and grenades. Bloc 1's gun turret jammed and could no longer be rotated. At 1425hrs Bloc 3 was attacked by a flamethrower squad.

The situation was now desperate. Fort Battice, also under heavy attack, no longer answered calls for help. Captain d'Ardenne sent them a farewell telegram and thanked them for their support. Bloc 3, Casemate 1 and Casemate 3 were still capable of engaging the attackers but they were running out of ammunition. Bloc 3 was still holding out but German explosions had caused the rolling bridge to move about 50cm from its slot into the postern, just enough space for soldiers to run across. Bloc 3 was again attacked with flamethrowers. One soldier was badly burned in the face when he opened the flap to drop a grenade down the chute. There was a powerful explosion near the main doors to the bloc. One of the double doors was damaged. The Germans were still unable to enter the bloc because a wall of steel beams and sandbags had been dropped behind the door. Grenades were brought up to Bloc 3 from other blocs.

The commander convened the Council of Defence. D'Ardenne wanted to fight to the end. He proposed that Bloc 3 be blown up and sealed off and that steel beams and sandbags should be prepared inside the fort if it became necessary to fight inside the tunnels. The rest of the council did not agree with him. One of the men stated that they were now 200km behind enemy lines and there was no chance at all of relief and no point in wasting more Belgian lives. They agreed to continue the fight until the defence of Bloc 3 was no longer possible.

At 1500hrs German Stukas were back in action. Casemate 1 and Bloc 3 were still holding out. At 1552hrs there was another explosion at the main door of Bloc 3. In the command centre all radio and telephone equipment was destroyed by the operators. The men were ordered to prepare to leave the fort and to gather one change of clothes. They were issued chocolate, food and cigarettes. The garrison was assembled in the underground barracks. Captain d'Ardenne congratulated the men for their tenacity and bravery. He asked them to trust him to defend their interests. The men gave him a standing ovation. Soon after, two of the four diesel engines were sabotaged. All handguns were thrown inside the diesel fuel tanks. All rifles were disabled. The fort's paperwork was set on fire. All alcohol was dumped. Finally the diesel fuel was flushed into the sewage system. At 1645hrs the grenade supply in Bloc 2 ran out. The fort could not fight any longer. Commandant d'Ardenne proceeded to one of the MG cloches, opened up the periscope cap and hoisted a white flag. The Germans ceased fire.

A few moments later a German officer opened up the main door and helped d'Ardenne over the steel beam barricade. He was informed that Colonel Runge was on his way to negotiate the handover of the fort. At 1700hrs Runge arrived and shook the commandant's hand. D'Ardenne reported to Runge[1] that 'the fort's means of defence were all expended. Before carrying on a fight that can only be a desperate one now, and because you have twice spoken to me about humanity for my garrison, I offer the surrender of the fort if all three of my requests are accepted.' Those conditions were:

Commandant d'Ardenne departs Fort Aubin-Neufchâteau after the surrender. Colonel Runge (with Pour la Mérite *medal) stands on the right.* (Copyright Amicale du Fort d'Aubin-Neufchâteau)

- A decent burial for the dead Belgian soldiers currently in the fort's morgue.
- That all wounded be tended to.
- Twenty-four hours of rest outside for the garrison that has just fought hard, for eleven days underground.

Colonel Runge answered: 'Commandant D'Ardenne, you have been a loyal and chivalrous adversary. All your conditions are accepted.'

At 1730hrs General Körner arrived with his staff. He returned Commandant d'Ardenne's sword, which he would be allowed to bear in captivity as a sign of his bravery in combat.

The garrison was authorized to come out of the fort in formation, bearing arms. The German troops were lined up along the outer wall and on both sides of the bloc's entrance to honour the garrison. The Belgian flag was only lowered when the last Belgian soldier left the building. The garrison was then disarmed and led away toward a farm in Warsage where they were allowed to rest for 24 hours. Colonel Runge honoured all three of his promises. This was the end of the war for Fort Aubin-Neufchâteau and its garrison. It truly fought until the very end of its capability – to the last grenade.

At 0210hrs Fort Tancrémont placed a call to the Mont casemate but received no response. An observer at Tancrémont raised up a periscope to see if Mont would be launching a signal flare. A few moments later a multi-

Commandant d'Ardenne and Colonel Runge discuss arrangements for the Belgian fortress troops.
(Copyright Amicale du Fort d'Aubin-Neufchâteau)

coloured flare flew into the sky to indicate the position was being attacked. The shelter was to be given fire priority and the turrets opened fire along with mortars. One hour later a flare signifying 'Cease Fire' had not yet been fired. The casemate had been forced to surrender. The guns moved on to other targets.

For the past three days Tancrémont was following the action against Aubin-Neufchâteau on the TSF. The command staff knew that the end was near and finally they received a moving farewell message from Commandant d'Ardenne: *'Bonne chance …'* On the same TSF channel they followed the bombardment of Fort Battice. One of Battice's blocs was very badly damaged and they were experiencing ventilation problems. Thirty of the crew had been killed in Bloc 1.

Fort Battice was shelled by heavy artillery and bombed by Stukas. The fort was rocked by a bomb or a shell every ten to twelve seconds. To the men inside it felt like a continuous earthquake. The damage inflicted on Battice after several hours of bombing by what was estimated to be seventy Stukas, was enormous. This also had the effect of shutting down Battice's ability to support Aubin-Neufchâteau. At 1645hrs a heavy bomb hit the entrance to the fort at Bloc 1 and set off a supply of ammunition. A major explosion followed, causing thirty deaths and four injured. At 2100hrs German envoys arrived at the fort to demand surrender. Guéry refused to surrender but requested a ceasefire to move the victims out of the rubble. They were given nine hours. Two forts remained at Liège.

Namur: The Fall of Forts Saint-Héribert and Malonne

211 ID's plans for Namur called for attacks on Forts Malonne and Saint-Héribert to begin at 0454hrs on the morning of 21 May. The forts were still a nuisance to the Germans. Fort Maizeret guarded the road leading from Liège to Namur down the Meuse Valley, Fort Andoy the road leading to Namur from the south-east, and Forts Malonne and Saint-Héribert impeded all traffic to and from the south-west of Namur and down the Sambre valley. The German Army used this route to send supplies to troops fighting in Flanders. Travel on these roads took extra precious time and even the back roads and bridges were exposed to the guns of the forts.

211 ID was equipped with three 88mm and two 20mm batteries. Reconnaissance units from 317 and 365 IR reported that the undulating and partly covered terrain provided a good opportunity to approach very closely to Saint-Héribert. Malonne also had several concealed approaches. General Renner decided to attack and capture Fort Saint-Héribert first and to launch the attack on 21 May. Malonne would be taken the following day. The attack on Saint-Héribert was to be carried out by 33/211 AR in cooperation with 365 IR, 1/211 AR with 317 IR, and 2/19 Flak Regiment in coordination with 317 IR.

The operation against Fort Saint-Héribert would begin with a 15-minute barrage from 1/19 Flak Regiment along with 14/317 IR. The Flak would target the armoured turrets and cloches to paralyze defensive fire and to allow the infantry to move to its jump-off position. This was to be followed by ten minutes of smoke shells and fire from 1/211 AR. Under cover of smoke the wire obstacles would be cut and the troops would work their way towards the fort. The artillery would then be pulled back and used against the adjacent forts to pin down flanking fire. 3/211 AR was also to be used to suppress fire from Fort Malonne. Smoke shells would blind the observers and gunners, also giving 365 IR the opportunity to work towards the fort and prevent observers from seeing what was going on at Saint-Héribert. The Saint-Héribert attacking force (called the Kohnert Group after its leader Hauptmann Kohnert) included 2/317 IR, with two flamethrower and demolition teams, and 211 Pi. Bn. 3/317 IR, in reserve in the Mont du Garde area, remained available for use. 1/211 AR was positioned 1,500m south-east of Six Bras.

Over the course of the night of 20/21 May the Kohnert Battle Group worked its way towards the forested area south and south-west of Fort Saint-Héribert. By daybreak the Germans were hiding in the forest and folds of the terrain approximately 300m from the fort. 5th Company of 2/317 IR was on the south-east front of the fort, 6th Company on the south. 7th Company was in position on the western side. The Flak regiments were 800m south of the fort, concelaed behind a hedge to take direct shots at the fort.

Dawn came after a starry, dry and cold night. The attack was to start at 0515hrs but when the morning came a heavy fog formed in the depressions of the ground and around the fort, so artillery fire was delayed until 0530hrs. The AA guns opened fire on schedule. The retracted turrets of the fort stood out in the last of the waning fog. The PAKs shots were excellent. 20mm tracer rounds could be followed to impact. But the fire only had a suppressing effect. It was only when the turrets and cloches responded to the German fire that the hits were more successful. The Flak guns' high-velocity shells ricocheted off the armour and flew up into the sky. The fort was soon covered with smoke and dust. 1/211 AR now also opened fire on the fort. Flak fire ceased at 0545hrs.

After a few minutes of silence the ground fog had not yet completely burned off and had thickened in some places so the view of the fort was not good. A breeze was also not favourable to further artillery fire. 211 Pi. Bn. formed two assault teams for the attack. Each consisted of one NCO and fourteen men equipped with one MG, flamethrower, smoke grenades, explosives, mine detectors and ladders. As the fog continued to dissipate the two teams worked their way forward. They went to work on the obstacles, one moving from the east and the other the west. Their task was to move into the ditch using ladders and blow the entrance to the fort after the ditch casemate guns had been neutralized.

The blasting of the wire obstacle proceeded without any problems. The pioneer team coming from the east was hit by heavy MG fire and had to remain prone. The team advancing from the west reached the entrance ramp to the fort. Heavy MG fire poured out of the *Corps de Garde*. The Germans hit the embrasure with MG fire and a blast from the flamethrower but were unable to move ahead. The team leader and one other man moved towards the gate and while attempting to climb it were hit and wounded.

Forts Malonne and Dave provided supporting fire on Saint-Héribert which also fired at its attackers from every possible embrasure. The Flak fire had not been as effective as hoped. To prevent the neighbouring forts from firing, Forts Dave and Malonne were blanketed by shells from 3/211 AR. But as soon as the German guns stopped firing the turrets of both forts popped up and fired on Saint-Héribert. As a consequence, 365 IR was ordered to advance on Fort Malonne and to fire on the gun ports to prevent them from firing.

Reconnaissance carried out by 2/365 IR troops on the evening of 20 May from east of the village of Malonne revealed that the external defences of the fort were either very light or non-existent and that the forested area to the east provided favourable cover for an advance. Despite the plans to delay the attack on Malonne, the order was given to launch an attack from the cover of the forest with about 100 men from 3/365 IR. 3/211 AR opened fire on Malonne and as soon as the shelling ceased the attackers moved forward and reached the ditch. However, the fire support from 3/211 AR switched back in support of the troops at Saint-Héribert and the Germans advancing on Malonne were forced to dig in. After a short time the squad used grenade launchers from the cover of the woods. German artillery was ordered by the division command to reopen fire on Fort Malonne, so that the German troops there would not get pinned down. The commander of 365 IR was not getting any news at all from Fort Malonne's assault teams. The only thing that could be concluded in light of the shooting that was going on near the fort was that the assault troops were still there. Finally at 0630hrs he was informed that his men were close to the entrance. The division needed to be informed as soon as the attack was carried out to prevent the men from being hit by their own artillery fire.

Meanwhile, the situation at Saint-Héribert was very unclear. Hauptmann Kohnert did not receive any news until 0725hrs when it was reported that shock troops were believed to be inside of the fort. Fort Dave also continued to fire at Fort Saint-Héribert and the Germans continued to respond but it did not have any lasting effects on Dave's ability to provide support. Fort Saint-Héribert also fired its own close-proximity weapons. The artillery fire on Fort Malonne was discontinued so as not to endanger the German troops who were somewhere near or inside the fort. Two of the 88s were redirected to fire on Fort Saint-Héribert and Dave.

At 0800hrs a report was received from the adjutant at 317 IR that German troops were in Fort Saint-Héribert and were trying to penetrate but a turret was still firing. 7th Company was in the western part of the fort, 5th Company east, and 6th Company south. The regiment sent a staff member to 2nd Battalion. Kohnert had been wounded so Hauptmann Muller had taken over and reported that the two combat groups had reached the outer slope of the wall. No one had reached the inside. The leader of the squad that attacked the gate was wounded and the squad pulled back. 5th Company also came under heavy MG fire and had to pull back. At 0820hrs another attack on the fort was ordered by the battalion. This time 6th Company would be moved out of the south front and over Ri de Flandre to reach the forest north of the entrance and to attack there. 7th Company was ordered to send its troops forward again while 5th Company was to mount a diversionary attack on the fort from the south.

Meanwhile, from 0830hrs to 0920hrs the regiment reported heavy fire from Fort Saint-Héribert as well as from Forts Malonne and Dave. The crew of the Flak batteries continued to fire at the turrets to suppress their fire. Ammunition supply from the battalion was kept up and every time the Flak guns fired the forts fell silent. Finally one of the turrets was pierced and three others badly damaged. But as soon as German fire let up the fort's guns and MGs opened fire just as heavily as before. 19th Flak Regiment reported to Hauptmann Muller that the arrival of five more Flak batteries was expected at 1600hrs. These would be used to destroy the armoured turrets and cupolas and permit the infantry to advance. At 0920hrs Muller suggested that the renewed attack be postponed until the additional batteries arrived.

However, in the meantime, at 0850hrs, Lieutenant Kanolzer and three men from one of the assault groups managed to get into Fort Malonne. They found that it had suffered terribly despite its ability to continue to provide artillery support. A mushroom-shaped concrete MG tower standing to the east side of the fort presented an extreme threat to the German troops. The fire from this position had not been silenced. In addition, Forts Saint-Héribert and Dave continued to land shells at regular intervals. At 1030hrs the regiment commander requested that Flak guns be made available as soon as possible. Two 88s were already on the way to 365 IR.

Since no new information about the situation at Saint-Héribert had been received by 0920hrs General Renner drove to the command post of 317 IR. He also heard that troops from 2nd Battalion had pulled back. No news was coming into the 317 IR command post so Renner decided to continue on towards Fort Saint-Héribert to find out what was happening. He headed for 2/317 IR HQ. Finally some updates were received at 0950hrs, although they seemed to be a continuation of the news from earlier.

- German infantry was in Fort Malonne.
- Fort Saint-Héribert was firing in support of Malonne.
- Fort Malonne was firing its guns again after some time of silence.
- Infantry in the vicinity of Fort Saint-Héribert have caused German troops to pull back.

In the meantime the AA batteries continued to fire on the armoured turrets of Fort Saint-Héribert with no let up. The guns themselves were about 800m from the fort in a completely open position but they were able to fire direct shots as soon as the turrets popped up to fire. By 1000hrs three of the armoured turrets were out of action. All 88mm ammunition that could be found was brought up to the gun positions and the 88s did not cease firing. Finally at 1100hrs, the fire coming from Saint-Héribert began to slacken. However, around noon the news from 2/317 did not appear to be good. The regiment commander asked for a new attack to be launched in the afternoon but reports indicated that the infantry was moving away from the fort and the attack was failing. It had become much quieter around the fort. Only machine-gun fire could be heard back and forth with occasional shots from the Flak guns.

It was not possible to determine if the reports received were accurate. They only presented small pieces of the puzzle; there was no overall picture of the battle situation. One report indicated the possibility that enemy infantry had advanced from somewhere between the forts and was pushing back the infantry attacking Fort Saint-Héribert. This could not be confirmed but had to be taken seriously. At 0710hrs 317 IR had received reports of an enemy battery firing from the north of Saint-Héribert. Another report at 0800hrs claimed that heavy artillery was firing towards Malonne. These reports had to be investigated but they later turned out to be wrong.

1 and 2/317 IR were ordered to dig in along the Ri de Flandre–Saint-Héribert line and to hold this line. The division would send out patrols to try to discover the truth and then prepare accordingly for another attack. An adjutant from the regiment was sent to 365 IR to determine its situation. If the attack could no longer be advanced with the means available so far, he would deliver the order to return to the starting position and dig in to defend against a possible infantry attack from the intervals. The adjutant met with the 365 IR commander at his HQ which was in front of the regiment and very close to the fort. He had been to the fort and described the situation very well. He believed that when the assets from 42nd Flak Battery were put in place in the afternoon, the fort would fall. While the adjutant was looking for a phone to call the commander the telephone operator shouted that, 'The white flag is waving on Saint-Héribert.' The AA fire on Saint-Héribert must have had a greater effect than imagined. Almost all of the guns were put out of action. The attack on Fort Malonne continued.

Commandant L'Entree, according to the German account written after the battle, stated that the German artillery fire had a strong moral and physical effect, and the shells made the air inside unbearable. Around 1100hrs the fort ceased fire and, after the destruction of the most important files and sabotage of the weapons, the white flag was shown at 1300hrs.

All reports received about the actions of the Belgians later turned out to be false. There were no enemy infantry troops attacking from the intervals. The blame for this was placed on Hauptmann Kohnert and he was accused of bad leadership of the battalion. Despite the poor communications and hesitation, the Germans had unwittingly captured the fort.

Around 1400hrs 12th Battery of 42nd Flak, with 88mm guns, was set up to assist 365 IR and opened fire with very good results against Fort Malonne's armoured components. The PAK guns of 14th Company that penetrated as far as the entry ramp of the fort turned their fire on the iron entry gate and *Corps de Garde*. The gunfire coming from the fort weakened and at 1430hrs the white flag was hoisted. Here too the shelling from 3/211 AR had a very strong moral effect on the crew. The anti-tank guns and the action to move up the PAKs helped to bring down the fort. Perhaps the surrender of Fort Saint-Héribert was also very discouraging and accelerated the surrender of Fort Malonne.

365 and 317 IR received orders to occupy the two forts and to send engineers from the Pioneer Battalion to clear mines and unexploded shells. In the evening the division commander visited the Krieger Battle Group in Chateau d'Assesse to discuss the initiation of the attack on the three remaining forts on the south-east front. Colonel Siry, the artillery commander, was tasked with eliminating the guns of the forts. The Krieger Battle Group was tasked with attacking and capturing Forts Maizeret, Andoy and Dave. The operation was set for 22 May. The necessary reconnaissance was made and the battle group moved closer to the forts on the night of 21 May. During

A 75mm turret of Fort Malonne. The cap of the turret has been blow off by a shell. (Digital History Archive)

the day the 2nd, 3rd, and 5th Batteries of 19th Flak Regiment arrived in the vicinity and were available to support ground combat against the forts. Immediately after the fall of Fort Saint-Héribert and Fort Malonne the artillery was reassigned. 2 and 3/211 AR were tasked with cooperating with 365 IR and then to advance further north to proceed against Namur, where the situation remained unclear. 1/211 AR remained with 317 IR. 4/211 AR changed position to support the attack of 306 IR against Fort Dave.

Patrols sent out on the evening of 21 May reported that it was almost impossible to approach Fort Dave from the east and north-east due to the surrounding terrain. From Fort Andoy the terrain fell on all sides, to the north and west without much cover except for small valleys and a few farms and orchards, but from the south-east the wire obstacle was deep but clear of shrubbery and undergrowth. Fort Maizeret sat at the top of a ravine rising from the east out of a deep gorge in which the road led from Goyet to the Meuse Valley and dominated the Meuse Valley to the north and the sparsely covered area of Stiden and west. A small section of forest in the west, about 200m away from the fort, in which small hollows could be found, extended towards the fort.

The fighting on 21 May showed that a fort being attacked did not fire on its attackers – at least with its artillery; it was the other forts that provided support. It was therefore assumed that the three forts on the east bank also formed such a mutually-supporting system. If one of the forts was taken out the remaining forts would begin to suffer.

Due to the difficulties presented by the terrain in the vicinity of the three forts, General Renner decided to launch the 22 May attack on Fort Andoy, reduce the fort by Flak fire and then assault Fort Maizeret while Fort Dave was pinned down. 211 Pz. Jag and 211 Pioneer Battalion reinforced by 1/306 IR would attack Fort Andoy. The shells to be used by the Flak batteries were delivered to the gun positions in the dark in order to have a sufficient supply ready to go at dawn.

21 May from the Belgian point of view

Fort Maizeret continued to fire on the roads and railways. The howitzer fired on a German column at Samson and provided counterbattery fire.

Fort Andoy provided counterbattery fire on behalf of Forts Malonne and Saint-Héribert. The Germans set up 37mm guns in the village of Andoy. These pieces were targeted by guns from PO BM 24b but without success. They were finally silenced by the guns of the fort.

The night of 20/21 May began calmly for the men of Fort Dave, but very early in the morning the fort was shaken by an extremely violent bombardment whose purpose was to cover the investment of Malonne and Saint-Héribert. The shelling had a disastrous effect on the already shaken garrison. Inside the fort the men were able to distinguish the 'music' made by the various enemy artillery – the dry fire of the anti-tank guns and the growling characteristic of the heavy-calibre pieces. The enemy batteries located on the left bank of the Meuse carefully regulated their fire on the fort. The observers were unable to locate the German batteries due to the smoke hanging over their neighbours. Malonne and Saint-Héribert continually called for support on the perimeters and especially the access ramps. It was evident that the Germans had launched an assault on the two forts.

Despite the terrible shelling, Dave, along with Andoy, was still able to provide ample protection to its neighbours. From the observation post near the intersection of Six Bras with Bois-de-Villers, General Renner watched the guns fire. When the German guns fell silent in preparation for the infantry assault, Dave and Andoy increased the firing of their own guns on the German guns and attackers. As a result, German pioneers attempting to break into the two forts were pushed back. However, the close defences started to cave in. German artillery had destroyed all of the turrets and ventilation systems – the Achilles heel of the forts. Saint-Héribert raised the white flag at 1210hrs and Malonne at 1430hrs.

At Dave, one of the heavy German guns hit the advanced armour surrounding the gun turret, forcing the evacuation of the crew and causing serious damage. The bolt heads were sheared and flung into the interior of the turret. The technicians attempted to fix the problem but could only make minor repairs. Concrete powder jammed the rotation mechanism. All around the fort debris was piled up and the surface dotted with craters. The shells dislodged the POC, rendering it unusable.

At 0426hrs (0526hrs German time) an intense bombardment of Fort Saint-Héribert began. One of the turrets fired *boîtes-à-balles* at a group of infantrymen who were spotted leaving the Bois Tonneau and advancing towards the access ramp. The Mi/LG and the machine guns of the *Corps de Garde* also opened fire on the woods and on the glacis of the gorge front. Other German squads followed. Observers in two of the observation cloches on the parapet reported the sound of MG fire around the fort. Shelling of the central massif forced the turrets to retract. A deluge of metal and fire rained down on the fort. Commandant L'Entree remarked that it sounded like hailstones pounding against a window in a heavy storm. Based on the sounds of the explosions it was easy to tell that the Germans were using a variety of calibres. The bombardment stopped at 0443hrs but picked up again with the same intensity at 0450hrs. This time smoke shells were deployed. A blanket of smoke began to envelop the fort. It was held down on the ground by a light fog. The visibility on the massif and the glacis soon worsened.

Other attack groups were soon reported coming from all directions. German infantry was running from the woods, headed towards the access ramp. The turrets fired *boîtes-à-balles* and the left Mi/LG turret and *Corps de Garde* opened fire. The Germans heading towards the ramp tried to hide in the ruins of the peacetime barracks but they were continually hit with shots from the howitzer at S-I. Howitzer S-IV fired on the gorge front with *boîtes-à-balles* and the two Mi/LG turrets fired continuously. Smoke was moving in from the direction of the Laquisse farm; apparently another assault underway. Fort Malonne was contacted and asked to fire on the fort. A group of about twenty Germans were heading towards the Saint-Héribert farm, the location of the abandoned AA guns. The turrets opened fire and only a small number of the attackers escaped. Another bank of smoke drifted closer to the fort and it was most likely that a new assault group was following behind it. The howitzers pounded the Laquisse farm road. By 0800hrs, as the fog lifted, German dead were spotted and it was believed the assault had failed.

The German bombardment intensified. The POC observers saw five men with flamethrowers on the edge of the ditch. They were hit by MGs and killed or driven back. German pioneers were also heard cutting through the barbed wire. Malonne, Dave and Andoy were asked to provide artillery support. The smoke now spread into the ditch. Nothing could be seen there and the howitzers and MGs fired blindly. The smokescreen finally dispersed around 0850hrs and the bombardment ended. It seemed as if a second assault had been stopped.

However, under cover of the smoke the Germans had moved anti-tank guns to within a few hundred metres of the fort, near the entrance, where they could fire precise, direct shots. The armoured cap of the 75mm turrets of S-I and S-II were blown off and put out of action. The 75mm of S-III was also hit and the left gun received a direct hit and could not be repaired. Then the right barrel was damaged. The gun of one of the Mi/LG turrets was hit and destroyed and the other turret was knocked off its axis and unable to move. All of the periscopes were destroyed. Finally the S-III turret, the last gun firing, was completely dislodged and rendered unusable. The bombardment caused cracks to form in the ceiling inside the fort. The ventilator motors, their exhaust shafts filled with debris, began to fail and were unable to clear the air inside the fort. Finally, the ammunition had nearly run out.

Damage to the top of the ramp leading to Fort Saint-Héribert. Note the Cointet gate, anti-tank rails, and chevaux-de-frises *that protected the ramp.* (Copyright @Fortsaintheribert.be)

The Council of Defence was convened by Commandant L'Entree. It was composed of the oldest officer at the fort (Lieutenant Fisette), the youngest (Adjutant Thibaut) and the head doctor (Sous-Lieutenant Vandervael). Each man was informed of the situation and was asked to give his advice. The council decided to continue the resistance against German troops in the ditch since the casemate MGs were still operational. Just before noon, the electrician Sergeant Gosset entered the *Bureau de Tir* and announced that the motors were failing and in a short time there would no longer be any light or ventilation. The lights began to dim little by little and the emergency lighting also failed. The ventilation probably was the most serious problem. In one of the machine-gun casemates, without ventilation, the removal of carbon monoxide would be impossible and deadly. Gosset declared that there was about 15 minutes of service left. At the same time the commander was informed that the left MG turret was no longer in operation.

To continue the fight under these conditions would be to doom the men to a certain and senseless death. The commander, with complete conviction that each man had done his job to the last possible limit, made the decision to surrender the fort. The order was given for all remaining weapons to be destroyed as well as documents and communications equipment. All of the remaining food was distributed amongst the men. At 1210hrs a white flag was hoisted and the fort surrendered. The garrison waited with mixed emotions in the tunnel near Salients I and III; sad about the surrender but relieved because their lives had been spared. The men marched into the ditch and then up the access ramp to the summit. General Renner wrote a dispatch saying that Fort Saint-Héribert did not raise its hands in surrender until after a courageous defence.

In early afternoon the Germans had occupied the central massif of Fort Malonne after crossing the partially filled ditches bombed by aircraft on 14 May. All of the fort's weapons were employed against the German attack, including the air tower FMs. Forts Dave and Andoy were called upon to clear the central massif and finally the Germans were driven off. After this the 75mm gun turret fired in support of Fort Saint-Héribert.

Around 1330hrs 88mm Flak guns came into action. One by one they picked off the weapons on the massif, including the turrets of S-I and S-III and the south Mi/LG turret, and caused many casualties. The crew of S-III turret was killed – Victor Du Bois, Arthur Colet, Jean Closset, Victor Grolet and Adelin Pâquet.

The embrasures of the air tower were hit by 88mm shells, causing the exhaust fans to suck smoke and concrete dust into the fort, making breathing difficult. The Council of Defence met and decided to surrender the fort. This took place at 1415hrs.

Only five Belgian forts now remained in operation, Forts Battice and Tancrémont at Liège and Forts Maizeret, Andoy and Dave at Namur. The Allied armies' situation was even less encouraging.

Strategic Situation in Belgium at the End of 21 May 1940

The encirclement of the Northern Armies was complete. It was in those tragic circumstances that Gamelin, the Commander-in-Chief, was replaced by General Weygand, who immediately held a conference at Ypres with King Leopold, General Billotte and General Gort. General Weygand proposed a counter-attack on the line Arras-Albert in order to reconnect the front. The Belgian Army would extend its front and cover the offensive operations by an all-out defence of its positions. If obliged to withdraw it would take position first on the Lys, afterwards on the Yser.

As soon as he arrived at the meeting, General Gort explained that he did not believe he would be able to remain on the Escaut. It was decided that during the night of 22/23 May the gap would be abandoned, and that the Allies would occupy a line extended by the Lys, the Belgian Army prolonging its front to Meenen.

On the Belgian front, the Germans made contact between Neuzen and Ghent. In the Ghent bridgehead the enemy was thrown back at Quatrecht. On the Escaut, they were thrown back in the Syngem loop. Generally speaking, the positions were intact. In the British sector, Oudenarde was captured.

At Liège, Fort Aubin-Neufchâteau, and at Namur, the forts of Saint-Héribert and Malonne had fallen.

Chapter 15

Wednesday, 22 May to Wednesday, 29 May 1940: The Last Heroic Days

Forts Tancrémont and Battice held on at Liège, but not for lack of German attention. Both forts, especially Battice, suffered heavily from the German attacks and today would be its last day. In Namur, the decisive battle was yet to come.

Namur – 22 to 24 May

211th Infantry Division actions on 22 May 1940

The night of 21/22 May was dark, cloudy and cool. During the night 3/306 IR moved to within 600m of Fort Maizeret, encircling the fort from the east, south, and south-west. Third Battalion staff and the assault teams were positioned in a wooded area west of the fort. 1/306 IR was in less favourable terrain between Mozet and Wierde about 1,500m south-east of Fort Andoy. At Fort Dave 2/306 IR was about 1,200m south-west of the fort in the Forêt de Naninne.

It was not possible to move 3rd Battery of 19th Flak Regiment (88mm Flak 18 guns), attached to 2nd Battalion, close enough to fire direct shots at Fort Dave. The battery positioned itself on a high point 1,000m west of Maillen in order to make use of forward observers to direct fire on the fort. 2nd Battery of 19th Flak Regiment (also 88mm), to be used against Fort Andoy, was unable to find a position from which direct fire was possible. It was positioned about 3,000m south-south-west of the fort and would also fire indirectly. 5th Battery of 19th Flak Regiment was positioned south-west of Fort Andoy to target the observation cloches with 20mm Flak guns. 1st Battery (88mm) was south of Sart-Bernard to strike Fort Andoy with indirect shots. The 4th Battery (88mm) was located in the forest 1,500m west of Maillen in reserve.

The operation against Fort Andoy was scheduled to begin at 0500hrs. Ground fog again delayed the opening bombardment until 0550hrs. 2nd Battery of 19th Flak opened fire on the fort but the projectiles were missing their targets because of the long distance between the battery position and the fort. 3rd Battery was unable to make contact with the forward observers so it did not fire.

At 0800hrs shock troops of 1/306 IR moved out towards Fort Andoy but they were immediately pinned down by all of the turrets of Forts Maizeret and Dave. Suppressing fire from 4/211 AR and 15th Battery of 607th *Schwere Artillerie-Abteilung*[1] was not enough to hold down the other forts. 3rd Battery of 364 Reserve *Flakabteilung*, located 3.5km east of Fort Maizeret, was then brought forward and received orders to keep Maizeret from raising its turrets. All available batteries now opened fire but it was still having little effect. Each time the German shooting died down the turrets raised up and fired. 5th Battery moved to within 700m of Fort Andoy but could do little harm to the observation viewing ports. It was not possible to bring the 88s closer due to the fire from the other forts. At 1215hrs the decision was made to cease fire and to postpone the attack until the following day. All adjustments to the attack plan would have to be made during the night. Scouts were sent out to get a closer look at the forts. The revised plan called for a simultaneous attack on Forts Maizeret and Andoy. All three forts continued to fire on German movements throughout the afternoon and the Germans occasionally returned fire.

The German companies to be used against Andoy and Maizeret would function independently of each other. Only the opening of the attack would take place at the same time in order to ensure the greatest possible effectiveness. The assault would open with shots from the 88s in front of Andoy. An exact time was not set because of the fog on the previous day. The organization of the attacking troops remained largely the same. After the capture of the two forts, all operations would shift to Dave. For this reason, the German plan called for Krieger's troops to pivot their right flank in such a way to reach the bend of the Meuse at Lives. His mission was to sweep the terrain and push towards Jambes. The centre of his formation was to be placed in the Bois l'Évêque–Andoy sector in such a way as to be facing Fort Dave, which would be captured on 24 May following an artillery bombardment.

The attack on 22 May from the Belgian perspective
The Germans opened fire on Andoy at 0550hrs. The three German batteries pounded the fort but the effect of the shots was not optimal because of the distance from the target. When the assault teams attempted to approach Andoy, Maizeret and Dave laid down an impenetrable barrage around

the perimeter. The Germans went to ground, unable to move, and Andoy opened fire on the attackers and caused heavy damage to one of the German batteries firing from near the chateau d'Arville. From the Wépion heights, the heavy German divisional guns were unable to neutralize Dave.

During the morning, because of the decisive action of the three forts, the Germans realized that it was going to be impossible to carry out the plan. General Renner then decided to pull back his assault groups and to prepare for another attack the following day, 23 May. With the German infantry now out of the picture, the artillery exchange continued during the afternoon, and the guns of the forts fired on all German movements.

The German bombardment was taking its toll on Fort Dave. A shell scored a direct hit on the embrasure of one of the 150mm guns and the barrel exploded. During a brief lull in the bombardment a sortie was made to examine the condition of the fort. The news was not good. The top of the fort resembled a lunar landscape covered with pieces of concrete and deep craters. A concrete electrical pole had been shot through and lay on its side. Debris was blocking all of the viewing ports of the turrets and observation posts.

After the abortive German attack on the morning of 22 May, sporadic fighting took place throughout the afternoon and heavy guns west of the river continued to fire on Dave. Large-scale enemy infiltrations were reported by PO BM 24a. The Troonois shelter also provided observation reports throughout the day.

211th Infantry Division – 23 May 1940

The night was dark and hazy with light rain showers that continued into the morning. Overnight German infantry moved closer to the forts. Obstacles were removed in several places. 301st Pioneer Battalion was placed under the control of 2 and 3/306 IR to serve as shock troops for the attack on the forts. They carried explosives and other engineering equipment.

Artillery units included 1/19 Flak with 1st and 2nd Batteries (88mm); 3rd Battery (88mm) at Mozet; 5th Battery (20mm) and three-quarters of 4th Battery (20mm) south-west of Fort Andoy; and one-quarter of 4th Battery (20mm) in the Mozet area. Three 88mm batteries from 364 Flak Regiment were located 1,100m south-east of Fort Maizeret. The Flak batteries had been brought into position overnight along pathways soaked by rain. For the most part they were lightly camouflaged in open firing positions in order to hit the targets with direct shots.

Once again a ground mist lay over the forts so the German gun crews waited for it to clear. Fort Maizeret fired on the location of 2/364 AR despite the fog. At 0830hrs the fog lifted. The first shot of 1/19 Flak was fired at 0840hrs at Fort Andoy. 364 Flak opened fire on Maizeret. The moment the Germans guns ceased firing the turrets lifted up and opened fire on the Germans. Fort Dave in particular fired well-placed shots in front of Andoy. From 0930hrs the fire from Fort Maizeret began to weaken. One turret remained in the battery position, apparently stuck open. The turrets were suppressed by fire from 364 Flak. Andoy spotted the location of 364 Flak and several salvoes were fired on the position. One of the positions received a direct hit, causing casualties. The batteries on the west side of the Meuse kept up their volleys on Fort Dave, but without effect. After each bombardment Dave continued to land shots on 5th Battery of 19th Flak and the assault troops of 2/306 IR in front of Andoy. The fire from Andoy gradually subsided due to 1/19 Flak's counterbattery fire each time the turrets lifted up.

Around 1050hrs the turrets firing to the south and south-west were silent and only shots to the north-east continued. The MG turrets continued to fire towards the south and south-east. At 1055hrs the German AA guns stopped firing and the Krieger battle group's assault troops were ordered to move into the forts.

The assault troops of 1/306 IR advanced on Fort Andoy and were immediately hit and pinned down by artillery from Fort Dave. Heavy MG fire came from Andoy. The Mi/LG turret fired grenades to all sides in rapid succession. One of the pioneer teams found a way through the undergrowth on the south-east slope of the fort and from there was able to fire on the turret. Another assault team approached the entry to the fort. Mines and obstacles blocked the way and an MG fired from the direction of the entry. With shells still raining down from Fort Dave the team was forced to pull back.

Meanwhile 3/306 IR's assault troops had reached Fort Maizeret and penetrated to the ditch. The men dropped benzene and hand grenades into the ventilation shafts. Another team attacked the entrance, fighting through the MG fire and entered the fort. At 1425hrs Fort Maizeret showed the white flag. Under interrogation, Captain Hambenne stated that one of the first shots destroyed the main observation post of the fort, severely impairing the fort's defences.

Meanwhile, the shelling of Fort Andoy resumed. The fort managed to get off a few quick shots from the turrets. At 1430hrs assault troops from 1/306 IR again attacked Fort Andoy and once again they were repulsed by MGs and the grenade launcher. Around 1500hrs the division ordered another 100 rounds fired on the fort. Fort Dave's guns were hit by explosive shells, concrete rupture shells and smoke grenades from 607 Heavy Battalion firing from the west bank and they were unable to support Fort Andoy. One hundred shells from 1/19 Flak were fired on Fort Andoy from 1450hrs to 1530hrs and after that the fort stopped firing back. Fort Dave periodically fired some shots around Fort Andoy but each time it did its guns were struck by retaliatory fire from the west of the Meuse.

At 1630hrs German envoys appeared at Fort Andoy to request its surrender. At 1750hrs the German officer handed over the written surrender request to Captain Degehet. The commander of Fort Andoy asked for one hour to think about it but if the white flag was not displayed within that one hour period he would have chosen to continue the fight. The German envoys returned to HQ and there was a one-hour cease fire. By 1900hrs there was no white flag so the assault troops were again sent forward. They reached the fort unchallenged and at 1955hrs proceeded through the postern entry without any resistance. The fort had surrendered. Degehet stated he wasn't able to put out the flag in time. Most of the fort's turrets were disabled and could no longer be raised. The air inside the fort was unbreathable due to the penetration of smoke from the shells plus dust shaken loose by the explosions. For these reasons Degehet had chosen to surrender.

At 2000hrs General Renner sent an envoy to Fort Dave with the same request. The envoy returned around 2200hrs and stated that Captain Noel wanted to know if Dave was actually the last Namur fort that still remained. Meanwhile, artillery units no longer needed against Maizeret and Andoy were moved into new positions against the sole remaining fort – Dave.

The attack of 23 May from the Belgian point of view
Beginning at dawn, the observers at Fort Andoy spotted suspicious movement through the fog and requested Fort Dave fire around the perimeter, especially in the Bois de Jeumont. Andoy's observation post and Dave's *Abri* La Perche precisely guided the targeting. Around 0840hrs the fog lifted and the first gun shots opened fire to signal the attacks on Andoy and Maizeret. Flak fire was direct, steady and well-aimed at the turrets. Dave's counterbattery fire remained active and responded to requests from its neighbours despite continuous shelling from the heavy guns to the west. The turrets were retracted after every shot to protect the embrasures from the German guns.

Between 0930 and 1000hrs, while firing protective shots at Maizeret, Dave's long-range ammunition ran out. From that moment Fort Dave was confined to the protection of Andoy and to its own close defence. Stripped of support from its neighbours, Maizeret gave up the struggle at 1400hrs after a strong resistance.

Meanwhile a violent bombardment continued against Fort Dave. The assault troops attempted to approach Andoy and force their way in. Several times they were stopped by Andoy's approach defences and fire from Dave. During the waves of attacks against Andoy, enemy guns of all calibres continued to pound Dave: 210mm, 150mm, 88mm and several 37mm PAK pieces moving continually closer and closer. German machine guns swept the massif, searching for all of the weak points, in particular the observation ports and embrasures. The periscope of the POC was struck continuously. The Germans used an ever-increasing number of smoke shells to mask their movement and to hide the location of their guns.

However, Dave's howitzers fought back with fewer and fewer remaining shells, and swept the edges of the woods with *boîtes-à-balles*. All known artillery techniques and shell types were used. The moment a turret rose in battery it was hit full force by the 37mm PAKs and had to be retracted immediately after firing. In order to thwart the German strategy, the Belgians attempted to draw attention to one of the turrets, to raise it quickly and lower it just as quickly. While the German guns concentrated on hitting it while it was elevated, the 75s would pop up sporadically and fire in all directions, then drop down. Surprised by the game of peek-a-boo, the Germans switched over to counterbattery fire using the 88s.

Despite encouragement from Captain Noel, Captain Degehet, in a desperate situation, was finally forced to surrender Andoy at around 1730hrs. He also allowed PO BM 24a and BM 24b to decide on their own what to do. The cessation of combat at Andoy and at PO BM 24b left BM 24A isolated. In these conditions Noel ordered the twelve men inside the bunker to destroy everything and to surrender. All attempts to escape were impossible as the Germans had completely pinned down the casemate.

In the late afternoon, all German efforts were directed towards Dave. The POC was a main target as well as the 75mm turrets. The Germans attempted to surround the fort. Around 2000hrs Dave fired its final shells against the German batteries at Malvaux. As night fell, calm and silence fell over the fort. The reason soon became apparent.

At 2045hrs two German emissaries were spotted crossing the railway tracks and heading towards the fort. They stopped on the rise at the top of the access ramp. Lieutenant Fries, who understood German, was sent out along with Maréchal des Logis Jacquemain to speak to the Germans. One of the German officers passed along to Fries a written message and asked him to relay it to the commandant of the fort. The paper was taken to the command post while the sentries in the guard room next to the postern kept watch on the two men who stood waiting, not saying a word. The Council of Defence met at 2100hrs. Present was Noel of course, Lieutenant Rene Collin (second-in-command), Sous-Lieutenant Fernand Casse (the youngest officer) and Doctor Frank Fosseur. The German letter was read out. The situation was judged to be, not surprisingly, very critical, but each man hesitated to be the first to admit it. Despite this, the majority were leaning towards continuing the fight. Just when the commandant was about to send Jaquemain back to relay the message to the Germans, Maréchal des Logis Bouvier, from the guard room, said that the Germans yelled down to him that 'All of the forts of Namur have fallen and all means we have at our disposal will be put to work against you.'

Text of the letter handed to Lieutenant Fries:

To the Commandant of Fort de Dave
The forts Saint-Héribert and Malonne surrendered 21.5.40. The forts of Maizeret and Andoy 23.5.40.

Namur is occupied by German troops and you are surrounded. Most of Belgium is in our hands. To resist further is useless. You, my commandant, and your soldiers have done their duty.

I [ask] you to surrender in a half hour. Otherwise I will attack you with all of my forces and you will bear the consequences.

Signed, Renner
Commandant General of the occupation troops of Namur

Twin 75mm GP turret of Fort Saint-Héribert. (Emil Coenen Collection)

The officers were still in no hurry to give up and first wanted verification that Suarlée and Marchovelette were included in the definition of 'all of the forts …'. Lieutenant Fries, in the name of Captain Noel, wrote a letter to General Renner that stated, before giving a response, Dave wished to get written confirmation of the fall of these two forts to the north. He also asked to know the dates upon which the forts surrendered. The German officers were not authorized to respond to that question and would have to come back later with the answer. With that they left.

This brief respite gave the officers a chance to better assess the condition of the fort and its potential to continue fighting. It was important to note that the Germans had held their fire in respect of the truce. Throughout the night the members of the council discussed in detail the situation with the other officers. They quickly confirmed that the fort was no longer capable of an effective defence. The 75mm turrets, in bad shape for some time now, could no longer be raised and their armoured protective band had been chipped away by the anti-tank pieces. The long-range turret was out of ammunition. The other could only turn with great difficulty due to pieces of concrete lodged in the gears. The fort was now blind due to the blocking of the viewing ports and scopes. The casemates along the Meuse were completely isolated and this caused a grave danger to the continued protection of the ventilation inlet. Shelter BM 24a had fallen after the surrender of Andoy. There remained only one day of food supplies for the garrison. The men were exhausted from many sleepless nights, plus non-stop physical labour and nervous attention, along with alerts and continual bombardment. The atmosphere inside the fort was terrible from the smoke of the guns and the smell of diesel fuel. The ventilation showed signs of failure due to the blockage of the vent shafts from direct hits. After having done its duty without failing, this would be Dave's last day. The decision to surrender was made.

The fort's firing plans, secret documents, plans of defence and the commander's journal were prepared to be burned. The garrison sensed that the end was near. An atmosphere of worry and pessimism permeated the corridors of the fort. Everyone was aware of the damage they had inflicted on the Germans and had no idea what reception they would get when they left the fort. The men gathered their personal belongings and prepared for the surrender. The chaplain attempted to soothe the men's fears and to quell the rumours that were travelling around amongst the men.

The remaining ammunition in the fort was moved to the gorge front ditch and charges set to blow them up. Brigadier Billiard was sent to Troonois to order the destruction of the guns at that location. In the company of the chief of Troonois, he lit a very long fuse and with that Troonois blew up. The shock could be felt all the way to Fort Dave and caused the airlock doors of the air tower tunnel to blow open, spreading smoke inside the fort. Billiard and the chief of Troonois staggered into the fort covered in soot with burns and partial asphyxiation. After that it was decided not to use explosives for any further destruction.

The turret crews sabotaged the guns and machine guns. The radio antenna and the telephones were smashed with a hammer. The air became worse since the generators were put out of service, stopping the ventilator from working. One motor was left running to keep the air as fresh as possible in the infirmary and quadrilateral tunnels, where the garrison now waited.

Around 0800hrs the German officers returned to the top of the access ramp. Commandant Noel and Lieutenant Fries went out to meet them. The Germans relayed two messages. The first was a letter praising the brave resistance of the fort while at the same time making threats if combat continued. The second was a certification of the surrender of Suarlée and Marchovelette from General Renner:

To the commandant of fort de Dave – 23.5.40
I assure you that forts Suarlée and Marchovelette are in our hands. Fort de Suarlée surrendered 21.5.40[2] and Fort de Marchovelette 18.5.40.
Signed, Renner

Captain Noel then made known his decision to cease fighting. One of the Germans invited him to accompany them in a vehicle to meet General Renner at Sart-Bernard. Fries stayed behind with the other officer, who was much more relaxed than yesterday evening and was anxious to begin a conversation. He explained that he was Austrian and had won the Iron Cross in the 1914–18 war. Fries had been authorized by Noel to give a tour of the position so he led the delegation towards the fort.

At Sart-Bernard, Captain Noel was taken to the great hall of the Ferme Biel in front of a group of officers, some of whom spoke French. Renner stated to Noel that the conditions of surrender would be the same for Dave as for Andoy: surrender with honours rendered to the garrison who would then become prisoners of war. Captain Noel, attempting to take advantage of the good nature of Renner, asked if the wounded could continue to be taken care of by the medical staff of the fort and that the chaplain remain to comfort them. This was an attempt at letting these men escape capture but Renner quickly refused.

Upon his return to the fort, Noel noted that the orders given to his second-in-command, Lieutenant Collin, were perfectly executed. The fort was in a terrible state. The guns were destroyed, debris was scattered throughout the ditch and the corridors inside the fort, diesel fuel splashed everywhere and on fire, sending a thick, acrid smoke across the fort.

Around 1000hrs the moment had come to leave the fort after 15 days of an underground existence. The last food was handed out and placed in the men's knapsacks. In the gorge ditch Captain Noel addressed the men for the last time. He told them he was proud of the way they handled themselves, his voice full of emotion. He ended by bidding farewell to the garrison of the *Batterie de Dave*. He individually introduced the officers to the German colonel in attendance who stood at attention and saluted each one. The men marched up the access ramp, steering clear of the land mines. All of them were tired but calm. They watched as the victors filtered out of the woods, prepared for the assault that was not necessary. The Germans had already set up a phone at the top of the ramp to communicate with the fort and a team was ready to handle the wounded as they were brought out.

The garrison was given a short time to go into a nearby field to stretch their legs and to enjoy their first breath of fresh air in a long time. Belgians and Germans mixed together, attempting to talk to each other, exchange cigarettes and bottles of beer and to take photos to immortalize the moment. The officers also mixed together and discussed the artillery battles, making comments such as: 'You fired at that location but there was nothing there, but there, on the other hand, you caused some damage.' Funny moments that prove once again that war is an extraordinary revealer of sometimes surprising human behaviour.[3]

It was time to leave. The ambulance arrived to take away the wounded. The Belgians formed up to march away towards Naninne and the Germans formed rows on both sides to render honours. For the Belgians the war was over and they would not return home to Namur for five years.[4] For the Germans it was to continue for a few more weeks, after which time it would shift to the East.

Renner later wrote in his journal:

On 23 May at 2000 hours I sent a parliamentarian to fort de Dave. The commandant was invited to surrender. Around 2200 the envoy returned. The commandant of the fort wanted to know, with certainty, that fort Dave was the only garrison of Namur which still held out. I was able to give the commandant the assurance requested.

For prudence sake, we had prepared 1,200 Flak shells in case he refused the invitation. The artillery on the west bank of the Meuse shifted its position to Fooz to be able to hit Dave directly. The commandant realized the uselessness of resistance and he surrendered the fort on 24 May at 1000.[5]

The following day the 211th Infantry Division was ordered to move on to Maubeuge. They departed 26 May at 1600hrs on a partly cloudy day. Namur had fallen.

Liège – 22 to 29 May 1940

Battice ended its fight on the 22nd. During the nine-hour ceasefire the commandant and a team of officers went out to inspect the damage to the fort. They concluded that it greatly reduced the fort's ability to continue the defence. After a secret vote by the remaining officers, the surrender was decided by sixteen votes in favour and three votes against. A message was passed throughout the fort that it would surrender at dawn. The order was given to destroy all remaining guns and weapons. At dawn the white flag was raised and the crew of the fort was taken prisoner of war by 385 IR. Battice had fought for 12 days and lost the most men out of all of the forts of the PFL and PFN.

During the morning of 22 May, the command post at Fort Tancrémont received the farewell message from Battice, which also brought news of the explosion that had killed thirty men. The message arrived just as Commandant Devos was sending his own message to offer condolences and encouragement. A short while later the observers at Tancrémont could see a white flag flying over Battice. The news filled the garrison with worry. Why did our big brother fall? When would it be Tancrémont's turn, and how would it happen? Of the twelve forts of Liège that began the war, only Tancrémont remained.

At 0830hrs the fort was hit by shells coming from the direction of Spa. At 1100hrs a Stuka flew over and dropped several bombs on the fort. Forty-five minutes later German envoys appeared and were received by Sous-Lieutenant Detroux who told them that surrendering the fort was not a consideration. As if to underline this message to the Germans, Bloc IVs turrets lifted up and fired, as if the envoys were not there.

At 1500hrs the envoys returned, this time accompanied by Belgian officers. It was Commandant Guéry of Battice and one of his officers. Captain Devos, without leaving the confines of the fort, shouted from one of the observation cloches that the fort would not surrender. A short while later Lieutenant Weimerskirch placed a large Belgian flag on top of Bloc 1 with the intention of making the Germans realize that their efforts to intimidate the garrison would not work. The garrison received double rations that evening but they were in no need of encouragement. Being the last survivors brought on its own new responsibilities and for now the men wanted revenge for their friends who were killed and to show the 'Boches' that even though they were far from the front, apparently abandoned by everyone, the men of Tancrémont were going to do everything they could to disrupt the Germans.

On 23 May the shelling of the fort diminished. Tancrémont fired on German targets at Soiron. In the early afternoon Bloc 2 fired on a convoy at Cornesse and some cyclists at Spa. The radio officer made contact with two forts of Namur. They did not want to identify themselves but he suspected that one of them was Maizeret. Everything in the vicinity of the fort was very quiet. The fort was truly isolated. At this point perhaps the Germans were just going to ignore it.

At 0715hrs on 24 May Tancrémont fired in support of *Abri* VM 3, where German cyclists were passing by. The turret crews did not miss an opportunity to intervene wherever possible. The intervention lasted about 45 minutes but the shelter chief burned documents and maps and took off with his men. In reality the shelter was no longer providing information of value. This was the last external shelter remaining. Nothing but Fort Tancrémont was left.

The Germans approached Blocs O and P in groups of three, darting in and out of the woods. MGs, mortars and *boîtes-à-balles* sent them quickly in the opposite direction. One of the sentries in a cloche of Bloc P noticed a dead German lying about 100m away. Another was spotted near Bloc I, stuck in the wire but definitely dead. Why would the Germans have abandoned their dead?

During the night of 24/25 May an incident occurred at the turret of Bloc IV. The mechanism to raise and lower the turret jammed but quickly repaired by the technicians. The fort fired both turrets and the mortars in the direction of Wegnez, Banneux and Spa. In the afternoon an armoured vehicle and three trucks on the Spa road were hit by shots from Bloc 3. As night approached the Bois de Marmol, a nest of German field grey, was also hit by the cloche guns of Blocs P and O.

On 26 May Tancrémont fired on Louveigné, Wegnez and Haut-Regard. The forest of Mazures deliberately set on fire by the Belgians. Stuka bombers dropped bombs on the fort throughout the day. That night some men were moved to Bloc O in case of a German attack. Rumours were circulating that the French had recaptured Boulogne but the front was too far away for anyone to truly care.

During the morning the engineers worked to boost the signal of the TSF and reached IV Corps. Captain Devos passed on a message: 'Fort de Tancrémont continues to hold out and is the last to pass on salutations to the field army and the commanders. *Vive la Belgique!*' The reply was comforting: 'Congratulations! We will transmit your message to the King. *Vive la Belgique!*' The men in the command post listened to the message traffic on the TSF; discussions of envoys, discussions going on at GQG. There was a general recall of all Belgian officers as soon as possible to GQG. Was this the end?

On 28 May 1940 Fort Tancrémont learned of the surrender of the Belgian Army. A message was sent to Belgian Army HQ requesting instructions. The reply was, 'Received your message 1200.' After that – silence. There were no further instructions. The fort's Council of Defence met but made no decisions. Civilians began to return to the villages around the fort. A small delegation left the fort to look for a German negotiator to help make contact with GHQ.

Captain Devos met with a General Spang around 0900hrs to discuss the situation of the fort. The Belgians did not want to stop fighting but the Germans threatened its destruction. Spang gave his word of honour and ensured Devos that the Belgian army had surrendered. Devos returned to the fort and convened the council. Tancrémont officially surrendered at 1100hrs on 29 May 1940. The officers were permitted to keep their swords. The German flag was not raised until the last Belgian had left the fort. Tancrémont had held out for 400 hours and put many German soldiers out of action.

Strategic Situation in Belgium – 22 to 28 May 1940

In the last few days of the war for Belgium, the Allies were driven back on all fronts. The French and British retreated to Dunkerque. May 27th dawned with the realization for the Belgian Army that no help was forthcoming from the Allies and no more fresh troops were available. At 1230hrs the king cabled General Gort to report that the Army would be obliged to surrender in order to prevent a rout. At 1430hrs French authorities were informed that Belgian resistance had reached its limits. Furthermore, there was no chance for an embarkation of the Belgians.

At 1700hrs a truce envoy was sent to the Germans to inquire of the conditions for an eventual cease fire. At 2230hrs the envoy returned with terrible news: the Germans would only accept unconditional surrender. At 2300hrs the king, in agreement with the Chief of the General Staff, suggested the cease fire be fixed for 0400hrs on the 28th.

At 0400hrs the cease fire sounded on the Belgian front and Belgium's 18-day campaign came to an end. Belgium was once again under German occupation, this time all of it. Fort Tancrémont was still holding out and did not surrender until the following day. The evacuation from Dunkerque began on 28 May and continued, under heavy bombardment, till 2 June. The Battle of France began on the Somme on 11 June and then spread across the entire line, forcing the French into a series of withdrawals all the way to Alsace. The last French armies, with the exception of fortress troops in the Maginot Line, surrendered on 22 June and an armistice went into effect between France and Germany at 0030hrs on 25 June 1940.

Chapter 16

Conclusions

T he questions are now asked, after the forts have all surrendered, the garrisons marched off to Colditz Castle and the Stalags, and 80 years have passed – why and how and what, if anything, could have been done to make the outcome any different?

German MG squad marches outside Fort Boncelles entrance. The Corps de Garde *is on the left, heavily damaged.* (Digital History Archive, 'Bunkers of the Blitzkrieg')

One cannot argue that the Allies were simply not prepared for the German onslaught that hit them on 10 May 1940. The Belgians (and the French and Dutch) spent millions building permanent fortifications along their borders. But the defences were never meant to be used as the sole means of keeping the enemy at bay. They were built and designed to be used in conjunction with field artillery batteries and infantry units. By the time the Germans crossed the border into Belgium, plans had long since changed and only light covering forces patrolled the frontier. Very early on 10 May these units were in retreat, if not already long gone.

If there was anything at all to praise about Belgium's very short 18-day war, it was the performance of the fortress garrisons of Liège and Namur. There were of course many heroic stands by the Belgian Army in numerous instances in battles across Belgium, but the forts consistently, from their first to last days, fought bravely under horrible circumstances, through injury and death and destruction. The forts could have raised the white flag when the interval troops pulled out but they continued to fight and only surrendered when there was no conceivable reason to continue. In just about every case the forts did not surrender until after all of their weapons had been destroyed by the Germans, their structure was wrecked and further resistance simply a senseless waste of lives. After the swift fall of Eben-Emael – the only anomaly that occurred during the 18-day campaign – not one of the twelve forts at Liège or seven at Namur gave up the fight before they had no other choice. This is a testament to the leadership of the commanders, staff officers and NCOs of the fortress garrisons.

Since it was the first to fall, let's begin with Fort Eben-Emael. We have already seen the ease in which the German gliders landed on top of the fort, with open landing zones the size of football pitches, no defensive protection such as barbed wire or ditches in front of the combat bloc embrasures (*fossé diamants*), and much of the garrison occupied elsewhere while the only surface defences, two machine-gun blocs, remained unmanned. Eben-Emael was considered to be the strongest, most modern fort in the world. It was considered to be impregnable. But this, like the claim of the *Titanic* to be 'unsinkable', proved to be very sadly wrong, and it only took about 15 minutes to inflict a mortal wound upon it.

Would it have made much of a difference in the war if Eben-Emael had been better prepared for an airborne attack? If the fort's AA defences had been more robust and the crews better protected, and the surface covered by obstacles that made it less of a landing strip, then probably yes, but to what degree? If the gliders couldn't land or were destroyed in the air over the fort, what difference would that have made? First of all, the 120mm

turret had a range that could reach far beyond Maastricht to the north and a few kilometres to the east of Aubin-Neufchâteau, meaning it could interdict all of the roads taken by the Germans to the north and east of Liège. The 75mm, which could fire much more quickly than the 120mm, could also cover an extensive area. The 75mm Maastricht casemates covered an arc that included the Albert Canal bridges to Lanaken and the Visé casemates had the entire Meuse valley to Pontisse and the main Meuse crossing points in their sites. The only question was whether the vertical arc of fire of the guns allowed them to fire over top of the Montagne St. Pierre towards Maastricht. Perhaps a couple of 81mm mortar blocs could have done the job. But, this isn't what happened and in 15 minutes most of the guns were out of commission. Had they remained operational they most likely would have made 151 IR's task of securing the Albert Canal bridgeheads and Sixth Army's advance more difficult. But for how long? Within 24 hours the Germans were already bringing up their heavy artillery batteries and no doubt Eben-Emael would have been the first casualty of the Flak and anti-tank guns. Being the weakest of the new forts in terms of construction, and probably the weakest when it came to leadership, how long would Eben-Emael have held out then?

Eben-Emael was the first of the new forts to be built at Liège – a test case, so to speak – and it was full of design flaws. Each fort was built with a certain degree of protection against enemy bombardment. Oddly Eben-Emael was only built to resist 280mm shells. The Belgians knew as early as 1914 that there were already German guns heavier than that – 305mm, 420mm, etc. They only had to look at Fort Loncin to be reminded of that. Fort Battice, closer to the German border, was built to withstand 520mm shells. Tancrémont and Aubin-Neufchâteau 420mm. So how long would Eben-Emael last under concentrated heavy shelling and aerial bombardment once the AA defences were neutralized? Colonel Mozin, the former commander of Fort Fléron in 1914 and commander of III Corps, commented in a 1935 letter regarding Eben-Emael, that it was haphazardly designed; the turrets did not respond to military necessity (i.e., the guns could not reach the German border nor could they fire at Maastricht because the Montagne St. Pierre stood in the way), and the concrete blocs were weak and did not offer a significant degree of protection (see photograph opposite). Mozin quoted an unnamed officer who commanded troops in Belgian Limbourg: 'If a war starts, I would not put my men inside the fort, but line them up on the outside, because the fort will crumble after the third cannon shot.'

Unfortunately Eben-Emael did not last long enough to see if Mozin was right. What truly killed Eben-Emael, more than anything, was surprise and shock. The fort was 35km from the German border, an airborne attack was never imagined, and thus the Belgians believed they had plenty of time to put the fort in its maximum defensive state. Once the gliders landed, the surprise was achieved. It only remained to apply the shock. The pioneers landed close enough to their objectives to swiftly use their secret weapon. The shaped charges blew holes in the steel cloches and turret caps, killing or badly injuring the crews inside while powerful explosive packages destroyed the gun embrasures and tossed the defenders around inside the casemates like mannequins. The 50kg charge placed against the door at the base of Maastricht 1 caused such a tremendous blast force inside the fort that it destroyed the staircase leading to the surface and broke open containers of chlorine powder cleaning agent stored in the outer corridor. This created suffocating fumes in the tunnels that required the immediate donning of gas masks and sowed more panic among the garrison. The attack by *Sturmgrüppe*

Granit was the perfect storm and the Belgians didn't stand a chance. Fort Eben-Emael held out only 36 hours but in the first 15 minutes the fatal blow had already been struck and the fort could do nothing to prevent the German army from crossing the canal.

The other three modern forts also suffered from a lack of anti-aircraft protection. They were equipped with AA MG batteries but they were installed on the surface, out in the open, and were one of the first targets of the dive bombers and infantry attacks. Due to the speed and manoeuvrability of the Stukas it is doubtful they were touched by a single Belgian AA bullet. The older forts practised a type of mutual anti-air defence which fared somewhat better, firing shells with fuses set to explode at various altitudes above the adjacent forts. This supposedly caused the bombers to fly at higher and higher levels where their bombs would not be as effective. This unfortunately was not a very long-term measure and the Stukas flew and dropped bombs at will for days on end.

The concrete of the new forts stood up well to the powerful bombs and shells. On 20 May alone, the Germans fired 589 heavy shells of 150mm, 170mm, 280mm, 305mm and 355mm calibre against Fort Aubin-Neufchâteau. While the experience was terrible for the men, at least they were fairly safe underground. The forts shook like in an earthquake as each bomb or heavy shell struck the surface, but there were no reports of significant damage to the underground structures. This was good for the men but if the crews were unable to move to the combat blocs and fire the guns then the shells and bombs had done their job in another way. When the Belgians fired back, the fortress guns performed magnificently. In coordination with external observation posts and adjacent forts, targets were pinpointed, guns assigned and shells were underway in a matter of minutes. The results were much more than a nuisance to the Germans. Convoys were diverted, vehicles destroyed, troops killed and gun batteries neutralized.

The forts did amazingly well when defending against infantry attacks. Machine guns, mortars, FMs and the 75s effectively stopped dozens of assaults. There are many examples of this in the book but Fort Battice and Aubin-Neufchâteau are prime examples. But after a few days the guns broke down or were hit by heavy shells and they kept the technicians far busier than expected. From the very beginning the turrets suffered mechanical breakdowns even before any shots were fired. It was a miracle and testament to the skills of the technicians that the equipment continued to function as long as it did.

The Germans had outstanding success picking off the embrasures and hitting the gun barrels while the turrets were raised. The most powerful weapon wasn't the 420mm or the Stuka bombs, it was the 88mm Flak gun. The shell flew towards the target at such high velocity that it penetrated the walls of the steel cloches, destroyed the embrasures and chipped away at the reinforced concrete, punching holes in the walls. The 37mm PAK AT gun was also very effective against the concrete and steel.

The older forts fared much worse. Shelter in the upper massif was useless and even the quadrilateral was no safe haven, with instances of ceiling and tunnel collapse. The escarp and counterscarp walls suffered numerous breaches from bombs and shells, creating natural scaling ladders for German pioneers to access the ditch and the massif. The refurbished turrets, made of 'rolled steel' from 1890, proved to be very fragile during the fighting of 1940, especially against the 37mm PAK and 88mm Flak guns. Many soldiers died inside turrets in which the top was blown off by the pinpoint accuracy and power of the 88mm shells. The performance of the 150mm turret was not good. These pieces, mounted in the old 210mm turrets, lacked a recoil mechanism, throwing the gun carriage off track by the sheer shock of firing the gun. The 75s, housed in the old 57mm turrets, performed very well. The 105mm, on the other hand, worked quite well but the supply of ammunition was exhausted fairly quickly and the gunners were forced to sabotage the guns. The concrete surrounding the turrets cracked, throwing the pieces off balance so they could not be raised or turned. Small pieces of debris lodged in the openings between the outer housing and the turret, contributing to the frequent jamming and breakdown of the equipment.

The ventilation systems were a primary target of the German guns. In a couple of cases, the air tower bunkers of the old forts were attacked with explosives, creating a massive amount of smoke that was drawn through the air ducts back into the fort, hastening its surrender, much like 1914. Nevertheless the air towers performed the unexpected function as observatories and defensive bunkers. They became the eyes of the fort after the loss of the external observation posts and the FMs chased off many German infantry attacks.

Another important element in German tactics was the use of troops specially trained to attack the embrasures, the weak points of the fortifications. These troops were called Pioneers or Stösstruppen. German experiments on the Czech fortifications had shown that only an explosive charge placed near the opening (niche, embrasure, support ball or closure flap) was capable of causing decisive damage. Aside from the shaped chargers, the Germans used powerful explosives in the openings or in the gun barrels. The flamethrower, another terror weapon, was also used to clear the Belgians from the inside of the blocs.

The Stuka was a powerful instrument of shock and terror, but it was not enough in and of itself to reduce the forts. The single-engine bomber was equipped with a 250kg bomb and four 50kg bombs under its wings. The concrete held up well but the bombardments wore heavily on the morale of the garrisons. The bomber also scored a very lucky (or unlucky, depending on your perspective) hit on Bloc 1 of Fort Battice. The bomb struck an unknown object, perhaps a tetrahedron tank-trap that changed its trajectory. The bomb ricocheted into the entry corridor, where it exploded, setting off ammunition and killing thirty Belgians inside the bloc and wounding several others. The explosion destroyed the staircase to the lower level and blocked all access from below. This single event was the deciding factor in the surrender of the fort.

This combination of German weapons and tactics – aerial bombardment, heavy shelling, high-velocity shells against the observation ports and embrasures, explosives, shaped charges, flamethrowers, machine guns and smoke – contributed in one form or another to bringing about the surrender of all but one fort. Tancrémont held out until the very end but neither did it receive the same degree of pounding as the other forts.

In truth, the defence establishment doomed the forts before the war began. The original plans called for the forts to perform a supporting role for the infantry, but they quickly became isolated, arresting or delaying forts, a role for which they were not designed. Before the PFL was completed, the Army knew that III Corp, which would occupy the PFL, did not have enough troops or MGs to hold the 60km-long forward line of 179 bunkers. For that reason the bunkers of PFL 1, with the exception of the observatories of Aubin-Neufchâteau, Battice and Tancrémont, remained empty. The Belgians waited in the interval trenches along PFL 2 for the Germans to attack in the centre like they did in 1914, but instead they headed north and south of Liège. When the Germans began to outflank Liège the staff of the III Corps ordered all its troops to retreat to the left bank of the river during the night of 10/11 May. The situation deteriorated very quickly. In the afternoon of 11 May, fearing encirclement, the staff of III Corps gave the order to evacuate the PFL. On the morning of 12 May, the Koningshooikt–Wavre (Dyle) line became the main line of resistance.

The PFL was designed to be the hinge of the Belgian defensive system in which the Albert Canal was to play the main role, where the Belgian army would hold back the enemy as long as possible while waiting for French and English reinforcements. However, the French did not think it possible to join the Belgian army in time. Therefore, the KW Line was chosen as the main battle line. Thus, the Belgian army modified its plans for defence. The

Albert Canal and the PFL lost their importance. They would only serve to contain the enemy while the Allies gathered on the KW line and the Meuse below Namur. The fortress troops stayed behind and fought on to the end of their ability.

- 7 days – Fort Boncelles and Flémalle – 16 May.
- 8 days – Fort Fléron, Chaudfontaine, Embourg – 17 May.
- 9 days – Fort Pontisse, Barchon, Marchovelette – 18 May.
- 10 days – Fort Evegnée, Suarlée – 19 May.
- 12 days – Fort Aubin-Neufchâteau, Saint-Héribert, Malonne – 21 May.
- 13 days – Fort Battice – 22 May.
- 14 days – Fort Maizeret, Andoy – 23 May.
- 15 days – Fort Dave – 24 May.
- 18 days – Fort Tancrémont – 29 May.

Was it all worth it or should the forts have surrendered after the army pulled out? If nothing else, the fortress garrisons gained the respect of the Germans who fought against them. The majority of the fort commanders, as indicated in Belgian and German documents, were permitted to keep their swords and personal weapons. One German lieutenant colonel, addressing a surrendered garrison, exclaimed that if it were up to him he would have allowed all of the officers to keep their weapons.[1] On 29 May Von Reichenau, commander of Sixth Army, accompanied by Paulus, presented himself before King Leopold III to accept the surrender of the Belgian Army. Von Reichenau commented to the king – 'The Belgians fought well – We pay tribute to the Belgian army and its leader. We also praise the amazing tenacity of the forts.'

As to casualties, several Belgians remarked that they saw dead German soldiers in the vicinity of the forts after the surrender. While leaving Fort Saint-Héribert by the access ramp, one soldier spotted two bodies next to the Cointet gate and several others on the edge of the woods across from the entrance. A German doctor asked the fort's doctor if any medical supplies were left in the fort because 'We have none left to treat our wounded'.[2] Numerous German soldiers were buried throughout the local communities – along the road outside Bois-de-Villers; in the Parc du General Nicotte at Arbre. A stretcher bearer for the fort, Private Schotsaert, ran into a German NCO near Bioul who told him that the fort cost them at least 500 casualties. A year after the capture of Fort Saint-Héribert, a German officer visiting there and claiming to have directed the attack on the fort stated: 'I wanted to revisit Fort de Saint-Héribert and above all to see the MG turrets that caused so much damage. The Belgian soldiers were very brave; they defended very well. After the first assault we had 129 dead and 602 wounded. During the course of the attack practically the entire 317th was decimated. It was a veritable inferno for us, especially the machine guns.'[3]

After the war was over the same conclusions were reached as at the end of the First World War: that fortifications, especially forts left all to themselves, could not offer prolonged resistance. One would now think that was certainly true in 1945. The era of fortifications had finally come to an end. None of the Belgian forts were refurbished after the war. They remained in the same dilapidated

An ammunition lift left behind in the buried Fort Fléron. (Renaud Mayers Collection)

condition as on the day the garrisons marched into captivity. Over the years they were used as military storage depots, or simply left to rot, covered in vegetation, the remaining metal taken by salvagers. Some were sold to private enterprises. Sadly, three of the forts, Boncelles, Fléron and Saint-Héribert, were completely buried. The only thing remaining of Boncelles was the entry gate and some structures in the centre. Fleron was completely gone; a park. Only the air tower remains. Saint-Héribert was completely covered over. There was only one way into the fort and only spelunkers went inside. But there is a silver lining to that particular cloud. Several of the forts at Liège, including all four of the new forts, are now museums. Some have been magnificently refurbished, in particular Fort Lantin. Namur did not enjoy the same fate, with one noted exception. Fort Saint-Héribert, in an action that no one would ever have thought possible, was literally brought back from the grave – excavated, cleaned up, and now open as a museum, where visitors can once again stroll down the entry ramp and through the portal and see the central massif and perhaps reminisce about the incredible stand that took place there over 80 years ago.

Perhaps it's not so much what the forts accomplished in 1940 but the legacy they left to the nation. That even in defeat a nation, or a town, or a village, can look back and remember a moment of glory that took place there, long ago, and the men who were the cause of that glory.

Notes

Chapter 1: 10 and 11 May 1940: The Tragedy of Fort Eben-Emael

1. The Albert Canal was widened in the 1960s to accommodate larger vessels, so the width in 1940 was slightly less.
2. Armoured gun turrets were referred to as 'eclipsable' or 'non-eclipsable', meaning the guns were either permanently in battery or the turret mechanism had the ability to be raised to the battery position to fire or lowered for protection below an armoured 'collar'.
3. *Abri* PL 19 was demolished during work at the quarry located on this spot.
4. Explosive charges used by German pioneers included:
   - 1kg (*Sprengbuschse* – detonator), a pressure-resistant zinc container filled with TNT or picric acid;
   - 3kg hollow, or shaped, demolition charge (*Hohlladung*);
   - 4kg charge filled with enthrite explosive;
   - 12.5kg hollow charge – to blast holes in steel plates in permanent fortifications;
   - 50kg hollow charge – made in two parts; the lower part, provided with a separate carrying handle, contained a hemispherical cavity. The upper part contained both an explosive charge and a standard cap socket. The hollow ring charge was used principally for the destruction of gun barrels (US War Department, *Handbook on German Military Forces*, pp. 478–80).

Chapter 3: Friday, 10 May 1940: Opening Action at Liège

1. On 10 May 1940 Sixth Army included 1, 11, 63, 216, 223 ID; 20th Motorized Division; 3rd Panzer Division; IX Corps with 19, 30, and 56 ID; XI Corps with 7, 14 and 31 ID, IV Corps with 18 and 35 ID; XXVII Corps with 253 and 269 ID and 4th Panzer Division. Army Artillery included *Artillerie-Regiments-Stab z.b.V.* (Special Purpose Regiment) 720 with I and II/84 AR; *Artillerie-Regiments-Stab z.b.V.* 780 with *Artillerie-Abteilung* (typically meaning 'Battalion') (E) 695 and 696; *Artillerie-Abteilungs-Stab z.b.V.* 676 with *Eisenbahn-Batterie* (Railway Battery) 655 and Eisenbahn-Batterie 717 and 718, equipped with the 17cm Kanone (E). Also assigned was *Schwere Artillerie-Abteilung* (Heavy Artillery Battalion) 820, equipped with the 42cm mortar and two subordinate batteries, 779 and 810, with 30.5cm and 35.5cm mortars, respectively. (Source: *Lexikon der wehrmacht. de* website, and L.W.G. Niehorster, *German World War II Organizational Series, Vol 2/II, mechanized GHQ Units and Waffen SS Divisions (10 May 1940)*, Germany, 1990).

2. *Aufstellungswelle* (Deployment Wave). The annual mobilization plan of 1938 called for multiple waves of active and reserve forces. The First Wave was the peacetime army; the other three were raised in anticipation of the invasion of Poland. The Third Wave consisted of divisions numbered 201 to 250. Third-wave divisions had about 17,900 men, about 600 more than those of the first wave.

3. The smoke was caused by the garrison burning the wooden barracks.

4. Sixth Army was in direct command of the *Brücken-Bau-Bataillons*, including 548, 646, and *Heeresgruppen* Reserve Battalions 624 and 552.

5. Captain-Commandant fell above the rank of captain and below major (see Table of Equivalent Ranks).

6. Commandant Pourbaix's post-war account to the Commission des Forts.

7. Which bridge is being referred to is not made clear. There is a small bridge on the Gieveld road north of Teuven but nothing significant.

8. Laurent Vanderhaegen, *Le Fort D'Evegnee en Mai 1940* (Carnet de campagne du commandant Vanderhaegen).

9. Located along the old Liège–Aix-la-Chapelle road.

10. Other units were listed in the message but not included here.

11. *Records of German Field Commands – Divisions* (National Archives Microcopy No. T-315, 223. *Infanterie-Division* (223rd Infantry Division). 2 Apr–19 May 1940, Ia, *Anlage zum Kriegstagebuch Nr. 1. Anlagen Nr. 188-264*. Division Orders and combat reports relating to the capture of enemy fortifications. T-315 Roll 1689, pp. 168–71.

12. Belgian Ministry of National Defence, *Campaign of May 1940*, published 1946.

Chapter 4: The Fortified Position of Namur from 10 to 14 May 1940

1. National Archives Microcopy No. T-78. *Oberkommando des Heeres, Die Befestigung Belgien: Die Festung Namur, 20 December 1939*, Captured German Records, Microfilm, T78, Roll 541.

2. *Revue Trimestrielle* No. 12 2001, 'Mai 1940: Le Fort de Dave Dans la Tourmente'.

3. Capitaine Léon L'Entree, *L'Historique du Fort de Saint-Héribert*, Wepion, 1972.

4. 211th Infantry Division *Kriegstabeguch 2: January 1 – June 30, 1940.*

Chapter 5: Saturday, 11 May 1940

1. Exact location unknown; probably the heights north-west of Hallembaye. The Rue de Tongres, which at this time ran over the Visé road bridge, was below these heights.

2. Probably bunkers NV 7 to NV 15.

3. National Archives Microcopy T-315 Roll 1689, p. 159.

4. Taken from a 'VIGILO' Amicale Nationale des Cyclistes-Frontière founded in 1977.

5. Records of German Field Commands – Corps – V Corps (V *Armee-Korps*). 10–19 May 1940, Orders and Reports I. Battle of Liège (*Befehle und Meldungen I, Gefecht Lüttich*). T-314, Roll 241, p. 15.
6. Possibly Rivage.
7. Today, 's-Gravenvoeren in Flanders.
8. It is said this Ju 87 was shot down by AA of the Aubin-Neufchâteau Fort and crash-landed in an orchard between Schophem (hamlet 'Schoppem'?) and Fourons-Saint-Martin (now Sint-Martens-Voeren), +/-8km east of Visé. The author, Mr Pierre Galère from Visé, remembered also another Stuka crashed near the villa Joassart in Argenteau-Sarolay, 5km south of Visé.
9. The location of Goffart farm is unknown.
10. Le Haut d'Evegnée (Carnet de Campagne de Commandant Vanderhaegen), Mai 1940.
11. Ibid.
12. Not to be confused with the small village of Liers north-west of Liège.

Chapter 6: Sunday, 12 May 1940
1. Divisional artillery included (all data from US War Department, *Handbook on German Military Forces*): 105mm light field howitzer (10cm *Leichte Feldhaubitze* 18), standard divisional field artillery howitzer (p. 326); 150mm medium howitzer (15cm *Schwere* FH 18), range 14,630 yds, ammunition HE, anti-concrete, AP, smoke (p. 332); 105mm medium gun (10cm *Schwere Kanone* 18), standard medium gun, range 20,850 yds (p. 334); 150mm gun (15cm K 18), range 27,040 yds, ammunition HE, anti-concrete (p. 335); 150mm gun (15cm K 39), later version of the above (p. 335); 170mm gun (17cm K *Mörser Lafette*), long-range mobile gun mounted on the 21cm *Mörser* 18 carriage, range 32,000 yds (p. 335); 21cm *Mörser* 18, standard heavy howitzer, range 18,300 yds, ammunition HE, anti-concrete (p. 336); 37cm PAK, reasonable penetration at up to 400 yards (p. 338). Anti-aircraft guns: 20mm AA gun (2cm Flak 30), standard light AA gun (p. 343); 88mm heavy AA gun 8.8cm Flak 18, 36/37. Flak 36 differed from the Flak 18 only in having a slightly different mount, while the Flak 37 was identical with the Flak 36 except for a slightly different data transmission system (p. 349).
2. Pioneer troops (*Pioniertruppen*). The pioneer battalion was organic in every German division, varying in strength and composition according to the type of division. They were first and foremost assault troops, tasked with overcoming man-made and natural obstacles. In the attack they supported the infantry as special assault troops, attacking fortified positions with demolitions and flamethrowers. Personnel in organic divisional engineer platoons belong to the arm of the unit, i.e., 223rd Pioneer Battalion. (US War Department, *Handbook on German Military Force*, pp. 155–6).
3. National Archives Microcopy T-315 Roll 1689, pp. 149–52.

4. Le Haut d'Evegnée (Carnet de Campagne de Commandant Vanderhaegen), Mai 1940.
5. Ibid.
6. Radio operator Digneffe's journal.

Chapter 7: 13 May 1940

1. *Lagekarten* West maps source: www.lexikon-der-wehrmacht.de/Gliederungen/.
2. Records of German Field Commands – Corps – V Corps (V *Armee-Korps*). 10–19 May 1940, Orders and Reports I. Battle of Liège (*Befehle und Meldungen I, Gefecht Lüttich*). T-314, Roll 241, p. 67.
3. Records of German Field Commands – Divisions (National Archives Microcopy No. T-315, 223. *Infanterie-Division* (223rd Infantry Division). 2 Apr–19 May 1940, Ia, *Anlage zum Kriegstagebuch* Nr. 1. *Anlagen* Nr. 188-264. Division Orders and combat reports relating to the capture of enemy fortifications. T-315 Roll 1689, pp. 160–1.
4. Probably the Route de Tignée and Rue sur les Heids in order to move towards Xhavée and into the Meuse valley.
5. Formed on 2 August 1939 with a battery of 10cm guns and two batteries of 30.5cm howitzers as an army force. By order of 13 February 1940, the division surrendered the 1st (10cm gun) battery to Artillery Division 631 and in return received the 3rd battery of the Heavy Artillery Division 624 with 21cm mortars.
6. The Mixed Artillery Division 624 was set up by Military District VIII (Silesia) in the Opole area before mobilization on 2 August 1939. The division was initially divided into one battery with 10cm guns and two batteries with two 30.5cm howitzers each. By order of 13 February 1940, the division surrendered its 1st Battery (10cm guns) to Artillery Division 631 and in return received the 2nd Battery of Heavy Artillery Division 624 with 21cm mortars.
7. Not true as Tancrémont had not fallen.
8. Pontisse was not in German hands. Liers and Lantin were not defended and Loncin was not armed in 1940.
9. National Archives Microcopy T-315 Roll 1689, pp. 158–9.
10. Not sure where this is or if it was property of FN Herstal.
11. Decarpentrie was the battery commander and adjutant. He gave the orders to the gun turret crews. Vanderhaegen was the fort commander in charge of overall operations.
12. Quoted in Commandant Vanderhaegen's Campaign Notebook (*Journal de Campagne*).
13. The exact one is not indicated.
14. 1940s 'Blue' campaign notebook from Fort d'Embourg.

Chapter 8: Tuesday, 14 May 1940

1. 251st Division Order of Battle: 1/,2/,3/451st Infantry Regiment; 1/,2/,3/459th Infantry Regiment; 1/,2/,3/471st Infantry Regiment; 1/,2/,3/,4/251st Artillery

Regiment; 251st *Panzerjäger* Battalion; 251st Reconnaissance Battalion; 251st Pioneer Battalion.
2. Quoted in Commandant Vanderhaegen's Campaign Notebook (*Journal de Campagne*).
3. This same process was used on the Maginot Line with the 75mm turrets.
4. Probably the Église St. Lambert, about 700m from the fort.

Chapter 9: Wednesday, 15 May 1940
1. 820th Battalion's subordinate units, Batteries 779 and 810, were equipped with 305mm and 355mm howitzers, respectively. From 19–21 May they bombarded Fort Aubin-Neufchâteau.
2. Light artillery pieces were usually towed by horses.
3. A good illustration as to why the ditch casemates were on two levels.
4. Quoted in Commandant Vanderhaegen's Campaign Notebook (*Journal de Campagne*).

Chapter 10: Thursday, 16 May 1940
1. National Archives Microcopy T-315 Roll 1689, pp. 93–4.
2. Quoted in Commandant Vanderhaegen's Campaign Notebook (*Journal de Campagne*).
3. Colonel Modard and his staff were captured along with the garrison. Modard later escaped and joined the Belgian Resistance.
4. National Archives Microcopy T-315 Roll 1689, pp. 93–4.
5. There was no connection between the mine and the fort.
6. National Archives Microcopy T-315 Roll 1689, pp. 75–9.
7. Ibid.

Chapter 11: Friday, 17 May 1940
1. National Archives Microcopy T-315 Roll 1689, p. 52.
2. Ibid., p. 53.
3. Records of German Field Commands – Corps – V Corps (V *Armee-Korps*). 10 – 19 May 1940, Orders and Reports I. Battle of Liège (*Befehle und Meldungen I, Gefecht Lüttich*). T-314, Roll 241, pp. 127–8.
4. Commandant Pourbaix's post-war account to the Commission des Forts.
5. Quoted in Commandant Vanderhaegen's Campaign Notebook (*Journal de Campagne*).

Chapter 12: Saturday, 18 May 1940
1. National Archives Microcopy T-315 Roll 1689, pp. 40–2.
2. Records of German Field Commands – Corps – V Corps (V *Armee-Korps*). 10–19 May 1940, Orders and Reports I. Battle of Liège (*Befehle und Meldungen I, Gefecht Lüttich*). T-314, Roll 241, pp. 157–61.
3. Report concerning fortifications and terrain obstacles in eastern Belgium and southern Netherlands. Oct 20, 1939. Records of Headquarters German Army High Command (OKH), Microfilm T-78, Roll 542.

4. National Archives Microcopy T-315 Roll 1689, p. 53.
5. *Koluft – Kommandatur Luftwaffe.*
6. National Archives Microcopy T-315 Roll 1689, p. 49.
7. 'Flamethrower, portable Model 35. Type with which German started the present war. It is a modified version of the 1918 model. Both fuel and compressed nitrogen containers are housed in one cylinder. The nitrogen is used for propulsion of the fuel, which is ignited at the nozzle by a jet of hydrogen flame. Both ejection and ignition of the fuel are controlled by the same trigger placed on top of the gun. It can fire ten one-second bursts as far as 30 yards. Weighs 79 pounds; too heavy for a single man in action. Later model 40 weighed 47 pounds' (US War Department, *Handbook on German Military Forces*, p. 533).
8. National Archives Microcopy T-315 Roll 1689, pp. 40–2.
9. Ibid, p. 22.
10. Commandant Pourbaix's post-war account to the Commission des Forts.
11. US National Archives. Captured German Records. (MS # P-203 – ATTACKS AGAINST FORTIFIED POSITIONS. GERMAN ATTACKS AGAINST PERMANENT AND REINFORCED FIELD-TYPE FORTIFIED POSITIONS IN WORLD WAR II by General der Infanterie a.D. Rudolf Hofmann with Co-Workers: Generalleutnant a.D. Friedrich Schlieper, Generalmajor a.D. Friedrich Wolf, Generalleutnant a.D. Walter Botsch, Historical Division, Headquarters United States Army, Europe.
12. National Archives Microcopy T-315 Roll 1689, pp. 14–19.

Chapter 13: Sunday, 19 May and Monday, 20 May 1940
1. Quoted in Commandant Vanderhaegen's Campaign Notebook (*Journal de Campagne*).

Chapter 14: Tuesday, 21 May 1940
1. From Commandant D'Ardenne's campaign journal.

Chapter 15: Wednesday, 22 May to Wednesday, 29 May 1940: The Last Heroic Days
1. One battery 15cm and two batteries 21cm mortars
2. The actual surrender date was 19 May 1940
3. L'Entree, *L'Historique du Fort de Saint-Héribert.*
4. Belgian enlisted men spent the war at Stalag IVb Muhlberg sur Elbe; officers in Colditz
5. L'Entree, *L'Historique du Fort de Saint-Héribert.*

Chapter 16: Conclusions
1. L'Entree, *L'Historique du Fort de Saint-Héribert.*
2. Ibid.
3. Ibid

Bibliography

General-Major Boulouffe served as President of the Commission des Forts at Namur Belgian after the war. The commission's report was published in 1947. It included the testimony of the surviving commanders of the forts of Liège and Namur. Bibliography is as follows:

Boulouffe, General-Major, *Rapport sur la defence du fort de [Name of Fort] en mai 1940*. Bruxelles: Ministre de la defence Nationale, 1946 (Testimony of [Rank and Name of Commander] before the Commission des Forts at Namur).
Name of Fort and Rank and Name of Commanders: (Note: Captain Charlier of Fort Boncelles was killed therefore there is no testimony):
Fort de Pontisse – Captain Fernand Pire.
Fort de Barchon – Captain-Commandant Aimé Pourbaix.
Fort d'Aubin-Neufchâteau – Captain-Commandant Oscar d'Ardenne.
Fort d'Évegnée -Captain-Commandant L. Vanderhaegen.
Fort de Fléron – Captain A. Glinne.
Fort de Chaudfontaine – Captain-Commandant Raymond Clobert.
Fort d'Embourg – Captain-Commandant M. Jaco.
Fort de Tancrémont – Captain-Commandant Abel Devos.
Fort de Flémalle Captain-Commandant Barbieux.
Fort de Battice – Captain-Commandant Guery.
Fort Marchovelette – Captain Georges De Lombaerdt.
Fort Maizeret – Captain Léon Hambenne.
Fort Andoy – Captain Auguste Degehet.
Fort Dave – Captain Fernand Noel.
Fort of St-Héribert – Captain Leon L'Entrée.
Fort Malonne – Captain Edgard Demaret.
Fort Suarlée – Captain Fernand Tislair.
Brock, Jean, *Le Fort de Fleron 1888-1998*, Liège: Centre Liègoise d'Histoire et d'Archeologie Militaires, 1992.
Coenen, Emil and Franck Vernier, *La Position Fortifiee de Liège Tome 4, Les Nouveaux Forts*, Erpe: Editions de Krijger, 2008.
——, *La Position Fortifiee de Liège Tome 5, Les Forts de la Meuse Modernises*, Erpe: Editions de Krijger, 2005.
Gonzalez, Oscar, Thomas Steinke and Ian Tannahill, *The Silent Attack: The Fallschirmjager Capture the Bridges of Veldwezelt, Vroenhoven & Kanne 1940*, Barnsley: Pen & Sword Books Ltd, 2015.

'Fort de Barchon: Cent ans d'histoire – 1888 / 1940 – à travers les deux guerres'; rédigé par les membres de la Commission Historique du fort de Barchon et édité par l'ASBL 'Solidarité et Services Rémunérés – Blegny.

L'Entree, Capitaine Léon, *L'Historique du Fort de Saint-Héribert*, Wepion, 1972.

Saunders, Tim, *Fort Eben Emael*, Barnsley: Pen & Sword Books, Ltd., 2005.

Scaillet, Andre, *Mai 1940: Le Fort de Dave Dans La Tourmente (L'epopee du fort de dave en mai 1940)*, 2001: Revue 'Itineraires Wallons'.

US National Archives Captured German Records. (MS # P-203 – ATTACKS AGAINST FORTIFIED POSITIONS) GERMAN ATTACKS AGAINST PERMANENT AND REINFORCED FIELD-TYPE FORTIFIED POSITIONS IN WORLD WAR II by General der Infanterie a.D. Rudolf Hofmann with Co-Workers: Generalleutnant a.D. Friedrich Schlieper, Generalmajor a.D. Friedrich Wolf, Generalleutnant a.D. Walter Botsch, Historical Division, Headquarters United States Army, Europe.

Oberkommando des Heeres, *Die Befestigung Belgien: Die Festung Namur, 20 December 1939*, Captured German Records, Microfilm, T78, Roll 541.

Report concerning fortifications and terrain obstacles in eastern Belgium and southern Netherlands. Oct 20, 1939. Records of Headquarters German Army High Command (OKH), Microfilm T-78, Roll 542.

(Same) – Technical data concerning Dutch and Belgian fortifications, with sketches and photographs. Nov 1, 1939. (Same).

OKH, *Denkschrift Namur*. A description of Belgian forts, called 'Namur', with tables showing the armament and personnel strength of the forts of Namur. Dec 20, 1939. T78 Roll 541.

Records of German Field Commands – Corps – V Corps (V *Armee-Korps*). 10 – 19 May 1940, Orders and Reports I. Battle of Liège (*Befehle und Meldungen I, Gefecht Lüttich*). T-314, Roll 241.

Records of German Field Commands – Divisions (National Archives Microcopy No. T-315, 223. *Infanterie-Division* (223rd Infantry Division). 2 Apr–19 May 1940, Ia, Anlage zum Kriegstagebuch Nr. 1. Anlagen Nr. 188-264. Division Orders and combat reports relating to the capture of enemy fortifications. T-315 Roll 1689.

US War Department, War Department Technical Manual TM-E 30-451; *Handbook on German Military Forces*, Washington DC: United States Government Printing Office, 1945.

Vanderhaegen, Laurent, 'Le Fort d'Evegnee en Mai 1940 – Carnet de campagne du commandant Vanderhaegen' (Liège: Centre Liègoise d'Histoire et d'Archeologie Militaires, Bulletin d'Information Avril-Juin 2008 Tome X, Fascicule 6, pp. 21–35).

Vernier, Franck, 'Le Fort de Chaudfontaine en 1940' (Liège: Centre Liègoise d'Histoire et d'Archeologie Militaires, Bulletin d'Information Juillet-Septembre 2007 Tome X, Fascicule 3, pp. 64–8)

——, 'Le Fort de Pontisse en 1940. (Liège: Centre Liègoise d'Histoire et d'Archeologie Militaires, Bulletin d'Information Avril-Juin 2009 Tome X, Fascicule 10, pp. 27–30).

——, 'Le Fort de d'Evegnee en 1940' (Liège: Centre Liègoise d'Histoire et d'Archeologie Militaires, Bulletin d'Information Avril-Juin 2008 Tome X, Fascicule 6, pp. 16–21).

——, 'Le Fort de Embourg en 1940' (Liège: Centre Liègoise d'Histoire et d'Archeologie Militaires, Bulletin d'Information Avril-Juin 2007 Tome X, Fascicule 2, pp. 47–51)

——, 'Le Fort de Flemalle en 1940' (Liège: Centre Liègoise d'Histoire et d'Archeologie Militaires, Bulletin d'Information Janvier-Mars 2009 Tome X, Fascicule 9, pp. 53–7).

——, 'Le Fort de Boncelles en 1940' (Liège: Centre Liègoise d'Histoire et d'Archeologie Militaires, Bulletin d'Information Janvier-Mars 2009 Tome 2, Fascicule 12, pp. 57–62).

——, *1929-1940 Les Forts de Namur Tome 2*, Verviers: Editions du Patrimoine Militaire, 2018.

Vliègen, Rene, *Fort Eben-Emael*, Kanne-Riemst: A.S.B.L., 1989.

Index